A MOVEMENT OF MIND

PREVIOUS BOOKS BY TONY ROBERTS

Poetry

Peterloo Preview 1
Flowers of the Hudson Bay
Sitters
Outsiders
Drawndark
The Noir American & Other Poems

Essays

The Taste in My Mind
The Taste of My Mornings
Poetry in the Blood (ed.)

A MOVEMENT OF MIND

Essays on Poets, Critics & Biographers

TONY ROBERTS

All rights reserved. No part of this work covered by the copyright herein may be reproduced or used in any means – graphic, electronic, or mechanical, including copying, recording, taping, or information storage and retrieval systems – without written permission of the publisher.

Printed by imprintdigital
Upton Pyne, Exeter
www.digital.imprint.co.uk

Typesetting and cover design by The Book Typesetters
hello@thebooktypesetters.com
07422 598 168
www.thebooktypesetters.com

Published by Shoestring Press
19 Devonshire Avenue, Beeston, Nottingham, NG9 1BS
(0115) 925 1827
www.shoestringpress.co.uk

First published 2024
© Copyright: Tony Roberts
© Cover photograph: Tony Roberts
© Author photograph: Katy Roberts

The moral right of the author has been asserted.

ISBN 978-1-915553-39-3

for Theo and Louis

&

always for Chris

'To say that you won't be bothered with anything but the words on the page (and that you are within your rights, because the author didn't *intend* you to have any more) strikes me as petulant... If you cared enough you would.'

– William Empson, *Argufying*

He 'requires neither rehabilitation nor censure; there is no need to minimize, rationalize, or indeed valorize those aspects of his thinking that do not mesh with present-day values'.

– Evelleen Richards, *Darwin and the Making of Sexual Selection*

CONTENTS

Preface ... 1

I: THE AGE OF LOWELL

Lizzie, Cal & Dolphin: 'one man, two women, the common novel plot' ... 7
John Berryman & Robert Lowell: Letters from the Bottom of the World ... 18
Edmund Wilson & Robert Lowell: Bunny & Cal ... 29
Alfred Kazin & Robert Lowell: A Wary Friendship ... 40
Pioneers: The Iowa Writers' Workshop in the Early Fifties ... 50
Delmore Schwartz: The Unravelling Man ... 63
Intimate Distance: Robert Giroux & John Berryman ... 72
Alfred Kazin: American Outsider ... 81
James Atlas: The Shadow and the Poet ... 93
Richard Hugo & James Wright: 'Make it scotch and dirty river water' ... 100
Robert Hass: A Voice in My Ear ... 110
Review: Dave Smith, *Looking Up: Poems 2010–2022* (2023) ... 119
Discovering F.T. Prince ... 123
The Low Visibility of Norman Cameron ... 131

II: THE AGE OF ARNOLD

Matthew Arnold's Letters: A Bicentenary Portrait	145
The Soul of Christmas: John Forster's Charles Dickens	197
Leslie Stephen: Life, Letters & Lit.	216
Robert Browning: How it Struck a Contemporary	233
Looking for Lewes: George Henry Lewes's *Life of Goethe* (1855)	249
James Anthony Froude: The Biographer as Ardent Apologist	264
'Such a life': Elizabeth Gaskell & Her Charlotte Brontë	279

III: THE AGE OF TERROR

Edmund Wilson's *Patriotic Gore*	297
Weltschmerz: the Remarkable Remarque	317
Review: Louis Menand, *The Free World: Art and Thought in the Cold War* (2021)	327
Acknowledgements	334

PREFACE

A good part of *A Movement of Mind* brings together essays – largely biographical and commendatory – which I have published in literary magazines since my second prose collection, *The Taste of My Mornings* (Shoestring Press, 2019). I take my title out of its original context, a remark by Matthew Arnold to his mother regarding his status as a poet. Here it has a double function. Firstly it is intended to suggest that it may be time to re-evaluate the contribution of a number of writers who have been left behind: overlooked, misrepresented or diminished by fashion. And secondly – as befits autobiography – it indicates a movement of my mind from a fascination with mid-twentieth century American poets, to a more recent return to mid-nineteenth century British writers and a movement from poetry to prose.

To claim these essays as autobiographical (as I did in an earlier book), may seem eccentric. And yet I consider them autobiography in the sense that they reflect my preoccupations over the last five years. They discreetly pursue what Henry James described as the writer being engaged in 'a reaching out for the reasons of [their] interest'.

In the essay on Dickens I refer to modern biography as offering a 'steely corrective' to the often more evasive Victorian. I ought to acknowledge here as a prefatory point that our expectations of biography, that it be microscopically intimate, fearlessly honest (and often needlessly prurient), tend to obscure the fact that no life can be captured as anything more than the merest momentary shadow show. The genre is, in its quest for order, consolatory. As readers we collude in overlooking the fact that our lives lack a stable, core *self* and a linear direction. Biographers, of course, are story tellers and have to presume to give us both. Hence their attraction.

On the biographical front, when Noel Annan writes of Leslie Stephen, 'I still believe that his writings are of greater interest than his life', I can only agree. To later generations how could it be otherwise: the work half-endures and licenses the investigation of the life, not generally the other way around. And yet I hold with Stephen, the veteran biographer, the view that the life and work are inseparable and not simply because the former offers a better understanding of the latter.

The two poles of this book are Matthew Arnold and Robert Lowell. What they have in common is a voice that absorbs me. One died thirty years before the other was born. Each came to international prominence in a mid-century, the one as a nineteenth century poet turned essayist, the other as a twentieth century poet. Arnold and Lowell were interesting characters and eminent voices of their periods. They were also inveterate networkers, ideally placed to observe their peers and admonish the times. My interest in them consequently spread to include their contemporaries.

Part One, The Age of Lowell, is concerned with the poet, his relationship with his second wife, Elizabeth Hardwick, with his friendship with fellow poet John Berryman, and critics Edmund Wilson and Alfred Kazin. There follow considerations of other American writers and poets with whom he connected. I then consider the work of two currently underrated poets: a South African (F.T. Prince) and a Scot (Norman Cameron).

Part Two, The Age of Arnold, moves back to mid-nineteenth century England for an extended consideration of the Arnold who emerges from the six volumes of his letters. Then come studies of biographies of Dickens, Stephen, Browning and Brontë, all written by intimates, plus Lewes's Goethe biography and Froude's Carlyle, which address the German literary critic Marcel Reich-Ranicki's theory: 'If you write about other people you cannot avoid writing about yourself at the same time.'

Part Three, The Age of Terror, provides a grim conclusion, with two pieces on war and the civilian – very much a modern theme – focusing on the work of Edmund Wilson and Erich Maria Remarque. I end with the Cold War.

What do the members of the cast of *A Movement of Mind* have in common? Ultimately, I suppose, it always comes down to voice, to that near-ineffable quality which draws one in. Our preferred writers are the ones whose voices correspond most closely to our tastes. These, then, are the most recent tastes in my mind.

Tony Roberts
Manchester 2024

I: The Age of Lowell

LIZZIE, CAL & DOLPHIN: 'ONE MAN, TWO WOMEN, THE COMMON NOVEL PLOT'

> 'Surely good writers write all possible wrong –'
> – 'Summer Between Terms'

'It is far more difficult to live one's life than to write about it,' remarked Nadezhda Mandelstam in a letter to Robert Lowell. This observation was perhaps least appropriate to Lowell, for whom the life and the work were largely synonymous. Over his last seven years – his English years – life and poetry clashed head on.

Greatly influential through his career, and often depicted, were his three marriages: to writers Jean Stafford (from 1940 to 1948), to Elizabeth Hardwick, 'Lizzie', (1949 to 1972) and to Lady Caroline Blackwood (1972 to 1977), Lowell's 'dolphin'. All three marriages had floundered, their problems compounded by the bipolar disorder that dogged Lowell's life. The first had been strained by Stafford's injury in a serious car accident caused by Lowell, as well as by his bout of extreme Catholicism, and then infidelity.

The second, the long marriage to the loyal Hardwick, has been the subject of some speculation. After a blue-collar Kentucky childhood, Hardwick (1916–2007) dropped her university studies to concentrate on a writing career. Eventually she found her way into the circle of the anti-Stalinist left *Partisan Review*. As an essayist she showed an impressive critical intelligence, her work stylish, experimental – and tough. She met Lowell in January 1949. Their eventful marriage helped shape her thematic concerns and doubtless promoted her highly regarded career. She has been viewed by biographers – ever since Ian Hamilton's brilliant but tart *Robert Lowell: A Biography* in 1982 – as offering a stabilising relationship. There have been dissenting opinions heard since. Hardwick's *New York Times* obituary referred to the marriage as 'restless and emotionally harrowing'.

Lowell's friend and collaborator Frank Bidart suggested that the Lowell/Hardwick relationship was a difficult one: 'Lizzie was supportive but she could be incredibly difficult too.' Bidart said of his time with them during the publication of Lowell's *Notebook*, 'They absolutely did not know how to talk to each other' (I should add here – in the interest of fairness – that Hardwick at least on one occasion revealed real antagonism toward Bidart.) Lowell's third marriage, to Blackwood, intense and chaotic, effectively ended shortly before Lowell's death in 1977 when he had returned, chastened, to New York to share his time with Hardwick.

Lowell was, after all, a thoroughly American poet, despite his grounding in the classics. It is evident in his thematic and prosodic preoccupations and his 'all-outness'. The trajectory of this Boston Brahmin's career had been from the explosive *Lord Weary's Castle* (1946) – an 'American version of heroic poetry' according to Frederick Seidel – to the epoch-making *Life Studies* (1959), which won the National Book Award and confirmed Lowell's status as the premier post-war American poet, a position which would be consolidated by *For the Union Dead* (1964) with its mix of public protest and private angst.

Problems had accelerated for Lowell when the 'tranquilized Fifties' turned into the divisive Sixties and the poet – by now a leading literary liberal conscience – became exhausted by the demands made upon him, as well as the wearying manic episodes. In a poem to their daughter, 'Harriet' (from *Notebook 1967–68*), he recorded with irony the premature ageing that had become his posture: the depredations of alcohol and cigarettes, the need for tablets and glasses, a reference to 'our leathery love'.

The commitment to protest continued when Lowell participated in the March on the Pentagon, his efforts lauded in Norman Mailer's *The Armies of the Night* (1968). Amused by the depiction, Lowell reported, 'Later, I wrote him I hoped we'd remain as good friends in life as we were in fiction.' In 1968 he moved less anonymously into politics, campaigning for his friend Eugene McCarthy in his bid for the Democratic nomination, and then becoming briefly intimate with Kennedy family members.

Some argued – in error I believe – that the first signs of Lowell's descent came in 1967 with *Near the Ocean,* which contained his last classic, overtly public poem, 'Waking Early Sunday Morning'. Then came the sonnet sequences of *Notebook 1967–68* and its various manifestations from 1969–1973. With Lowell, to write poetry was to publish and often rewrite and publish again. The unrhymed blank verse sonnets he adopted divided the critics, while he himself felt they allowed more latitude. The form 'can stride on stilts, or talk', he reported in interview. Equally importantly it could capture something of the flux of life and memory, with the division between public and private experience porous. So the poem 'Anne Dick 2. 1936' begins with the Anschluss, touches on Lowell's intention to marry and then – via the view from her family's bay window to M.I.T. – the painter Claude, Nero and Christ (I am reminded of Lowell's suggestion in a 1949 letter to George Santayana that for the 'cryptic' poems of his peers, 'It might be profitable to go into illogical associative structures.')

On leave from teaching at Harvard in 1970, the Lowells visited Italy. While Hardwick and their daughter Harriet returned to New York, Lowell flew to England to take up a fellowship at All Souls College, Oxford. He explained in conversation with Ian Hamilton in 1971 that this was no 'protest against conditions in America, though here there's more leisure, less intensity, fierceness. Everyone feels that; after ten years living on front lines, in New York, I'm rather glad to dull the glare.' The glare he referred to – the violence in the city itself – extended to strained race relations, the aggressive opposition to the Vietnam War that had polarized society, and his own dabbling in politics. Coming to England was tantamount to taking a vacation from his Furies, he reckoned. As he expressed it to Hardwick on arrival: 'Almost everyone understands how one would want to leave America temporarily.'

England, then, seemed to offer Lowell a breather – that is until a week after his arrival when he met Caroline Blackwood. This would be no passing infidelity. In her late short story, 'An Influx of Poets' – a thinly veiled recounting of her tempestuous early marriage to Lowell – Jean Stafford offered the shrewd insight that 'infatuation acquires its history and literature in minutes'. It seems to have been the case in Lowell's meeting with Blackwood. Appealingly aristocratic, a member of the Guinness family, Blackwood was also married for the second time. The thirty-eight year old, a self-destructive socialite and writer, remembered that after the Faber party in his honour Lowell moved into her Chelsea house in Redcliffe Square 'instantly, that night'. Subsequently he took up a teaching position at Essex University and two years later, after the birth of their child, they married.

The following year, 1973, *The Dolphin* appeared, bringing with it controversy that has lingered. *The Dolphin: Two Versions, 1972–1973* and *The Dolphin Letters, 1970–1979* (Farrar, Straus and Giroux, 2019), both edited by the indefatigable Saskia Hamilton, encourage the reader to explore the last seven years of Lowell's life. While the poems offer his view of events, the letters, like the biographies, redress the balance somewhat, giving Hardwick her own impressive voice. On the other hand Caroline Blackwood, whom the Lowells had known briefly in New York as a young mother of three, enters almost exclusively as subject (One might go to Nancy Schoenberger's *Dangerous Muse*, published in 2001, for a lively account of Blackwood's eventful life and 'ragged beauty.')

Critical attention was and still is focused on the use of Hardwick's letters and phone calls in *The Dolphin*, lines from which appear in some form or other in as many as fifteen of the poems. Most seem voiced by Lowell to shape the narrative. There is cold logic in a poet who is looking for verisimilitude in voicing his wife when writing about their break-up, though it is a temptation many would stifle as being a further betrayal. Hence Hardwick's anger. She would much later distance herself, referring to these poems as 'quite silly' and offering the sly observation that 'they seem to have been under the reign of Lowell's famous habit of revision'. Yet he had subtly altered what he took. Where in 'Marriage', for example, she is quoted as saying '*not that I wish you entirely well, far from it*', we learn from Hamilton that her line actually was, 'I don't entirely wish you well, far from it, of course.' While the casual reader may not notice, the poet has moved the 'entirely' to add force to it.

Why then did Lowell pursue publication when he knew the damage it could do to those he loved? The answer lies in a letter to Christopher Ricks in March 1972: 'My new book is a small one, some eighty poems in the meter of Notebook – the story of changing marriages, not a malice or sensation, far from it, but necessarily, according to my peculiar talent very personal. Lizzie is naturally very much against it. I am considering publication in about a year; it needn't be published, but I feel fully clogged by the possibility of not.'

As Mary McCarthy observed at the time, 'People in fact are sacrificed to *it* [the poetry], to keep the flame burning. It is a Jamesian subject, I guess.' To other friends Lowell's behaviour was also a second betrayal: Stanley Kunitz ('There are details which seem to me monstrously heartless'); Elizabeth Bishop ('*art just isn't worth that much*'). Adrienne Rich savaged the published collection in review ('bullshit eloquence, a poor excuse for a cruel and shallow book'). In response to Bishop's supportive but critical letter of March 21st, 1972, Lowell had remained wilfully blind, though he reported it to Bidart as 'a kind of masterpiece of criticism'. To him it seemed as much a technical as an ethical problem: 'I could say the letters are cut, doctored part fiction; I thought of it (I attribute things to Lizzie I made up, or that were said by someone else. I combed out abuse, hysteria, repetition.) The trouble is the letters make the book, I think, at least they make Lizzie real beyond my invention.'

It is difficult to tease the two Elizabeths apart. In 'Hospital 11' he writes as her, 'You left two houses and two thousand books, /

a workbarn by the ocean, and two slaves'. Although this is apparently a reference to an August 1970 letter in which Hardwick listed some of the things he would miss by not returning (apartment, work barn, friends) her words do not correlate with those in the poem and the 'slaves' comes from another context. Almost broken-hearted in 'Records', Lowell ventriloquizes Hardwick again, envisaging his future as an equivalent of her own past:

> you doomed to know what I have known with you,
> lying with someone fighting unreality –
> love vanquished by his mysterious carelessness.

And yet *The Dolphin* is nominally a celebration of the mythologized Blackwood. Re-reading it, I begin to wonder how much room it has to express the wonder of this new love. There is awe and there is joy, but these are compromised by the break-up of the old marriage, his responsibilities and all that is alien in a new life. The undertone is to be heard in 'Flight to New York': 'a feeling, / not wholly happy, of having been reborn'. Worst is the indecision because it cripples. Lowell sees himself as Hamlet in one poem. In 'On the End of the Phone' it is his hypocrisy, his 'side-stepping and obliquities' that defeat him.

In 'Doubt' he names his problem: 'From the dismay of my old world to the blank / new – water-torture of vacillation!' As if to confuse things, poems often recount dreams or move like dreams. There is a plethora of rhetorical questions ('What shall I do with my stormy life blown towards evening?') The poet is lost and not only in wonder ('If I cannot love myself, can you?') Then there is the concern about his adopted family ('how do I know I can keep any of us alive?) and, in another poem, a waking into tears.

All these concerns are contained within a plot, as Saskia Hamilton reminds us in her introduction to *The Dolphin: Two Versions*. The poet falls in love, undergoes a manic episode, leaves hospital, vacillates, flies to New York to see his current wife, then makes a choice and remarries. Somewhere in there he and his new companion have a baby. In the first version (the manuscript circulated to friends) the baby's arrival comes at the end, in the published version earlier, where it helps to clarify his thinking.

Reading the manuscript one can see the power of Lowell's first thoughts, for example, in placing the poem 'Burden' (essentially 'Marriage' in the published version) in the penultimate spot behind 'Dolphin'. Its last line 'Darling, / we have escaped our death-fight with our lives', allows the poet to turn in the final poem to his awe of his new love and rueful consideration of his own behaviour. Conventionally, the birth requires the marriage.

The manuscript version of the poem 'Dolphin' has Lowell's plea – rather Shakespearean – for indulgence for the book, after all he has acknowledged of himself and his behaviour ('yet ask compassion for this book, half fiction'). In final form the adverb 'yet' and 'this book' are omitted, the sense being now that he will ask no compassion for his *behaviour*. The published versions of key poems like 'Fishnet' and 'Dolphin' are clearly superior, however, and most readers would be satisfied with this published collection – its notoriety aside – since there is a limit to one's willingness to keep attending to changes.

'My old life settles down in the archives', he writes and 'archives' reminds us that Lowell is self-consciously writing about his writer's life as well as the lived one. In 'Dolphin' he refers again to 'this book, half fiction'. As Hamilton observes, 'He thinks of his pursuit of Caroline and of his own art as continuous.' We are dealing with an element of fiction, at least a tidying up of fact. In her preface to *American Fictions* (1999) Hardwick quoted Ivy Compton-Burnett on finding real life no help to a writer because it has no plot. Besides, as she remarked in an April 1972 letter to Lowell, 'We always think we are writing our autobiography, but life is not willing to assure us which part of ourselves is the main one, which action is telling and what it tells.' Lowell thought differently, but not too differently.

Throughout his so-called confessional career he was given to rewriting life where it suited. In a *Paris Review* interview of 1961, for instance, speaking of *Life Studies* he had told Frederick Seidel, the poems are 'not always factually true. There's a good deal of tinkering with fact. You leave out a lot, and emphasize this and not that. Your actual experience is a complete flux. I've invented facts and changed things, and the whole balance of the poem was something invented. So there's a lot of artistry, I hope, in the poems.' What counted, he went on to say, was that 'the reader was to believe he was getting the *real* Robert Lowell'. In 'Marriage', from 'The Dolphin', he admits, 'the fiction I colored with first-hand evidence, / letters and talk I marketed as fiction'.

Reading *The Dolphin Letters* we see there is something impressive in the way Hardwick endured the pain, humiliation and financial chaos resulting from their break, despite the occasional bitterness expressed. (The abuse, having been 'combed out' of the poems, must have been mostly edited out of the letters at some point, if Hardwick were to be believed when she told Ian Hamilton that she wrote lengthy vitriolic letters at the time.) Lowell too emerges with some eloquence and conscience, despite his wilful blindness. To Hardwick he writes on one occasion 'you couldn't have been more loyal and witty. I can't give you anything of equal value.' 'Not having you,' he writes in another letter, 'is like learning to walk.'

Since both were professional writers we should not be surprised at how intellectually vibrant and cultured each can be, even in distress, witty too. In the early letters we are reminded also of the busyness of such public figures ('The phone rings all day with meetings one could attend, plays one is urged to go to in the freezing night, an occasional unwanted invitation, malignant growths of mail, bills.') We learn of the impressive liberal commitment of both Lowells during the national handwringing about Vietnam and the outrage at Nixon's muddled and then criminal response to civil unrest. There is also a deal of agonising over money, taxes, over selling Lowell's papers (what to include, to which institution, for how much). Then 'book-keeping and housekeeping and child-raising details', all of which fell to Hardwick in Lowell's absence. There is also good old gossip ('character analysis' as Hardwick would wittily style it later) and interesting illustrations of social and political conditions in England and America at the time.

Emotionally, though, the early letters make excruciating reading: the knowledge that Lizzie's loving notes inspire only silence; then Lowell's uncharacteristic reticence followed by the inevitable leaking of the news of his affair; the realization that this is not simply another flirtation, followed by Lowell's equivocation as to the future. By the sixteenth letter, where Hardwick writes innocently about England, sounding delighted at the prospect of Lowell's current happiness and the imminent arrival of herself and daughter Harriet, the reader's heart sinks, knowing that Lowell has already moved in with Blackwood.

In a poignant prolonged series of exchanges, Lowell is clearly ambivalent about both relationships ('I too can't state my feelings even to myself. The past is almost more with me than today') and vacillates chronically. 'Maybe you could take me back,' he writes to Hardwick at one point, 'though I have done great harm'. Blackwood, being mostly at his side, rarely makes a direct appearance. She loves ('I think about you every minute of the day, and I love you every minute of the day') and is loved ('I've never been so happy, nor knew I could be,' writes Lowell) but appears almost exclusively as subject. Frank Bidart, in the Chapman interview, stressed that Lowell loved her very much even in his months when he returned to Hardwick 'though he couldn't live with her'. Even 'Caroline', a poem early in *The Dolphin*, reads like an epitaph.

Third party letters, those written to and from friends, help to give context in the wider world. Lowell seeks advice relating to his manuscript. Hardwick picks up the pieces, writing as she does frequently to Mary McCarthy. Immediately after the revelation of the affair with Blackwood she reports that she felt such relief and burst out laughing when she heard who he had chosen because 'I cannot take her seriously for Cal'. To Hardwick she is a chaotic home-wrecker. One thing Blackwood seems to have in common with her partner is carelessness. Weeks later Hardwick tells McCarthy, 'I believe one cannot win with Cal. He will spare you nothing, least of all that terrible breeziness and casualness about the deepest feelings of your own life and, also, of his own.'

Things are said back and forth. There is a great deal of suffering ('We are utterly miserable, unbelievably wounded.') Time passes. Hardwick grudgingly accepts the inevitable, focusing on the welfare of their daughter, Harriet, and resumes her own work: her writing and teaching. Slowly the two find another level for their relationship, built on the foundations of the years of their marriage. The arrival of Lowell and Blackwood's baby, Sheridan, breaks the uneasy peace. Then, with divorce, Lowell is naturally upset at the 'barracuda settlement' (the loss of the Castine, Maine, house they had inherited and his trust fund). It is publication of *The Dolphin* that does most harm. Though he assured her she would not 'feel betrayed or exploited' that is exactly what she feels, especially after the review by Marjorie Perloff in *New Republic*, which is a scathing indictment of Lowell's book, his 'taste' and his wife and daughter who 'seem to get no more than they deserve'.

Lowell acknowledges in a letter to Elizabeth Bishop that his 'sin (mistake) was in publishing'. His defence again – dramatically expressed on this occasion – is 'I couldn't bear to have my book (my life) wait inside me like a dead child.' If his misappropriations lead to a lawsuit, he tells his American editor, Robert Giroux, then he has no money to fight it. It does not, though Hardwick expresses her feeling in a letter to Bishop: 'somehow it has hurt me as much as anything in my life'.

Hardwick does not write for months. Eventually a new note enters the renewed correspondence: concern about Lowell's increasingly poor health. In December 1975 Hardwick writes to McCarthy of his premature ageing and his turn to acupuncture from lithium. There is a measure of harmony and of regret on his part. He writes of his last and poignant collection, *Day by Day*: 'Autobiography predominates, almost forty years of it. And now more journey of the soul in my new book.' Finally, with seemingly terminal problems in Lowell's relationship with Blackwood (fears of his mania and her drinking), he and Hardwick achieve a comradeship when he returns. As she explains to Mary McCarthy in mid-June 1977, 'We, together, are having a perfectly nice time, both quite independent and yet I guess dependent.' Three months later Lowell died.

I have been reading the poetry and the life of Robert Lowell for forty years (and writing on him for twenty). I thought for much of *The Dolphin Letters* that it, rather than *The Dolphin*, is 'the most unkindest cut of all'. True it dramatizes the issue of the boundaries of art and illustrates the process of composition. Yet these letters are shockingly intimate – not in a prurient sense – in a way that even biography cannot match. Biography protects the reader by offering an intermediary to do the prying. Here our only defence is to remind ourselves that the authors sold their story with their papers; they too made out of it. I refer once more to Hardwick's view, that it is all an 'appropriation':

> I can't tell you how I dread the future with biographies and *Lizzie*; to say nothing of "Cal" who will never be even touched with the truth of his own being and nature. Fortunately I'll be dead before most of them come. It is such a violation, like a wound.'

We readers are the intruders, the 'violators'. And there is something Lowell-like in the thought that for those of us who are still moved by the work of one of the great American poets of the twentieth century, then *The Dolphin* and *The Dolphin Letters* – once published – are inescapable.

JOHN BERRYMAN & ROBERT LOWELL: LETTERS FROM THE BOTTOM OF THE WORLD

In a June 1947 letter to Katharine White at *The New Yorker*, John Berryman suggested that, in comparing a passage in Robert Lowell's magisterial 'The Quaker Graveyard in Nantucket' to its source material in Melville, the magazine may have unintentionally given the suggestion that something time-honoured – the use one writer makes of another – might look like plagiarism. In defending his recent friend, Berryman signalled the supportive nature of what would characterize their long friendship, one built on admiration and empathy. Implicit would also be an energizing, if submerged, competitiveness and – shrouding it all – their bouts of mental instability.

Their correspondence – available in separately published collections – is essentially concerned with celebrating and commiserating on matters of poetry and health. There is assistance with employment efforts; talk of awards and news of the poetry scene; quotations from reviews; advice and arrangements to meet; and acknowledgements of the power of new directions in each other's work. In a word their correspondence provided encouragement.

Each poet confronted in himself the madness of the other (Lowell's bi-polar breakdowns, Berryman's alcoholism and incapacitating depressions). There is little doubt, for example, that Lowell was to a degree unnerved by Berryman's drive, since it mirrored his own. He referred to it in a letter to Adrienne Rich at the time of Berryman's suicide in January 1972: 'I was thinking of Berryman, his troubles and his power, and with what smash and vehemence he carries himself. It's too near me, I would crumble in a minute… Parts of his character are so close to me that I cannot look on him even in the imagination without a drowning feeling.'

On the other hand, the friendship – tortured at times – brought literary rewards. Although their poetic territory differed, Berryman acknowledged the influence of Lowell's *Lord Weary's Castle* in later poems from *The Dispossessed* and, of his *Homage to Mistress Bradstreet*, he explained, 'I sort of seized inspiration, I think, from Lowell, rather than imitated him.' And when Lowell came to free up his own metres and then turned to loose sonnets – from *Notebook 1967–1968* onward – he had the example of Berryman's groundbreaking experiments in *Bradstreet* and the *Dream Poems*. Paul Mariani, biographer of both Berryman (1990) and Lowell (1994), was clear on the point: 'In an unpublished draft of his "Afterthought" to the completed volume [*Notebook 1967–68*]… he would acknowledge Berryman's influence before erasing his tracks: "I can think of us working in much the same way: the intense shaping of a short section, free yet dependent, in that it pointed towards sections already written and suggested others half intuited.'

'What appealed,' according to Ian Hamilton, Lowell's first biographer, 'was the illusion of structure: the predetermined sectioning… the freedom to break lines at will, to be prosy, talkative, discursive, jokey, and yet still have the constraint of being "boxed up" by the "machinery" of a repeated line count.' Lowell saw early what would make Berryman's mature poetry so recognizable, if so different from his own: 'John could quote with vibrance to all lengths, even prose, even late Shakespeare, to show me what could be done with disrupted and mended syntax. This was the start of his real style.'

Their influence on each other, then, lay more in technique than in terrain. John Haffenden, in his biography *The Life of John Berryman* (1982), distinguished between the two when writing that he left it to time and study to answer the question of 'how much Lowell's work speaks to a sense of cultural and social history, and how much Berryman's is a function of moral and spiritual preoccupations'.

Both poets were relentlessly ambitious. Consequently,

competition drove them on. Berryman seemed ever to be aware that he stood partly in Lowell's shadow in the poetry world. In a letter of March 1963 he refers to friends and strangers calling him the greatest living American poet, 'as if it mattered and as if it weren't obvious that Lowell in fact is, since Mr. Frost's death, if it matters', which of course it did, to Lowell and Berryman at least. To his mother, Jill, he wrote of being perturbed with such comments: 'I've been comfortable since 1946 with the feeling that Lowell is far my superior... But now' others championed him. He adds, 'I can't tell what the story is. And we will never know. And who cares?' To Haffenden, Berryman's remained 'implacable, though innocuous, competitiveness'.

The 1940s proved to be the decade of the emergence of the two on the poetry scene. After leaving Harvard to study with Southern *Fugitives* Allen Tate and John Crowe Ransom, Lowell had married aspiring author Jean Stafford in 1940, converted to Catholicism, first volunteered and then refused conscription (serving five-months in prison), left the church, developed obsessive symptoms, and published his heralded *Lord Weary's Castle* in 1946. He would be hospitalized for the first time in 1949.

Early in his career. Berryman also suffered variously from ill health and professional uncertainty. In March 1942 Delmore Schwartz described the problem to his friend's Columbia mentor, Mark Van Doren, as 'some kind of hysteria. The fainting fits he has occur when he is spoken to sternly or contradicted'. He would publish his first collection, *Poems*, and marry that October.

Four years later the two met – the year in which he reviewed *Lord Weary's Castle*, concluding 'a talent whose ceiling is invisible'. The first significant reference to Lowell in *The Selected Letters of John Berryman* (2020) is in an April letter to Schwartz. It records their first meeting at a party at *The Nation* offices and his liking him 'extremely', despite his discomposure: 'I find I'm a fool at parties, they make me want to climb up the chimney with nervousness.' That July he suggested that he and his wife, Eileen, with Richard and Helen Blackmur, call for an overnight visit at the Lowell's Damariscotta Mills home in Maine, as Lowell had invited them to do.

Eileen Simpson wrote of the visit in her absorbing memoir of marriage to Berryman, *Poets in Their Youth* (1982). They had met Lowell and his novelist wife, Jean Stafford, on an earlier occasion, over an unsuccessful Princeton lunch with Caroline Gordon (Allen Tate's wife). This time, however, the two couples gelled and in the absence of the squabbling company of the Blackmurs, who withdrew from the visit, they remained a fortnight, the poets exhausting themselves in poetry discussion, quotation and literary gossip. Berryman delighted at the visit with Lowell and the entertaining Stafford. He would tell his mother that he had not met 'anyone so pleasant since Delmore in 1939', though his own marriage would effectively end a couple of months later.

As Simpson indicates in her book, the two poets had a great deal in common aside from their complete commitment to poetry. They were both impractical, as well as being short-sighted. Each suffered mood swings and had endured a domineering and disappointed mother. Their fathers had been ineffectual (Berryman's a suicide). To both, the advocacy and influence of Allen Tate was intermittently important. Later, infidelity, breakdowns and alcoholism would be added to this grim list.

On February 13, 1948, Berryman recorded four poems for the Library of Congress in Lowell's office there, Lowell being Consultant in Poetry (U.S. Poet Laureate) for the year. Over the weekend they visited Ezra Pound in St. Elizabeth's Hospital near Washington, where he had been incarcerated after his wartime fascist broadcasts. An exchange of letters in March 1948 described the fall-out from that Washington weekend. Lowell had misunderstood Berryman's interest, assuming he preferred to hear *his* work rather than have Berryman's read. As the latter noted placatingly, 'I took it as a corollary of your work, and got used to it. Friends anyway, with exceptions, don't read friends'. Lowell offered in reply the apology, 'I do intend to read your new poems with friendly care and be one of [the] exceptions who does read his friend's work. Randall & Ransom agree with me that they're a great stylistic development.' Lowell also apologized for making him what he described as a 'link' at the time of the visit, since Berryman had also met with Jean Stafford and Gertrude Buckman who, as former lovers, naturally discussed Lowell with him.

Replying to the April gift of Berryman's second collection, *The Dispossessed*, in late August 1948, Lowell wrote with slightly puzzled admiration: 'The new difficult poems seem to me the most wonderful advance that anyone has made. I rather agree with Randall [Jarrell] that they exist in bits and passages... You seem to have the equipment to do almost anything now. I think it needs to be docked in some overwhelming and unifying object.' He added carefully, 'Maybe this is stupid criticism.'

There are letters in November/December 1953 – the year of the breakthrough collection *Homage to Mistress Bradstreet* – regarding Berryman's deputizing for Lowell's second term at the Iowa Writers' Workshop the following year, which turned out disastrously. In October 1954 Lowell wrote consolingly, sidestepping the alcoholic dimension of Berryman's dismissal (and rescue by the University of Minnesota): 'You got a lousy deal, and it looks as though the whole business was impossible from the start this fall... You are too good a writer to fit their system, and too much of a scholar and professional teacher to find much in a stop-gap job. I can see that Minnesota is a hundred times better, and am awfully glad all has ended serenely.'

Serenity would hardly last. Lowell wrote again at the news of Berryman's second marriage, in March 1957, to a graduate student, Elizabeth Ann Levine. The marriage lasted less than three years, pushing Berryman further into alcoholic turmoil, though his teaching continued to be either brilliant or a little distressing, depending on the perspectives of his students. On March 15, 1959, Lowell wrote supportively, just before Berryman's divorce and with the latter recently out of hospital. He mentioned the troubles poets of their generation had to live with and turned to admiring some of the more recent poems in the pamphlet, *His Thought Made Pockets & the Plane Buckt* (1958). He felt they had 'a strange heart-cutting poet *maudit* and late Elizabethan tragedy quality'. He wondered – as he always did – 'if you need so much twisting, obscurity, archaisms, strange word orders, &-signs for *and*, etc.? I guess you do. Surely, here as in the *Bradstreet*, you have your voice. It vibrates and makes the heart ache.' Lowell acknowledged that writing in this 'graveyard way' seemed ironic, given the Berryman's reputation ('from all we hear you are top of the world, stunning audiences, milling our work'). He ended the letter in the hope that Berryman could attend the publication party for *Life Studies*.

Berryman replied in spring 1959 with an alarming, 'I've been so sick & sunk in misery since I got out of hospital, and there too, I haven't been able to write any letters or anything except some sections of my poem and a short poetry review a magazine wanted… I can't thank you properly yet for yr good letter abt my little book, much less write properly about your big one.'

Lowell could be particularly empathetic to friends in mental distress and in September wrote (in words that echo his support for the troubled Theodore Roethke), 'we have gone through the same troubles, visiting the bottom of the world. I have wanted to stretch out a hand, and tell you that I have been there too, and how it all lightens and life swims back.' He commiserated on Berryman's separation from his son, Paul, reminisced about Berryman's impact in performance, of his current poetry, their meetings and years of 'fellow feeling'. His letter ends with, 'I still haven't at all said what I want to, but our hearts are with you and we love you very dearly.'

When buoyed by both poets inclusion in Al Alvarez's *The New Poetry* anthology in 1962, Berryman remembered his own contribution to Lowell's success. To Edward Hoagland he wrote, 'I try to remember that I helped him in Maine on the proofs of Lord Weary fifteen years ago & helpt make his Amer. reputation

w. an endless review in Partisan & held his hand many times, between marriages (his & mine)'. In a 'Note' prefacing *For the Union Dead* (1964) Lowell acknowledged, '"Beyond the Alps" is the poem I published in *Life Studies*, but with a stanza restored at the suggestion of John Berryman.' That stanza begins, with characteristic Lowellian relish: 'I thought of Ovid. For in Caesar's eyes / that tomcat had the Number of the Beast'.

Berryman's current state, however, seemed pitiable to Lowell who described it to Elizabeth Bishop as 'utterly spooky, teaching brilliant classes, spending week-ends in the sanitarium, drinking, seedy a little bald, often drunk, married to a girl of twenty-one from a Catholic parochial college, white, innocent beyond belief, just pregnant'.

In September 1963 Berryman wrote him a short letter reporting that he had taken Lowell's advice at long last and sent his editor, Robert Giroux, seventy-seven of the hundred Dream Songs they had talked about. He added with affected humility, 'But why publish verse anyway? It's all right for you to do, but why the rest of us?' The two read together on the 31st October, 1963, at the Guggenheim Museum, where Lowell expressed his admiration, calling Berryman one of the three poets people were now talking about (the others being Theodore Roethke and Sylvia Plath – neither of whom would live another year). He commented on the fact that obscure poetry, such as that of Hart Crane, William Empson and Dylan Thomas, had seemingly been replaced in popularity by more accessible work until Berryman's came along and made the prevailing clarity seem 'tired' and 'mannered'.

Berryman had less cause to be satisfied by his friend's reception of *77 Dream Songs*. Lowell reviewed it in *The New York Review of Books* (May 28, 1964), referring to it as 'a conglomeration of high style, Berrymanisms, Negro [sic] and beat slang, and baby talk'. He acknowledged his mystification: 'After a while, the repeated situations and their racy jabber become more and more enjoyable, although even now I wouldn't trust myself to paraphrase accurately at least half the sections.' Lowell ends his review of this 'sloppier' book with a recognition of its power to unsettle, missing something of its comic dimension: 'As it stands, the main faults of this selection are the threat of mannerism, and worse – disintegration… And yet one must give in. All is risk and variety here.'

Having read the proofs Berryman requested his editor Robert Giroux to intervene. Elsewhere he wrote, 'I expected only the perfunctory from Allen [Tate] and so am not disapp't'd, but I could not foresee that both Cal & Mark [Van Doren] – in many words & in few – would wholly fail Henry… For many reasons he never should have reviewed the book – for one, he does not understand it AT ALL – he thinks Henry is only 'one' of the characters and thinks Mr. Bones is distinct fr. H.' A permissible blunder, we might think, though not nearly as trying as the continuing eliding of poet and protagonist. Lowell dutifully published a correction in a letter to the *NYRB*.

The mitigating factor may have been Lowell's uncertainty about his feelings about the book at that time. Privately he had confessed to Randall Jarrell he thought *Bradstreet* his friend's best work and had described *Dream Songs* to Bishop in April as follows: 'The poem is spooky, a maddening work of genius, or half genius, in John's later obscure, tortured, wandering style, full of parentheses, slang no one ever spoke, jagged haunting lyrical moments etc.' To William Meredith, late in the year, he had written of his 'uncertainty and distress' at reading the book. Yet he hedged his bets: 'A handful of the songs now seem part of what we are proudest of.' His last comment on *77 Dream Songs* came in his obituary for Berryman in 1972, where he mentioned having 'misjudged them', having been 'rattled by their mannerisms'.

Lowell wrote to Berryman on March 10, 1966, the year after Berryman received the Pulitzer Prize, about the latter's reminiscences for *Randell Jarrell: 1914–1965*, a collection Lowell, Peter Taylor and Robert Penn Warren had edited for publication the following year. He mentioned the memorial service and reminisced, urging Berryman to take care of his 'fragile' health ('If anything happened to you, I'd feel the heart of the scene had gone.') Earlier in the same short letter, Lowell refers to what Berryman had offered in his poetry: 'freedom for us too, if we had the nerve'. The line rings with sensitivity to Berryman's gift of outlandishness.

Lowell sent a telegram that September calling Berryman's 'Op. Posth.' series which were appearing in print 'a tremendous & living triumph', though to Elizabeth Bishop he worried that the poems 'really seem ex humo, from beyond the tomb. I thought he was gone, but the experience seems to have resurrected him'. They met two years later for a memorial reading for Jarrell, Roethke and Schwartz and that September, responding to *His Toy, His Dream, His Rest* (1968), Lowell offered a comment on what they shared: 'rough iambic lines... short sections that are not stanzas; wife, wives, child, old flames, new ones, sex, love, loves...'. What he liked, he said, 'is your ease in getting out everything – I mean everything in your experience, learning, thought, personality etc... mills thru the poetry.' He then pointed to the crucial difference that Berryman's world was 'rather more comic.'

It was Berryman's turn in September 1969, after 'your formidable and gorgeous' *Notebook 1967–68*. His initial reservations, he wrote, had been that, 'I suppose I always expect you to come on like King Kong and in this poem you often don't.' He had worried about chattiness in the poems and the form ('the expectation of rhyme'). All were reservations he dropped, he said, at a second reading. Lowell's reply came four days later. They had just returned from a summer in Castine, Maine. He expressed his usual concern about his friend's health, mentioned the twenty or so new poems and Berryman's appearing in the 'Advocate', ending with a wish to meet up and acknowledging Berryman's praise as most important to him.

Then everything changed for Lowell. The final letter to Berryman published in *The Letters of Robert Lowell* is from the following December, written on a visit home to Lizzie and Harriet. He gives his London address, since he had now moved in with Caroline Blackwood. This time, in praising Berryman's *Love and Fame* (1971), he singled out the prayer 'Eleven Addresses to the Lord', describing it as 'one of the great poems of the age… Along with your posthumous poems, to my mind, the crown of your work.' We could perhaps read this judgment as motivated by discomfort. They met again, unsatisfactorily, before Berryman's suicide.

Lowell's obituary for his friend appeared in the *NYRB* on March 30th, 1972. To Elizabeth Hardwick he wrote sadly: 'I was on a program for him in London. It centered on a movie interview with Alvarez – John, close-up, just off drunkenness, mannered, booming, like an old fashioned star professor. His worst. I think of the young, beardless man, simple, brilliant, the enthusiast… buried somewhere with the older.'

Eileen Simpson described her reason for divorcing Berryman as 'his need to live in turbulence'. Lowell's obituary does not dwell on his friend's incapacitating alcoholism and ragged lifestyle, though it does chime with his aggressive obsessiveness. It offers a nuanced portrait with anecdotes: of a visit with Jarrell for an unsuccessful dinner at the Berryman home; the trip to visit Pound at St. Elizabeth's; and that final meeting in New York a year or so before his death. Lowell's portrait offers two views of Berryman, the first from his early days ('humorous, learned, thrustingly vehement in liking') and then later, 'As he became more inspired and famous and drunk, more and more John Berryman, he became less good company and more a happening.'

Lowell stressed their commitment to poetry in 'For John Berryman 1': 'I feel I know what you have worked through, you / know what I have worked through – we are words; / John, we used the language as if we made it.' Finally, nostalgically, 'For John Berryman' appeared in Lowell's last book, *Day by Day* (1977). Had the order of their deaths been reversed,

Berryman might have written of Lowell and himself as he had written for Jarrell:

> In the chambers of the end we'll meet again
> I will say Randall, he'll say Pussycat
> and all will be as before
> whenas we sought, among the beloved faces,
> eminence and were dissatisfied with that
> and needed more.
> Op. posth. no.13

EDMUND WILSON & ROBERT LOWELL: BUNNY & CAL

Edmund Wilson and Robert Lowell met in Cambridge, Massachusetts, at the beginning of April 1957. It was to be – from time to time – both an inspirational and a supportive friendship. Wilson had long before established a considerable reputation, though he lived in danger of its being marginalized. Lowell, on the other hand, was still building his. The forty year old Lowell, a decade after his Pulitzer Prize for *Lord Weary's Castle*, had become a well-connected force on the poetry scene, currently teaching at Boston University. He was also moving toward completion of his ground-breaking *Life Studies*, which would appear to considerable acclaim in 1959.

Wilson, a formidable critic since 1922, had published a succession of critical works, novels and plays, which included his well-timed introduction to Modernism, *Axel's Castle* (1931); his Marxist-Freudian readings in *The Triple Thinkers* (1938) and *The Wound and the Bow* (1941); his study of socialism, *To the Finland Station* (1940); and essays collected as *Classics and Commercials: A Literary Chronicle of the Forties* (1950) and *The Shores of Light: A Literary Chronicle of the Twenties and Thirties* (1952). The year before the two met *A Piece of My Mind: Reflections at Sixty* had appeared. It included an autobiographical glance in which Wilson portrayed himself as a man resolutely behind the times ('I have ceased to try to see at first hand what is happening in the United States, and my movements are all along a regular beat, which enables me to avoid things that bore or annoy me.') He did not acknowledge there his deep commitment to what would be his controversial *magnum opus*, *Patriotic Gore* (1962), a highly atmospheric study of the literature of the Civil War and the lives of some of its white participants.

The meeting of the two men occurred during the Wilsons' four months in Cambridge, where the critic worked in the Harvard library and spent time browsing local book stores. He took to the poet immediately, as was recorded in *The Fifties: From Notebooks and Diaries of the Period* (1986): 'Pleasant to see someone – Lowell – who is more like the friends of my youth and not like the Partisan Review et al.' The 'et al' doubtless included some members of the Harvard faculty, since Wilson expressed initial disquiet at the 'traditional mannerisms for the Harvard intellectuals', which according to him included a thrusting head, a pointing finger, and a way of disguising the passion in the voice. Six years later he remained dismissive of all. In a comment praising George Saintsbury's *Miscellaneous Essays*, which he had picked up at Blackwell's in Oxford, he wrote: 'If these essays were ever read by the Partisan Review boys and the other New York writers of the same breed, they would either not understand them or, if they did, be reduced to despair.'

Common interests drew Lowell and Wilson to each other: the classics and American history, literature and literary gossip, a revulsion and fascination with wars and outspoken pacificism, the state of the nation and, shortly after, each other's work. They both exhibited a confidence, a decisiveness of tone in their writing, plus a similar (fallen) world picture. And as Jeffrey Meyers explained, in *Edmund Wilson: A Biography* (1995), Wilson 'admired Lowell's imaginative strength, rhetorical force and technical skill', while Lowell admired Wilson's imperiousness, his knowledge, his exhaustive reading and his thirty-five years as America's pre-eminent literary critic. Not incidentally, they both had New England worthies among their ancestors, whose influence manifested itself often as a kind of indifference of manner, courteous at least in Lowell' s case. They also shared a fondness for drink and pursuing women.

Wilson now divided his time between living with his fourth wife, Elena, in 'two-old fashioned country towns' – Wellfleet, Massachusetts, and Talcottville, New York – with sojourns in New York City and Boston. While he may have written in his latest book that 'Old fogeyism is comfortably closing in', this might have been his response to the institutionalization of criticism in the universities, which had left Wilson – ever an independent – on the outside. He prized the continuity of his life circumstances, he wrote, but no longer 'bothered with the kind of contemporary conflicts that I used to go out to explore'. He preferred, he reckoned, to return to the classics than keep up with the younger American writers. This again was in part a pose, since for one thing he took an active interest in such poets as Lowell, John Berryman and Elizabeth Bishop.

Wilson's work provided occasional topics in Lowell's correspondence with Bishop. In a January 1957 letter she responded to the autobiographical reflections at sixty by noting that she shared his view at forty-five and worried how she would be when reaching his age. Many years later, reading his *The Cold War and the Income Tax,* she mentioned being struck by the fact that Wilson had 'such a funny naïve streak', an understandable view given his intransigence (or negligence) with regard to filing tax returns. On another occasion Lowell wrote admiringly of Wilson's 'terrific review' of Pasternak in the *New Yorker* in November 1958.

The events of Lowell's disturbed life inevitably provided endless speculation for his friends, including Wilson, who was not above sharing the occasional titbit about marital discord and the Lowells. In April 1961 he informed Mary McCarthy that Cal (Lowell) and Elizabeth (Hardwick) were living separately now that Lowell had come out of hospital. In February 1967 he was telling an Anchor Doubleday editor, Clelia Caroll – on whom he had a Wilsonian, therefore engulfing, crush – 'Robert Lowell, the poet – a manic depressive – is in a Boston hospital and can only be seen when he is out "on parole"'.

Their convivial get-togethers also provided anecdotes of alcohol-fuelled evenings. On October 25, 1957, Lowell wrote to Bishop of a drunken party at the Schlesingers, of Wilson's talking of being a Calvinist and how the Lowells planned a visit to Wellfleet about two weeks hence. To J.F. Powers he reported after the event: 'What a visit. Wilson drinks like an ox, like Ted Roethke, and yet it does no harm. Only at about 11:30, he becomes rather speechless. The rest of the time conversation pours back and forth. I know no one who has read so much and is so good company about what he has read.' Again literary gossip seasoned with admiration.

On his part it took Wilson some time to appreciate that there might be a dangerous side to Lowell's enthusiasm. The poet appears in Wilson's *The Fifties* in this light in December 1957 when Edmund and Elena Wilson returned a visit to the Lowells. Initially, Lowell's company took him back to heady days: 'I was so pleased to find someone who talked like an old friend of the twenties – I kept telling him that I was a man of the twenties.' What Wilson meant by that is explained in *The Sixties: The Last Journal 1960–1972* (1993). When ruminating on Hemingway's suicide in 1961 he offers a definition: 'As a character in one of Chekhov's plays says he's "a man of the eighties" so I find that I am a man of the twenties. I still expect something exciting: drinks, animated conversation, gaiety: an uninhibited exchange of ideas.'

In considering Lowell as a friend of the twenties, then, Wilson meant high praise: 'he seemed to me perfect'. There were 'accelerating conversations, going off in all directions, interrupting one another,' he reported. They shared 'a range of interest and reading, flares of imagination, general freedom of the world. I didn't know that he was getting into his manic phase.'

Wilson's comments came after an impromptu and notorious party where he certainly saw the effects of Lowell's bipolar condition. In his account Wilson described the poet as being 'very exhilarated' after having recently returned from a reading in the South. He had confided to the Wilsons about a student he was sleeping with who looked 'like a Renoir' and urged Wilson to join him for dinner with the girl. He also discussed having $50,000 above his income to invest and later 'latched on' to Elena Wilson at lunchtime in the famous Parker House Hotel, effectively coercing her to spend the afternoon in his company.

Returning via an Episcopal church that had figured in his childhood, he began phoning people for dinner and drinks, including his 'Renoir'. Elizabeth Hardwick managed to put some of the invited guests off, being greatly concerned by Lowell's state. Nevertheless their 'dinner party' was soon oversubscribed. 'It was already impossible for him to talk to everybody without flying off into a "free association."' Included among the guests were Robert Frost and his wife, invited for devilment, Wilson assumed, since he had told Lowell he felt the old poet to be "a dreadful old fake". I.A. Richards, another guest, observed to Wilson that he could see Lowell 'was getting perverse and mischievous'. Elizabeth, upset, retired upstairs, and Lowell's 'Renoir', doubtless out of her depth, attempted to play hostess to the Schlesingers and the like.

Lowell's biographer, Ian Hamilton, talked to Dido Merwin – at times a disputed memoirist – then wife of poet W.S. Merwin. In Hamilton's *Robert Lowell: A Biography* (1982) she remembered the party: 'There was a table covered in glasses and Cal came up to this corner where a number of us were circulating, including Lizzie [Hardwick], and he sat down in a chair and dashed the glasses off the table with his feet and sat there, with his feet on the drinks table, surrounded by broken glass… There were punch-ups. There were insults. And Cal was just going round like the devil putting people against each other. It was the most extraordinary party – an absolute triumph for Cal… The extraordinary thing was that nobody seemed to realize he was mad.'

The behaviour certainly made an impression on the Wilsons and on Boston generally. In *The Sixties*, Wilson again refers to that evening and how it was immediately known about in Boston and Cambridge. (He also learnt that Lowell was aware of whatever was going on in Wilson's seminar. The master gossiper, while briefly in academia, had found an equal.)

The morning after the party Lowell remained high. At breakfast he talked at the same time as Wilson, saying it was a custom the other would recognise. He then intruded on the critic's rest, 'almost naked and covered with black hair, carrying an immense set of Macaulay's *History*, which he dumped on me – having discovered at breakfast that I had never read it – and announced that it was a present in return for the *Ingoldsby Legends* I had given him.'

The chapter in *The Fifties* featuring Lowell ends with a curiously childlike simplicity: 'Elizabeth took him to the doctor's, and we did not see them again. He was in hospitals most of the time from then till March. When I saw him again, he was quiet and orderly. Elizabeth said she hoped he was good for four years more.'

A manic episode would not be enough to distance the two men. They would enjoy each other's company over the years, whenever their schedules allowed. So, for instance, Lowell reported to Bishop in December 1958, that they had driven to Wellfleet from Boston for what another Lowell biographer, Paul Mariani, described as 'their annual "boozy" Wellfleet weekend in November, when Wilson, "loaded to the gills," discoursed eloquently on Pasternak and Mosby's Civil War memoirs.'

During an earlier visit Lowell had inscribed his poem 'Children of Light' on Wilson's Wellfleet window pane – a custom offered favoured guests. On May 19, 1959, he sent a new version to be diamond-pointed. This one came from McLean psychiatric hospital in Boston where Lowell was recovering from a manic episode. In the accompanying note, he declared himself feeling well 'and looking forward to tanking up again on your conversation'. As Harwick explained to Bishop later in the month, her husband had been busy 'doing poor rewritings of all his early poems in preparation for a Collected'. Wilson thanked Lowell for the poem and added diplomatically, 'When you come up here again, you must engrave it below the other one.'

On Lowell's part the friendly notes continued. In December of the following year he wrote to Wilson as critic and amateur magician: 'I've lately met about ten Englishmen who have been in

Boston. They all feel you are *the* living person in your new northern world. Or perhaps in any world – their reverence is incredible, though of course deserved. Meanwhile we sorely miss you [and] Elena. Wouldn't you like to come down here and perform for Harriet's birthday party on January 7th?' Wilson apologised for not being able to attend. Perhaps in recompense, at the end of the year he invited the Lowells to attend his Punch and Judy show, which he had made 'into a great ritual drama'.

Their most public meeting took place on May 11th, 1962, at the White House dinner, to which one hundred and sixty eight guests were gathered for an event hosted by the President and Mrs Kennedy in honour of André Malraux, writer, diplomat and recent recipient of the Nobel Prize. The Lowells, Tates and Warrens were among the invited, which also included Saul Bellow and Andrew Wyeth ('who has become the approved official American painter', Wilson noted). It was the occasion at which Kennedy quipped that there were more brains assembled that evening in the dining room of the White House than [at] any time since Thomas Jefferson dined alone.

Wilson naturally reported on the dinner. His wife, Elena, enjoyed a certain scepticism concerning the event, which Wilson ascribed to her 'atavistic reactions… The women of her mother's family were ladies in waiting at the Tsarina's court, and her grandfather was the Tsar's ambassador in Tokyo, The Hague and Washington.' Afterwards she had reportedly been unimpressed by the behaviour and dress of a number of people there, though she supposed events such as these were a good thing as 'they made those people take a bath for the first time'.

In a letter of mid-May, Lowell sketched the occasion for Elizabeth Bishop's amused cynicism: 'The White House! 200 guests, about a third maybe I think actually known to us – Schlesinger, absolutely top of the world squiring the Kennedy sisters, MacLeish, who told me the trumpets made his heart beat, New York types like Mark Rothko, Bundy drunk, Mrs. Lindbergh, Red Warren with whom I had a frantic search for the men's room, everyone rather drunk after dinner and cocktails and 3 wines and then more champagne, having to be told to give up their champagne and cigarettes and listen to Stern and Istomin play a long Schubert trio – and next morning we read that the President had ordered our 7th fleet to Laos. It was fun and a ball, but I think we all seemed rather silly, little colored bits of frosting.'

At the end of the month Lowell wrote to Wilson 'a little fan note after Washington. Except for you, everyone there seemed addled with adulation at having been invited.' He mentioned the 7th fleet again, adding 'I feel we intellectuals play a very pompous and frivolous role – we should be windows, not window-dressing... I thought of all the big names there, only you acted like yourself.' Despite the rather good image of window and window dressing, his report on the evening to Bishop does not mention Wilson, who had apparently so impressed him with his behaviour. Perhaps we might attribute that to his desire to flatter the other for remarks Wilson had recently made on Lowell's work ('I am very set up by your *New Yorker* interview. The part on me is a wonderful piece of picture – writing and judgment, and along with two early essays by Jarrell moves me more than anything that has been written on me').

Lowell had every reason to be thrilled by the remarks of such a regularly discerning critic – if one who tended at times to play favourites. 'As for poetry,' Wilson had written, 'aside from the older poets, the only one I really read is Robert Lowell'. Lowell has captured, materially and spiritually the 'dinginess and ugliness and vulgarity' of Boston, he said, adding, 'He is, I think, the only recent American poet – if you don't count Eliot – who writes successfully in the language and cadence and rhyme of the resounding English tradition.'

He then linked Lowell with Auden as standing alone within the English tradition and, given their 'stature' and ambition, 'they also have big enough talents to achieve poetic careers on the old nineteenth-century scale'. He also defended Lowell's license in his book of versions of European poets, *Imitations*. This defence had been particularly appreciated, since the book had 'got such a mauling from the popular reviewers', the poet acknowledged. By way of conclusion here Wilson paid fanciful praise to Elizabeth Bishop, which by default confirmed Lowell's status once again ('not a poet on Lowell's scale, but her poetry is perfectly delightful').

Lowell had had the opportunity to read a pre-publication copy of Wilson's *Patriotic Gore*. After having just taken a ten day vacation with his family to Puerto Rico, he wrote to Wilson on March 31, 1962, approving of his blistering attack on American foreign and domestic policy, which many believed an ill-fitting introduction – as an introduction – to *Patriotic Gore*'s celebration of American fortitude during the Civil War (though it is in-keeping with his theme of the abuse of American power). Lowell described this 'triumphant' book as 'a sort of Plutarch's Lives'.

The two men had never been closer in their preoccupations with the American experience. Lowell's own family had connection with that war, and he had read his 'For the Union Dead' before several thousand people in the Boston Public Garden in June, 1960, at the Boston Arts Festival. The poem deals in part with Saint-Gaudens's civil war bronze bas-relief of the doomed Colonel Robert Shaw and his black troops, killed at Fort Wagner. Shaw had been related by marriage to Lowell's abolitionist ancestor, remembered as a 'Beau Sabreur'.

Patriotic Gore also unfortunately resonated with Lowell's state of mental health later. On his trip to South America, supported by the Congress for Cultural Freedom in June 1962, Lowell re-read Wilson's book before he left New York. With its focus on power, courage and violence, it helped to fuel a manic episode. According to Ian Hamilton, 'Lowell spoke of the book throughout the trip; although as he got higher he became more thrilled than repelled by the "menace" of American imperialism.'

Lowell's career as a dramatist proved much more successful that Wilson's. The latter tried on numerous occasions, before consigning his playwriting to print in *Five Plays* (despite the wonderfully flat title of one: 'This Room and This Gin and These Sandwiches'). Lowell had some stage success with his 'Phaedra', 'Prometheus Bound', 'The Oresteia' and especially with 'The Old Glory', two thirds of which Jonathan Miller directed at the American Place Theater in 1964, winning five Obie awards.

In autumn 1964 Wesleyan University, Connecticut, had put on an essentially student production of a Lowell play. The Wilsons were in town for the rehearsals when they took a call from Richard Wilbur and his wife, warning that Lowell was high: 'It was like hurricane warnings on the Cape' wrote Wilson. They found, sitting next to the Lowells at the dress rehearsal, that he was indeed 'speeding up', talking uninterruptedly around the performance. Fortunately for Wilson he later had a perfectly normal conversation with Lowell over dinner.

When they met again at New Year, Lowell had apparently been 'heavily toned down with tranquillizers'. Wilson writes of how his wife felt uneasy in Lowell's presence: 'He has established a relation with her, as he does with everybody, and she worried about him afterwards.' There soon followed gossip about Lowell's living with a Latvian dancer named Vija Vetra, though by late September, when Wilson dined with them at the Princeton, the Lowells were reunited.

The poet reappears in *The Sixties* journal the following January when Wilson reported on a dinner at their home, with an uncharacteristically quiet Norman Mailer and a Japanese novelist: 'Cal [Lowell] had just emerged from wherever he had been. He was subdued and seemed aged, going gray; had just been going through a crisis of changing his analyst. This time, when he had gone off the deep end, he had bought for, I think, $3,000 a life-size statue of Tecumseh and had it painted red.' Then, in New York in mid-November 1966 Wilson recorded another meeting, one which 'restored my morale'. At this, Lowell paid the older man 'extravagant compliments: how much I meant to him, how much he had learned from me; that we were both "conservative radicals"'. Wilson had also gleaned that in Lowell's opinion Jarrell had committed suicide in North Carolina on October 14, 1965, when struck by a car at dusk, despite his wife's assertion to the contrary. Lowell also felt, he added, that Berryman 'would not last very long, was drinking heavily'.

Their occasional dinners continued. In February 1967 Wilson recorded finding Lowell a little more of a task: 'Cal at the dinner table was always as usual going off on a conversational tangent – though he often says brilliant things, this makes him rather difficult to talk to.' There is a note from November 5th of a dinner with Jason and Barbara Epstein (editors and founding co-directors, with the Lowells, of *The New York Review of Books*), Lillian Hellman, and the Wilsons. Lowell recounted his adventures on the Pentagon march with Mailer, Dwight Macdonald and 50,000 others in a protest against the Vietnam War ('Cal said that it had been one of the fine moments of his life'). The last sighting in Edmund Wilson's memoirs is in that same month when he reported that Lowell 'has found some drug' to stabilize his condition. Then, in March 1970, Lowell left America with Hardwick and their daughter. What began as an Italian holiday ended in divorce two years later. Lowell and Wilson did not meet again.

In *Robert Lowell: Interviews and Memoirs* (1988), Jeffrey Meyers quotes a letter of June 20, 1972 from Lowell to his editor Robert Giroux eight days after Wilson's death at the age of seventy-seven: 'My good angel must have told me to write Edmund, out of a blue sky, about three weeks before his death; I had an answer saying he had just had a stroke. He must have somewhat recovered to get to Talcottville. I'm re-reading almost all his books since I came back to England – he's the best bridge maybe for an American in Europe, and so much of him reads like great short stories for novels. Good-bye, dear old man!' Lowell was to die five years later.

ALFRED KAZIN & ROBERT LOWELL: A WARY FRIENDSHIP

Over the course of thirty years Kazin (1915–1998) and Lowell (1917–1977) learned to appreciate each other's considerable talent, despite their personal and political differences. After early setbacks, Kazin proved frequently effusive in his praise of Lowell – in public and in private – as we see from his books and *Journals* (2011). After the poet's death he would concede certain weaknesses in the work and particularly in the man. For Lowell, on the other hand, Kazin provided an interesting, discriminating reader and a friendly audience.

Kazin, the radical critic, and Lowell, the conservative poet ('I have never been a Liberal tho I have a liberal vein') shared an absorption in American history, which they romanticized in their different ways. The son of impoverished Jewish immigrants, Kazin saw America as rich with promise, though a promise perilously close at times to being broken. His greats were the isolated literary radicals of the nineteenth century – Emerson, Thoreau, Whitman and Melville – outsiders like himself.

> The past, the past was great: anything American, old, glazed, touched with dusk at the end of the nineteenth century, still smoldering with the fires lit by the industrial revolution, immediately set my mind dancing (*A Walker in the City*)

Lowell, a patrician New Englander, was also a patriot, but one who in his early work seemed to relish castigating America as a fallen world, rich in sin and violence, and in need of redemption:

> Our fathers wrung their bread from stocks and stones
> And fenced their gardens with the Redman's bones;
> Embarking from the Nether Land of Holland,
> Pilgrims unhouseled by Geneva's night,

They planted here the Serpent's seeds of light
    ('Children of Light')

A formidable networker, supportive of his many correspondents, Lowell kept a close eye on the literary scene, which included critic friends like Randall Jarrell, Allen Tate, William Empson, Al Alvarez, Edmund Wilson and his literary heir, Kazin. He prided himself on not losing any friendships (the delusional Delmore Schwartz's aside). As he remarked in a letter to Elizabeth Bishop in 1959, 'I think, perhaps I have more warm intellectual friends than anyone... But it's like walking on eggs. All of them have to be humored, flattered, drawn out, allowed to say very petulant things to you.' On occasion Lowell could even summon his part-Jewishness as a credential ('I'm one-eighth Jewish myself, which I do feel is a saving grace.') Despite his positive pronouncements on Jewish cultural influence, one comment obviously rankled with Kazin, since he referred to it twice in published work: 'Only Lowell was capable of saying of Jewish writers who were just as saturated in American life and literature as himself: "They have finally unloaded their European baggage."'

It is perhaps unfair to contrast Lowell's heartfelt letters to Bishop with Kazin's *Journals* ('The fact is that the journals scare even me when I look them over – so much longing, so much resentment' – July 27, 1989.) In fact, they are a tribute to his frankness and probably more in line with the *mea culpa* tone of Lowell's post-breakdown letters and certain poetic moods. Yet even a look in the index reveals repeated entries for insecurities, intellectual uncertainty, psychoanalysis, self-criticism, and social discomfort. Kazin, brilliant, doubtless charming, was ever troubled and always wary. His upbringing did not offer him the social insouciance Lowell could take for granted.

Politically the two had little in common. In a letter of Jan 15, 1949 to George Santayana, Lowell had written, 'I had a long argument the other evening with a fellow named Alfred Kazin. I said I couldn't imagine "Socialism" (he favors the liberal international kind...) has anything one could "believe in." It's a technique, necessary in various degrees, but depending on its context and qualifications for its value.' Lowell felt himself closer in 'sensibility' to T.S. Eliot. Kazin may have been nonplussed. He was later to write, concerning the poet's friendship with Hannah Arendt, 'I was never to understand what Lowell's politics were.'

They would meet cordially from time to time, but on two early occasions their views clashed dramatically. In 1948 Ezra Pound received the Bollingen Library of Congress Award for the *Pisan Cantos*. Pound at the time remained confined in a mental hospital for his anti-Semitic, Fascist propaganda from wartime Italy. The award committee, including Eliot, Auden, Tate and Lowell, had voted for him in the belief that his work rather than his behaviour had been worthy of the award. Their decision proved highly contentious. As one of those canvassed for his views by *Commentary* magazine, Kazin pointed out that most Jewish intellectuals were fascinated by the very modernists who were anti-Semitic: he mentioned Dostoevsky, James, Henry Adams, Gide, Santayana, Cummings, Céline, Eliot and Pound. He believed that the isolated modern writer hated the Jews for that same isolation (a condition that R. P. Blackmur also touched on in an essay on Joyce's *Ulysses* in which he described the Jew as Everyman the outsider: 'in each of us, in the exiled part, sits a Jew').

Writing eleven years later Kazin, who by now had followed his precociously brilliant debut, *On Native Ground* (1942), with the first of his admired autobiographical trilogy, *A Walker in the City* (1951), expressed his criticism of Pound more forcefully. While recognizing that the young might be drawn to the poet as 'aged hipster and clown', he offered the following: 'Any man of good will *must* be divided about Pound. For myself, surrounded as I am by inexpungible memories of the millions of dead, I cannot think of the purely literary case made out for Pound without horror.' In his 1961 interview with Frederick Seidel for *The Paris Review*,

Lowell posed the opposite view. The committee had believed in the book, he argued, and 'the consequences of not giving the best book of the year a prize for extraneous reasons, even terrible ones in a sense – I think that's the death of art'.

The following year Kazin and Lowell clashed publicly, this time over the allegiances of the director of Yaddo, the writers' colony in Saratoga Springs, New York. Lowell had enjoyed his first visit to the retreat in the summer of 1947. There again in October 1948, after his stint as poetry consultant to the Library of Congress, he had written cheerfully of it. He lived in rooms of the farmhouse, Yaddo itself being 'an enormous mansion'. Here he met his future wife, Elizabeth Hardwick, and befriended Flannery O'Connor. He ate and played ping pong with the other guests. However, all was to change shortly as Lowell entered a manic phase, his condition read as exhilaration by those who did not know him well.

According to Lowell's biographer Ian Hamilton, 'If, in his already "wound up" state, and with the Pound business in the air, Lowell needed an immediate target for his political hostilities, then Yaddo could hardly have been more obliging.' Agnes Smedley, a journalist with sympathy for the communist forces in China's civil war (a war nearing its end) had been a long-term guest at Yaddo and a friend of its administrator, Elizabeth Ames. In February 1949 *The New York Times* printed a false allegation that Smedley was a spy and Soviet agent. The army soon distanced itself from their report, which had prompted the accusation. The newspaper recanted; Smedley publicly thanked the army for clearing her name. Nevertheless FBI agents travelled to Yaddo to interview Elizabeth Hardwick and another guest.

Seizing this as an initiative, Lowell demanded the Yaddo board of directors dismiss Ames as 'a diseased organ, chronically poisoning the whole system'. In what he saw as his anti-Communist crusade, he threatened the public involvement of a number of highly influential literary friends. The following month Ames was officially exonerated, her reputation defended by a group including Kazin (for whom she had been 'a devoted friend to many writers over the years'). Lowell was censured. Shortly after this (and other highly wrought episodes) he had been confined in Baldpate, a private hospital near Georgetown, Massachusetts.

It seems ironic that during the war Kazin should have confided in his journal, 'I learned something at Yaddo – I learned a new sympathy for writers. I felt a new solidarity with all the lonely men in the lonely rooms' (June 1942). The world had changed since then; the war had turned 'cold'. If Lowell had been "wound up" for the Yaddo episode, Kazin himself – according to his autobiography *New York Jew* (1978) – hardly felt like tolerating what seemed to him a prevalent hysteria: 'The demand for orthodoxy suffocated me. Almost everywhere you looked now, the lies of Stalinists and the blood lust of super-Americans yelled down everything else.' Among the worst had to be the writers: 'The artist under political stress was an unforgettable picture of limitless self-regard.'

Lowell had been both dangerous and an irritant to Kazin: Though 'no longer a Catholic… he sounded like Evelyn Waugh rampaging against the wartime alliance with Russia. He objected more to Russia than to the war. It was a gloomy time for me; listening to Lowell at his most blissfully high orating against Communist influences at Yaddo and boasting of the veneration in which he was held by those other illiberal great men, Ezra Pound and George Santayana, made me feel worse.' He would describe it in a review of Hamilton's biography for *The Times Literary Supplement* (May 6, 1983) as his 'most jarring experience' with Lowell.

On a personal level, however, the matter would be dropped. In March 1953 the two met again at Oberlin College, Ohio, where Lowell deputized for Allen Tate. and where they both 'had made an effort to be civil', as Lowell mentioned in a letter to Tate. Their last reference to the Yaddo episode came on October 3rd, 1966, when Kazin records in his *Journals* in a conciliatory tone the dangers of Lowell's excitement: 'Lunch with Cal Lowell at Fleur de Lis. Cal very subdued, at the bottom of his cycle – terribly affectionate with me, full of intellectual fondness. He was talking about the old Yaddo business, and for a moment tried to indicate how strange his fanaticism of then seems to him now. I found myself saying how far the river of history has carried us, how much it has changed'. Kazin then mused on the universal tendency to demand coherence ('The cruelty of change on a mind seeking *constants*.')

The two men corresponded irregularly over the years. In the fascinating Bishop/Lowell correspondence (collected in *Words in Air*) we read Elizabeth Bishop's tart reference to Kazin (April 1st, 1958) after his recent piece in *The New York Times Book Review*, in which he had praised James Agee's *A Death in the Family* a little excessively for her taste: 'AK is getting just too sort of injured-sophistication for words – he sounds as if he were the only man in the USA who *appreciates* things.' While Bishop could be critical of Kazin, they had in fact been friends of sorts since her difficulties (with alcohol) at Yaddo in late 1950.

Kazin's *Contemporaries: Essays on Modern Life and Literature* (1963) drew their only sustained response, since the collection featured one essay of particular interest, 'In Praise of Robert Lowell', written at the time of the appearance of *Life Studies* in 1959. The essay began with an observation on the early poetry: 'Robert Lowell's poetic style has been marked by a peculiar force, one that might well have been called violence but for its learning, bookishness, and nostalgia for traditional order.' Kazin mentioned the poet's 'precision of passion', the 'formal beauty' of his style, and wrote of the literariness of the poems 'more intense about life than intimate with it'.

With *Life Studies* he saw the 'native elegance' retained even when the style has been 'stripped'. Henry Adams served as a comparison. Both 'have the gift of experiencing and expressing their own situations to the depths'. Pound and Pound's master, Browning, are also invoked as influences in their 'overliterary inflation' and 'dash and speed', in 'stylizing the communion with self that is the essence of dramatic monologue'. In sum, Kazin declared: 'In these poems twentieth-century poetry comes back to its great tradition as plain speech; comes back, in Pasternak's phrase, "to its sister, life".'

Inevitably flattered, Lowell wrote to Kazin in March 1962 of his delight at being admired, freighting it with the compliment, 'You seem to be the only critic beside Edmund [Wilson], who reads new books. I mean in some deep way they are relived inside you and come out again heavy with their old actuality, but reformed by your character and digestive system.' He suggested they get together the following spring and, in a postscript, reiterated the admiration: 'I can't read one of your pieces without feeling changed.' This could be called criticism *quid pro quo*, Lowell's reference to Wilson being intended to thrill Kazin, whose admiration for the master remained infinite.

It is somewhat deflating then – and a peril of searching private letters – to read that mid-April Lowell described the book to Bishop as a 'great heap of essays, surprisingly tougher and less long-winded than he is'. Bishop in her turn proved severe about them in her loyal response: 'The Kazin book I find infuriating but good in spots – the best spot being his review of you – the one really generous review in the whole book, I think. There must be thousands of "*I*"s in that book… and it's badly written, as well.'

Lowell received more generous treatment in Kazin's *Journals*. The first reference is a punchy one-liner from November 26, 1946: 'Robert Lowell: the triumph of talent over confusion.' This appeared in the context of an entry about how the atomic bomb had invaded the thinking of everyone in post-war America. This feeling would be captured years later in Lowell's 'Fall 1961', the immediate context now being the Bay of Pigs debacle, when nuclear extinction was again in everyone's thoughts: 'All autumn, the chafe and jar / of nuclear war; / we have talked our extinction to death.'

By the 1960s the relationship between poet and critic had

been established on a firmer foundation. There is intellectual exhilaration and hero worship ('my mad poet, my only genius') in one entry Kazin made in his journal in November 1965 concerning an evening visit with Lowell: 'Cal flitted easily from name to name and from subject to subject, but his sense of greatness, his sense of the great work, of the great moment in the great work, made me feel, again, as if I were breathing the unfamiliar, pure air at the mountain peak.' His last recorded sighting of the poet in the *Journals* is on November 19, 1967, where he enthusiastically reports the following: 'Here it is Sunday morning, gray and leaden, and suddenly Cal Lowell is on the phone talking about St. Paul and St. Louis and Cato the younger, moving in and out of history with what a perspective! Marvelous unprovincialism of the gifted man… Great to have him reading these poems on the phone just now. What a privilege.'

It was probably to be expected that, as the critic, Kazin would explore or at least reference the work of the poet, rather than that Lowell would write of him. Kazin hardly appears in the published Lowell letters after this time and Lowell left for England in 1970. There is a sighting when Hardwick wrote to him there in August 1970 regarding her social life: 'Ann and Alfred Kazin have spent the summer near Blue Hill, which seems odd, and are coming over this afternoon. Alfred has been unkind about M. McC. and so nothing communal can be planned' (In *Starting Out in the Thirties* (1965) Kazin had been scathing about her friend, Mary McCarthy.) The last reference in Lowell's published correspondence is admiring. In a letter of April 1973, he mentions a piece Kazin had written for *The New York Review of Books*, describing it as 'Alfred's nostalgic but beautiful picture of the New York that has disappeared'.

Lowell's death in September 1977 released Kazin from the need for discretion and his remarks after that date betray an ambivalence, especially about the man. He acknowledged Lowell's talent in *New York* Jew, describing him as 'the strongest poet of my generation' (though adding that he was 'given to mood swings that encouraged his gift for exaltation'). He also admitted that Lowell's instinct for language worked on him 'with the force of a jackhammer'. The use of 'strongest' and 'jackhammer' reveal Kazin's preference for the kind of muscular style characteristic of the poet through much of his career.

To him, Lowell's experience had been symptomatic of the national experience: 'Poetry in America could never be anything but "personal," for the only tradition it had was American energy rather than the classical art of harmony.' And then Lowell carried a lot of family baggage with him, tradition and pressures which fascinated Kazin: 'The Lowell attic – the world of things – heirlooms – all that stuff, all those ancestors and relatives, associations and quotations, almost too many people to write *to*.'

In his review of the Ian Hamilton biography (*TLS* May 6,1983), Kazin wrote his most negative assessments of Lowell as poet and man. Time had passed. His earlier enthusiasm had obviously cooled somewhat as fashions changed. He noted that 'Among the poets only "Cal" was so familiar to readers who never met him, who didn't need to in order to gossip about him.' He saw this as an 'over-valuation of Lowell's "confessional" tone'. He went further: 'A net of allusiveness, fame and anxious name-dropping surrounded his poetry.' Coming to the heart of this, Kazin reckoned that the famous poems 'are not so much moving as "impressive". The most important feature of Lowell's poetic line is its tricky grace, its need to surprise, its demonstrativeness… Lowell performed all the time, and soon it did not matter if the poem was weak so long as the line was "strong".'

This focus on the line in Lowell is, I think, accurate. What comes next, however, is severe: 'By nature he was a powerful, aggressive and altogether bossy person beset by manic depression and frightened even when, with his ventriloquist's skill, he wrote in a lordly voice alternating with a timid one.'

In his penultimate book, *Writing Was Everything* (1995), Kazin is kinder. While his ambivalence is clear ('Other poets needed praise; Lowell expected adoration'), he reaffirmed his faith in the poetry: 'I always forgave Lowell for taking on superior airs,' he wrote. 'His talent in a generation of poet wimps was vivid and strong, even if the learned allusions with which he began his career were derived from the southerners he adored so much.' Kazin admired too, 'Lowell's immensely sophisticated ease in knowing when to rein in, his upper-class training in controlled conversation.' The reference to 'upper-class training' brings us back, once again, to the essential distance in affinity between the two men.

PIONEERS: THE IOWA WRITERS' WORKSHOP IN THE EARLY FIFTIES

'We were pioneers, but did not know it', wrote author James B. Hall of the Iowa Writers' Workshop in the early fifties. It offered graduate fiction and poetry writing classes and its visiting faculty included John Berryman, Robert Lowell and Karl Shapiro, with appearances by Randall Jarrell, Dylan Thomas, John Crowe Ransom, Robert Penn Warren, Allen Tate and John Ciardi. These poets – several still building reputations in their late thirties – had in their classes some of the finest of the next generation of poet-teachers: Donald Justice, W. D. Snodgrass, Philip Levine, William Stafford, Jane Cooper, Robert Dana, Henri Coulette, William Dickey and others. The memories of that time and place of this younger generation, entertaining in themselves, are also illustrative of the nature of creative influence.

The founding director of the writers' programme had been Wilbur Schramm, but its fame resulted from Paul Engle's tireless efforts between 1941 and 1965. A native of Iowa and alumnus of the university, Engle clearly understood, as he later explained, that it took imagination on the part of the university to invest in creative writing. In fact, according to poet Robert Dana, an M.A. student there, 'in the 1950s, the writing program played no great role at the university. Kept on a short leash by a skeptical administration, it had at most only two or three assistantships to offer. It was a lean operation in lean times.' Warren Carrier, who taught there at the time, pointed to conflicts between the 'scholarly' members of the department and themselves.

Engle, however, proved adept at defending his territory. In his absences – often in pursuit of sponsors for the programme – he brought in rising names in the poetry world to take his place in teaching the appreciation and craft of writing. To Dana, 'He was sometimes the shrewd and hardheaded horsetrader he claimed his forebears had been. But he was also the scholar of literature who had won a Rhodes [scholarship] and crewed for Oxford, and who, at twenty-six, had been a poet of promise and of some achievement.'

Dana, later editor of *The North American Review*, also conceded that Engle could be 'enigmatic and contradictory and hard', a point W. D. Snodgrass took up elsewhere. He credited Engle's excellence as an administrator and acknowledged that he was at times a brilliant teacher: 'I remember him introducing us to Baudelaire, Verlaine and Rimbaud, and making us see ways of meaning we'd never even thought of.' Snodgrass remained critical of Engle's poetry though, while also feeling the director manipulated his students (cancelling grants – Snodgrass had been a casualty – and requiring menial tasks to be performed for him).

Against the uncertain background of the Cold War, aspiring and generally impoverished young writers, many with a service background, came to sit, learn and suffer (some offered a parallel with time spent on Devil's Island), in corrugated steel sheds, old barracks by the Iowa River. Robert Lowell later characterized the experience – on the dust-jacket of Snodgrass's stunning debut collection, *Heart's Needle* (1959) – as flowering in 'the most sterile of sterile places, a post war, cold war Mid-western university's poetry workshop for graduate students.'

Iowa City itself hardly proved to be the most exciting of places. On his first visit Lowell described it to Elizabeth Bishop as 'gray-white, monotonous, friendly, spread-out, rather empty, rather reassuring'. To Elizabeth Hardwick it seemed 'a strange place… it's so flat and ugly and somehow has the air and look of a temporary town. Actually, anything over fifty years old is a landmark.' Its cultural capital appeared to be in foreign movies and New Criticism. James B. Hall would remember it as more colourfully exasperating: 'Life in Iowa City was at once terribly high minded, demanding, and – always – no end in sight. Each spring there was a sensational murder of some kind; the divorce rate was too high to be exemplary. The period vice was drink, with no upper level stated on consumption, either.'

At the time Engle summoned them, Berryman, Lowell and Shapiro had been given a lot of attention from the literary world. Shapiro and Lowell had each won a Pulitzer Prize: for *V-Letter and Other Poems* in 1945 and *Lord Weary's Castle* in 1947. Berryman stood between *The Dispossessed* (1948) and 'Homage to Mistress Bradstreet', which appeared in *Partisan Review* in the fall of 1953, the year his first marriage effectively ended. He took over from Lowell for the first of two semesters at Iowa in spring 1954, when suffering both mentally and physically.

Randall Jarrell appeared first. He had been invited to give a reading of poems and discuss students' work in April 1952 and wrote, thrilled, 'Well, I've had a wonderful time here at the University of Iowa! I never saw such a pleasant, unspiteful, un-nasty-intellectual bunch of poets as here.' He mentioned Justice and Snodgrass. 'I talked to them and some others about 2 ½ hours yesterday afternoon about their poems and poetry. Last night I read… I've never in my whole life been so successful with an audience; by the time I was 2/3 through, there was such rapport that we were like mother and long-lost child… I've never, almost, felt more strongly what a wonderful thing it is to have made the poems and have moved people so.'

Iowa proved no such epiphany for Lowell and Berryman. There would be much discussion among the participants of the classes over the years as to the teaching of each. Lowell came first to the workshop in 1950 and taught there again in 1953. His first stint seems to have been the quieter. He had married Hardwick in July 1949, then been hospitalized until that December for what would be eventually diagnosed as bipolar disorder. At the prospect of teaching, he wrote to his college friend, the novelist Peter Taylor, that he might meet 'frightfully brilliant' students and so he was preparing as if for a PhD examination. Part of the fear, of course, had been Lowell's inexperience as a teacher, part his recent health and part, perhaps, teaching veterans on the G.I. Bill.

The class of twenty-five aspiring poets turned out to be much friendlier ('There are no fireworks,' he reported.) To Bishop he elaborated: 'O, and the poems! Everything from poetry society sonnets to the impenetrably dark – defended with passion, shyness, references to Kant and Empson mysticism. About six of my students are pretty good – at least, they do various things I can't and might become almost anything or nothing.'

Emboldened, the Lowells returned to Iowa in spring 1953. This time he had twenty-three students in their twenties, a workshop and courses in French poetry and Homer in the original Greek to teach (with classicist Gerald Else). Lowell did not make a great deal of the visit, writing to Allen Tate that he had good students, some confused and, like a psychiatrist, had offered 'banal worldly wisdom'. By the beginning of 1954 he admitted to Bishop they were 'sick of Iowa City' and were moving on to a teaching appointment in Cincinnati. After his mother's death early in the year, he would suffer another manic episode.

The students anticipated Lowell's arrival as a major event. He was after all something of a firebrand by poetic reputation. Among those waiting was Donald Justice, already well-travelled in the academic and poetry worlds. He knew Frost through Frost's grandson, Lowell and Jarrell through their college classmate, the author Peter Taylor (his wife's sister's husband). Having grown up in Florida, Justice had earned degrees at the University of Miami and North Carolina, before studying at Stanford, where he came under the influence of Yvor Winters. He had published a little, also.

Justice had arrived at Iowa at the suggestion of Taylor and Robie Macauley, taking up an assistantship to teach fiction writing. He would go on to teach at the writers' workshop for many years and win awards for his thirteen collections of poetry, from a Lamont Poetry Prize for his first collection, *The Summer Anniversaries* (1960) to a Pulitzer Prize for his *Selected Poems* (1979) and a Bollingen Prize in 1991.

Unlike the Lowells, Justice found the life of the town exciting. He remained equally positive about the classroom: 'I thought Lowell was an excellent teacher. He was someone of great intensity, to whom everything mattered. There was a distance, a decent and probably self-protective distance... As well, I liked him a lot personally, and he was always very kind to me. All the same, if I don't remember him quite the way Phil does, it's nevertheless true that Lowell was more interested in what he himself was writing than in what his students were doing... It's also true that there was a hint of condescension in his regard for student work.'

The 'Phil' he referred to was Philip Levine, a native of Detroit, who had had a tough working life from the age of fourteen. The opening of an early poem, 'On the Edge', is identifiably his:

> My name is Edgar Poe and I was born
> In 1928 in Michigan.
> Nobody gave a damn. The gruel I ate
> Kept me alive, nothing kept me warm,
> But I grew up, almost to five foot ten,
> And nothing in the world can change my weight.

After earning his B.A. at Wayne University in 1950, Levine had worked hard shifts in the automobile industry, before marrying and attending (without registering) at Iowa. He would also teach there, finally settling at California State University, Fresno, and win among other honours a National Book Award for *Ashes: Poems New and Old* (1979) and a Pulitzer Prize for *The Simple Truth* (1994).

Like Snodgrass, Levine was quite forthright about his teachers at Iowa: 'To say I was disappointed in Lowell as a teacher is an understatement', he wrote. He felt Lowell taught 'badly' (being competitive, playing favourites, misreading poems, imposing his own work on the class). He had – according to Levine – given the impression 'that there was a secret, a hidden key, to the reading of poetry', yet would never 'unlock the secret door to understanding' for his students. Instead, he stared at their incomprehension and rejected their efforts at explication of poems by Housman,

Ransom and Pound. (Ironically, on March 10th, Lowell had written to his mother regarding what was required of a new teacher and had stressed, 'To know how a poem is put together and what it *means* – no amount of enthusiasm or energy can relieve you of that duty.')

Levine had other charges to level: 'His fierce competitiveness was also not pleasant to behold: with the exceptions of Bishop and Jarrell, he seemed to have little use for any practicing American poet, and he once labeled Roethke "more of an old woman than Marianne Moore."' He offered a further damaging suggestion, 'Lowell was, if anything, considerably worse in the seminar; we expected him to misread our poems – after all, most of them were confused and, with a very few exceptions, only partly realized, but to see him bumbling in the face of "real poetry" was discouraging.'

Most of his students, Levine reckoned, failed to attend throughout the semester, though he remained: 'I stayed to the bitter end, and felt exactly as Lowell wanted me to feel: honored to be in his company.' He then 'discovered that one-to-one Lowell could be both helpful and encouraging'. Although he failed to push Levine in the direction he might have been expected to do (W.C. Williams, Hart Crane, Dylan Thomas), 'He prodded me to a rereading of Hardy – for which I am still thankful.' Levine did make another concession: 'In fairness he was teetering on the brink of a massive nervous breakdown... Rumours of his hospitalization drifted back to Iowa City, and many of us felt guilty for damning him as a total loss.'

Levine's seems to have been a minority view. Neither Dana nor Snodgrass accepted his perspective on Lowell's teaching, though all acknowledged the fact that he did not encourage familiarity. Dana, who was to teach at Cornell for forty years wrote, 'I recall neither his boredom nor overt acts of favoritism. If anything, Lowell permitted, whether from generosity or sloth, a wider range of what might be called "amateurism" than Berryman would allow later. In fact, Donald Petersen's description of Lowell's classroom manner seems to me entirely accurate. "... he praised what he could in our poems and diffidently suggested that we consult other poets' works, to see how it was done this or that way. He seldom suggested any specific revisions."'

His impact seems to have been, for Dana, more subtle: 'It may have been partly Lowell's influence that caused Henri Coulette and others to enroll in courses in the classics department, and which caused me later to undertake a translation of Rilke's *Letters to a Young Poet*. He had a way, however indirectly, of pushing you.' Dana also felt Lowell's influence when he came to drop 'uniqueness of idiom as a literary value' as Lowell had in *Life Studies*.

Snodgrass, the poet whose early work most resembled (and influenced) Lowell's, came to Iowa after war service in the navy. He later taught at a number of universities, winning the 1960 Pulitzer Prize for *Heart's Needle*. Both Jarrell and Lowell mentioned him in their letters, the former describing him as 'inspired', the latter acknowledging that he had written a couple of the best poems by his students at Iowa and, 'I now think he is incomparably the best poet we've had since you started.'

He had come from Empson to Lowell, after Eliot's 'etiolated language and attitudes', and remembered the students as 'ravenous' for the 'vigor' of Lowell's poetry. In person he had proved 'the gentlest of mortals, clumsily anxious to please'. Snodgrass went on to say, 'However high the expectations, almost no one was disappointed by Lowell's teaching – it was only years later, from comments published in *The Gettysburg Review*, that I learned of Philip Levine's resentment.'

Lowell's courses on masterpieces of English poetry continued to inspire him: 'For each session he picked a poet or even a single poem, then for several hours would free-associate to that work. Wyatt, Raleigh, Milton's "Lycidas", Landor, Tennyson's "Tithonus" – week after week we came away staggered under a bombardment of ideas, ideas, ideas…. Who could feel less than grateful for a mind so massive, so unpredictable, so concerned?'

Snodgrass's reminiscences of Randall Jarrell came from his time in Iowa and from a conference in Boulder, Colorado, which took place around the same time. As a teacher Jarrell delighted but surprised him: 'Slender and graceful, with a pencil-line moustache, he displayed the manners and vocabulary of a lively but spoiled little girl.' In contrasting their teaching styles, Snodgrass observed, 'Lowell's analyses had tended to the highly intellectual; Jarrell's, the emotional and personal.' He tended to discuss individual student's work in private, which did not always satisfy the class, though in these sessions he could be 'remarkably kind' about their poems. Snodgrass appreciated the fact that Jarrell helped change the direction of his work. 'Snodgrass, you're writing the very best second-rate Lowell in the whole country!' he once declared.

While there remains the difference of opinion on Lowell's teaching, there appears to have been general agreement on the startling effect John Berryman could have in class. His time in Iowa City did not begin auspiciously, however. After unpacking and drinking with old friends: 'Hall dark, steep stair down, travel blind, I crasht / & snapt a wrist, landing in glass'. The broken wrist and swollen ankles incapacitated him for days, though he went on to dazzle his class with the greats in poetry and poems by his contemporaries (Lowell, Bishop and Roethke). Donald Justice reckoned he was the best of his teachers there: 'He was full of a kind of fervour or fire, in class and out. In class he was a master of detail and care; he was in love with the whole business of reading and writing and talking about it, in love with teaching itself, though he had not done much of it.' To Justice, while not a model, Berryman showed genuine interest in the work of his students.

Justice was also, memorably, the young poet who stunned Berryman in class with the quality of his sonnet, 'The Wall', which begins:

The wall surrounding them they never saw;
The angels, often. Angels were as common

As birds or butterflies, but looked more human.
As long as the wings were furled, they felt no awe.

For this he received the astonished: 'It is simply not right that a person should get a poem like *that* as a classroom assignment.' The poem remains one of Justice's best and best-known. That year Berryman helped him toward an Iowa-Rockefeller grant in poetry ('I should place him very close to W.S. Merwin and Anthony Hecht, who seem to me the best American poets younger than Lowell.') He seems to have been most impressed by Justice of all the Iowa students, for his work and possibly for his reliability. In lieu of a will, he wrote instructions in 1959 naming Justice after Lowell as adviser on the publication of his 1947 sonnets. He recommended the younger poet's work to Dwight Macdonald – then a staff writer for *The New Yorker* – to Catharine Carver at *Partisan Review*, and he also offered to write to a senior editor at Scribner's on behalf of *The Summer Anniversaries*.

Jane Cooper, a poet who later taught at Sarah Lawrence College for forty years, remembered Berryman's speaking with 'great delicacy and warmth' of Roethke ('the only man who... *thinks* like a flower!'), though it was Philip Levine for whom Berryman was the greatest of teachers: 'He was the most brilliant, intense, articulate man I've ever met, at times even the kindest and most gentle, and for some reason he brought to our writing a depth of insight and care we did not know existed.'

Levine said that Berryman sensed and applauded the 'wonderful fellowship' among the students, burnishing it: 'These were among the darkest days of the Cold War, and yet John was able to convince us – merely because he believed it so deeply – that nothing could be more important for us, for the nation, for humankind, than our becoming the finest poets we could become.'

Two extraordinary high points, apparently, were Berryman's teaching of Whitman's 'Song of Myself' and Dylan Thomas's 'A Refusal to Mourn the Death, by Fire, of a Child in London'.

Berryman loved Thomas as a friend and poet. To Levine his performance remained unequalled ('Never again would I encounter so great a poem so perfectly presented.') There continued a friendliness and respect between the two, and Levine's enthusiasm never waned: 'No matter what you hear or read about his drinking, his madness, his unreliability as a person, I am here to tell you that in the winter and spring of 1954, living in isolation and loneliness in one of the bleakest towns of our difficult Midwest, John Berryman never failed his obligations as a teacher.'

On his part Snodgrass remembered, 'I could only get to an occasional class. As well as fighting to see my child, I was working as an aide in a hospital, so I didn't have much time left. But he *was* a very impressive teacher, and very different from anyone else I had had. I didn't always understand what he was saying. I couldn't work out what principles lay behind his judgments, couldn't even be sure that there were any such principles. But he was full of startling insights, and we learned a lot.'

Snodgrass credited his poem, 'A Flat One', to Berryman's assignment on death, which prompted him to a subject he would not otherwise have tackled. This unillusioned poem begins:

> Old Fritz, on this rotating bed
> For seven wasted months you lay
> Unfit to move, shrunken, gray,
> No good to yourself or anyone
> But to be babied – changed and bathed and fed.
>   At long last, that's all done.

Berryman's commitment had its more disturbing edge. Apparently he reduced the oversubscribed class he had taken over from Lowell to thirteen students – removing what, to Levine at least, were hangers-on who were 'just horsing around' – by being particularly harsh about a poem by a doctor's wife. As Levine put it, 'In his workshop John was ruthless and screamingly funny:

everyone… got leveled at one time or another.' He was given to sarcastic remarks: 'When I first saw your poems I thought you'd borrowed Cal's old portable Smith-Corona'; 'If you're going to write something this long why don't you try making it poetry?' 'Yes, yes, you have a genuine lyrical gift, but who encouraged you to never make sense, always to be opaque?'

Biographer John Haffenden quotes another student of Berryman's as saying, 'And there was even more to learn from him outside of class as he talked almost exclusively about writing and writers & always in his tense, nervous, paranoid bombastic manner. Thinking back I don't believe I've ever known a more gentle yet violent individual. In private, he was marvellously compassionate about his students and their work even though in class he was often devastatingly sarcastic, nasty and generally tough. But all of this was tempered by his brilliant wit and candid openness.'

In one letter Berryman described Philip Levine as 'a real tough guy & sensitive'. He had reason to know this from a drunken incident, which Levine did not repeat in his encomiums on his teacher, when he made a pass at Levine's girlfriend, hit him with a bottle and was punched as a result. The problem with Berryman, according to Snodgrass, was that 'as soon as he liked you he began making your life difficult by tampering in your love life and sometimes trying to tamper with your wife'. His total commitment to writing contrasted, according to another student, with 'his total desperation about himself, his relationships to others, and his compulsive daily self-assessment. And such awesome burdens of guilt about all aspects of his life!'

One incident illustrating Berryman's desperation involved his decision to take his own life, which was prevented only by Donald Justice, who had been summoned by him. Seeing his professor with razor blades, Justice almost fainted, thereby becoming the patient. To balance the record Justice pointed out that Berryman's 'emotional peak' was not the only one at the time and also that he had a 'capacity for joy as well as suffering', and that there were calm and enjoyable tavern meetings. Eventually though, like Lowell, Berryman would write that he detested life in Iowa City. His miseries, he reported, included colitis, malnutrition, dyspnoea and insomnia.

Karl Shapiro, doubtless in better physical shape, had less of an impact in Iowa. He joined the faculty for a semester, commuting from Chicago one day a week. Justice found him less interesting as a teacher, though 'some of us were very fond of his new Adam and Eve sequence of poems, which had recently come out in *Poetry*'. He felt that perhaps Shapiro's sequence had influenced his own 'The Wall', but remembered only one remark from the classes, 'to the effect that we should never use anything literary as subject matter' – a remark occasioned, probably, by his proposed sonnet on Hamlet's father.

Snodgrass had less time for Shapiro ('oddly noncommittal, almost evasive'): 'Considering his position as editor of *Poetry* and the rambunctious heresy of his recent critical dicta, we were astonished at how vague he seemed about student poems.' Unsurprisingly, Snodgrass remembered Dylan Thomas at Iowa: 'We had the usual longed-for scandals: the stevedore's language, the crush on a dumpy local waitress, the Tournament of Insults at the chairman's party.' At a reading, 'Before and between poems, his speech was slurred, shambling, obscene; suddenly, for the poem, he would shift into that sonorous, nearly Shakespearean voice still so familiar on recordings. The effect was so electrifying that one couldn't help wonder how much it might be calculated.' At his meetings with the workshop, he passed over the students' poems, instead, reading 'marvellously' his favourites'.

Snodgrass remembered also the New Critics, who made brief visits: Brooks, Tate, Warren, Ransom. He seems to have been underwhelmed by these Southern Agrarians, as 'dialect problems sometimes developed' and Warren, moreover, 'paced and mumbled'. He saved his strongest criticism for John Ciardi, translator of Dante, who 'brought a sense of emptiness and intellectual posturing', while 'his own poems, when he read them, seemed null or pretentious'.

In a depressing coda: John Berryman returned to Iowa for the fall term, only to be dismissed. This time he was to teach a course focusing on the idea of voice in the novel and a short story workshop with novelist Marguerite Young. A combination of heavy drinking and Young's approach led to Berryman's immediate disaffection. Gertrude Buckman – his friend Delmore Schwartz's first wife, now auditing the course – described late-night phone calls from Berryman in 'a drunken, revved-up state, assuring me of his genius, and reading his latest verses'. An argument erupted during only the second shared workshop, which caused Berryman to drink even more aggressively that night and led to his arrest for disorderly conduct. When the local paper picked up the story, he was dismissed. Fortunately, his career was saved by Allen Tate, who found him a teaching post at Minnesota, where he remained.

The Iowa Writers' Workshop boasts seventeen Pulitzer Prizes, six recent Poet Laureates and dozens of other awarded alumni over the eighty-six years of its existence. Its graduate writers' programme has become a place of myth as much as history, given that post-war record. As Paul Engle wrote with satisfaction of its poets in 1961, 'Their talent was inevitably shaped by the genes rattling in ancestral closets. We did give them a community in which to try out the quality of their gift.'

DELMORE SCHWARTZ: THE UNRAVELLING MAN

What is left of a poet? Delmore Schwartz figured so largely in his time in American letters (chiefly the 30s and 40s), that if one is to focus on his better remembered peers (Lowell, Berryman, Roethke) it inevitably brings him into the wings. Today his poems, stories and essays are probably little read except for study, though his brilliance, his charisma and particularly his ghastly later life story have the power to draw the reader in. James Atlas wrote a stunning (and stunned) biography in 1977, *Delmore Schwartz: The Life of An American Poet*, a page-turner about a manic authentic artist unravelling. And he returned shortly before his death in 2019 to the subject in the excellent *The Shadow in the Garden: A Biographer's Tale* (2017). One might sigh about the fact that what begins as art dwindles in the end to biography, but as Atlas argued – correctly in my view – a balance should be struck, because 'Art and life didn't just coexist: they enriched each other.'

So what is left of Delmore Schwartz, enriched or impoverished? First the life story. Schwartz was born into a difficult family life in New York City in December 1913. His Romanian parents split up early, his father, preoccupied with success, made and lost a million in real estate, then died. His disappointed mother lived to wreak emotional vengeance on him via her two sons. Schwartz discovered Eliot – his lifetime's obsession – early, and as his biographer tells us, 'Erratic as a student, Delmore drew on his arrogance and a fund of intuitive knowledge to get by.' He escaped home to the University of Wisconsin in 1931 and switched to New York University when his money ran out. His financial woes were endless. Graduating in philosophy in 1935, he turned to Harvard which he left without a degree but having impressed his brilliance on his professors. Only gradually did his bipolar disorder become evident, though he had been capable of unpredictable behaviour early on.

Schwartz married in 1938, the year his *In Dreams Begin Responsibilities* (fiction, poetry and a play) appeared to massive literary acclaim (A number of the finest critics reckoned with Allen Tate that Schwartz's style was 'the first real innovation we've had since Eliot and Pound'.) He returned to Harvard (1940–7) to teach advanced composition, translated Rimbaud's *Une Saison en Enfer* in 1940 to some critical dismay (especially given his barb that earlier translators confused translation with paraphrase), became a literary consultant to New Directions for James Laughlin, publisher and friend, then was embraced as an editor for *Partisan Review* (1943–55), the left-wing periodical, home of 'The New York Intellectuals' (to Irving Howe a pejorative code for 'Jews'). They were more political than Schwartz, though they often shared his conservative literary views.

Meanwhile he published *Shenandoah* (1941), *The Imitation of Life* (1941) and *Genesis, Book 1* (1943). These three – a verse play, essays and autobiographical long poem – hardly received the same critical adulation as his first work. *The World is a Wedding* (1948) showed a return to form, followed by *Vaudeville for a Princess and Other Poems* (1950). Subsequently more poems appeared, some new, in the Bollingen prize-winning selection *Summer Knowledge* (1959). *Successful Love and Other Stories* (1961) was his last completed book. Obsessed in all his writings with himself, his fate, his background and his psychological state, Schwartz kept journals, doubtless with one eye on posterity. As Eileen Simpson noted, in *Poets in their Youth*, Schwartz's 'life was his subject. He was frankly and unashamedly autobiographical. Long before the word came into fashion, he was "confessional."'

There were two unstable marriages to writers: to Gertrude Buckman, in 1937, and then Elizabeth Pollet in 1949. By then Schwartz was the most anthologized poet of his generation. Despite two years as poetry editor and film critic for *The New Republic* (1955–7), various false starts teaching here and there (including Syracuse University) did little to reverse a grinding decline. An inspiring but increasingly unkempt and finally uninterested teacher, Schwartz held on longest to the critical talent evident in his first rate essays. The barbiturates and drink he used to cure insomnia and then to cure each other led to hospitalization and persecution mania. Yet his journals show also the remorse Schwartz could feel about his behaviour and his talent – and his victimization (He wondered on one occasion whether, 'I am unread because of having turned to the theme of the Jew after my first book.')

Until his last years Schwartz was an exacting but magnetic friend to writers like Irving Howe, Saul Bellow (who recreated him in *Humboldt's Gift*), John Berryman (who captures his decline in *The Dream Songs*) and Robert Lowell ('To Delmore Schwartz'). Howe, in his superb autobiography, *A Margin of Hope* (1982), wrote of him: 'I heard in his stammering rhetoric, at once worldly and naïve, a note almost familial; and in all his work I found, even when it started crumbling under the pressure of madness, a straining toward a shy nobility.' Dwight Macdonald wrote of the 'genial shimmer over Delmore's talk… generous, easy and, no matter how outrageously exaggerated, never envious or malicious'. He described him as 'egoistic without vanity'. To them all he was, in Bellow's words, 'simply the Mozart of conversation'.

Unsurprisingly Schwartz's letters make interesting reading. Their trajectory is from the diplomatic to the paranoid via the forthright, the self-deprecating and the defeated. To Berryman he wrote as editor: 'I like your poem so much less than most of your other poems… that I had better send it back to you, hoping against experience than I can get some of the songs you showed me two years ago' (January 1945). To Karl Shapiro: 'Let me know if you come to New York, or just ring my bell. You'll probably find me illustrating to myself the inexhaustible maxim I mean to use for future contributors' notes: "DILIGENCE IS NOT ENOUGH"' (May 1945). To Howard Moss, sometime in 1961: 'The enclosed poem is typical, I'm afraid, of all that I have written in verse for more than a year, so I will spare you the other examples of the results of complete chastity.'

Schwartz was always most critical of himself. There is a sighting of him in his story 'New Year's Eve' for example (in the guise of his character Shenandoah Fish): 'when he spoke, he spoke with such passion and contempt and with so many speech defects that it was difficult to imagine that he would ever be successful and well-to-do'.

According to the editors of his essays, Dike and Zucker, Schwartz eventually loosened his grip on his literary ambition: 'Increasingly, his own anguish and the measures he took to endure it became for him the important reality' and Alfred Kazin gave a bleak description of him in his last years: 'He was buried up to his fine eyes in accusations of "betrayal," unbearably sicker than in the forties, not so much talking as accusing, erupting, plotting, demanding, suffering. Everything was vehement and tragic at once.' In 1966, after having alienated his second wife and all these friends, he died alone in a New York hotel, undiscovered for three days.

Bellow's Von Humboldt Fleisher (Schwartz) died, suddenly remembered by the press as Schwartz was: 'For after all Humboldt did what poets in crass America are supposed to do. He chased ruin and death even harder than he chased women. He blew his talent and his health and reached home, the grave, in a dusty slide.' Bellow's cynical conclusion is that poets are no longer seen as being in touch with the miraculous in this business and technologically driven America. 'So poets are loved, but loved because they just can't make it here.'

For some the Delmore Schwartz of the short stories is the memorable one. His most famous – the story which delighted his *Partisan Review* colleagues and featured in their first issue – is 'In Dreams Begin Responsibilities'. It treats of the conflict between Jewish New Yorkers and their immigrant parents. The central character dreams of witnessing his parents' courtship on a cinema screen – Schwartz was a lifelong moviegoer – and failing to intervene in preventing the union. Billed now as 'the foundation for all post-World War Two American-Jewish fiction', it introduced anxiety as a dominant theme.

Among other anthologized stories, satirical and poignant, are 'America! America!', 'The World is a Wedding' and 'New Year's Eve' (a take on the *Partisan Review* crowd). These are driven by character and dialogue rather than plot, and still entertain. It is questionable whether they universalise experience, though the generational conflict remains at their heart. In 'America! America!' the first generation is thrilled: 'a thing more marvellous than fulfilment had transformed their expectations. They had been amazed to the pitch where they knew that their imaginations were inadequate to conceive the future of this incredible society.' Unfortunately these same lower-middle class parents had raised children 'full of contempt for every thing important to their parents'.

Whatever angst was apparent in Schwartz's conversation and stories, the critical essays he wrote are notable for their authority. He was proudest of being a poet and, on one occasion at least, infuriated at being described as a critic. Philip Rahv pointed out, also, that he 'put no particular emphasis on his critical work'. However Schwartz was an excellent critic, as he privately recognised. So careful was he in collecting his essays that he prevaricated about their appearance in book form. In the event they appeared posthumously. He was also alert to the shadow of the poet behind the words of the critic, as he pointed out when writing on Eliot: 'there is, as everyone knows, a natural tendency upon the part of a poet who writes criticism to try to justify and praise in his criticism what he attempts to accomplish in his poetry'.

Some of the long ones hold up as well as anything he wrote, such as those on Hemingway as a moral historian, on Allen Tate's poetic honesty, on T.S. Eliot's reversals of position. All Schwartz's criticism testifies to his defence of what was then 'high culture'. These essays are long, sober, logical, insightful, conservative – and personal. They reveal Schwartz's commitment to Modernism and tradition, his Cold War patriotism ('To criticize the actuality [of American life] upon which all hope depends thus becomes a criticism of hope itself') and conservatism (for example his view that the Beats are indulged by the system, their rebelliousness merely shadow boxing). As a good modernist Schwartz committed himself to the times he lived in and to the new tradition, about which he wrote exclusively.

His admiration for Eliot as *the* major modernist did not blind him to the man's limitations as a sage. An essay 'On Literary Critics: An Appreciation' included the observation that it might be nice 'if more [critics] shared the social and moral values of Van Wyck Brooks and Edmund Wilson, instead of those of T.S. Eliot'. He was naturally sensitive to Eliot's patrician manner and anti-Semitism, especially given the academic climate of his times, which was unwelcoming to Jews. He also revealed himself obsessed – curiously – with interpreting Eliot's private life.

Schwartz ruminated a great deal on poetry and culture in his essays. In 'The Isolation of Modern Poetry', for instance, he explores the irrelevance of poetry to the average American, seeing that the contemporary, more scientific world view marginalises culture. In 'Views of A Second Violinist' he reckons the poet himself renounces a popular audience, being magnetised by 'a consciousness of the powers and possibilities of language'. One curious result of all this, according to 'The Present State of Poetry', is paradoxical: 'When a poet is asked to teach, or to act as an editor, or to write book reviews and critical essays, the basis of his employment is such as to enable him to earn a living. When, however, he writes a poem, this is not true in the same way: for the most likely result of the writing of a poem and its publication is that he will have one or another opportunity to earn a living in some other way than that of writing poetry.'

Yet Schwartz himself never stopped writing poetry. According to Atlas, he found 'a characteristic voice that could provide an effective vehicle for his self-dramatizing imagination. This was a sonorous, faintly archaic, uneven blank verse' with 'deliberately inflected rhetoric'. His best-known poem is possibly the Freudian self-portrait, 'The Heavy Bear Who Goes With Me':

> That inescapable animal walks with me,
> Has followed me since the black womb held,
> Moves where I move, distorting my gesture,
> A caricature, a swollen shadow,
> A stupid clown of the spirit's motive,
> Perplexes and affronts with his own darkness

Crucial to Schwartz's poems is this critical self-examination and a baffled view of the human condition that emerges from it. Mirrors most often tell the tale, as do the poet's photographs, which reveal beauty and fame, abuse and alienation. The symbolic shot, one that can be seen on the cover of my 1978 chunky little Avon paperback ($2.95) and on Atlas's *The Shadow in the Garden*, is of the twenty-five year old fresh from the triumph of his first book. It was taken at a 1938 *Vogue* magazine session and shows him staring into a mirror. It is a behind-the-shoulder shot of a handsome man whose inclined, intense gaze confronts itself.

One thinks of a number of these confrontations: the early dialogue, 'Father and Son' ('Be guilty of yourself in the full looking-glass') or 'The Sin of Hamlet':

> And when it comes, escape is small; the door
> Creaks; the worms of fear spread veins; the furtive
> Fugitive, looking backward, sees his
> Ghost in the mirror, his shameful eyes, his mouth diseased.

Ever Freud's student, Schwartz is nothing if not self-accusatory, as in the late poem 'The Fear and Dread of the Mind of The Others':

> They thought I had fallen in love with my own face,
> And this belief became the night-like obstacle

> To understanding all my unbroken suffering,
> My studious self-regard, the pain of hope,
> The torment of possibility

This poem, with reference to a statue, ends bleakly with 'Do you not understand me now, and how / The words for what is my heart do not exist.'

The idea of the constraints of fate is also central to Schwartz's poetry. 'Experience', not 'truth', he argued is the poet's mission. He is a man trapped by the 'inevitable' past, which subverts the living. In 'The Ballad of the Children of the Czar' he plays on a contrast between the Czar's fated children rolling a ball and his own two year old self losing a potato, in order to illustrate 'The wheeling, whirling world / Makes no will glad.' The poet here is 'Thinking of my father's fathers, / And of my own will.' Again in the dialogue 'Father and Son', he sees the inescapability of one's identity: 'Do not look past and turn away your face. / You cannot depart and take another name'.

And yet, as Schwartz sank, he countered with hope, as he did in 'The World Was Warm and White When I Was Born', which seems to see early promise redeemable through love and truth. While these later poems are shot through with the philosophy he trained on, many have a grandeur often too generally expressed. They rest on big nouns: 'love' and 'death' and 'eternity' and 'pride' and above all 'time'. Writing on Schwartz, in *Poetry* in 1966, the critic M.L. Rosenthal saw the best poems as having 'an anguish so unbearable that only a very pure poetry could handle it'. He cited, for its vulnerability and near whimsy, the unusual 'A Dog Named Ego' in which innocence vies with ego in the poet:

> A dog named Ego, the snowflakes as kisses
> Fluttered, ran, came with me in December,
> Snuffing the chill air, changing, and halting,
> There where I walked toward seven o'clock

The playfulness of the opening hardens into something lost at the poem's end with the refrain, 'And left men no recourse, far from my home'. Rosenthal quoted also from the moving 'All the Fruits Had Fallen' in which the poet wishes for innocence, the desire to be:

> Free of the future and past
> – Until, in the dim window glass,
> The fog or cloud of my face
> Showed me my fear at last!

Rosenthal might also have cited Schwartz's monologue 'Jacob' ('Love is unjust: justice is loveless') or 'Seurat's Sunday Afternoon along the Seine' with its moving conclusion echoing Flaubert ('Yet with a wild longing for forbears, marriage, and heirs: / They all stretch out their hands to me: but they are too far away!').

It was Irving Howe's opinion that 'What matters are the stories, poems, essays Schwartz wrote, perhaps most of all his stories, five or six of which are lasting contributions to American literature.' That was the view forty years ago. I am not so sure. Posterity qualifies, promotes, forgets. Schwartz will be remembered for a handful of work perhaps, but a couple of poems, a couple of essays, a story. The biographical interest in Delmore Schwartz will survive: troubled lives are memorable. And in the end who can draw the line at where the reader should stop. Not the writer. Like an actor, the writer is saying look at me. Enter the fan.

INTIMATE DISTANCE: ROBERT GIROUX & JOHN BERRYMAN

'Every good thing that comes is accompanied by trouble' is a line attributed to the legendary editor of Fitzgerald, Hemingway and Wolfe: Max Perkins. It is particularly applicable to the dealings of another great editor, Robert Giroux, with his client John Berryman.

Readers are familiar with Berryman's fêted yet frantic life – the brilliance, the destructive alcoholism, the manic depression, the periodic infatuation with suicide – and especially with the idiolect of his Dream Songs protagonist. We may not be as familiar with Giroux, whose talent took him from a modest background into the, then, country club world of publishing, where he eventually became the third partner at *Farrar, Straus*, founded in 1946. With unfailing admiration, patience and encouragement, he was to edit over a dozen books by the poet.

The two met in Mark Van Doren's Shakespeare class at Columbia University in the early 1930s. Van Doren, a Pulitzer Prize winning poet ('the great teacher in my life', according to Giroux) was admired for his 'technique of pretending that you were his intellectual equal'. Berryman remained equally impressed: 'It was the force of his example that made me a poet.' Giroux came under another influence also, that of biographer and editor Raymond Weaver who had helped pluck Melville from posthumous obscurity. Their serious commitment to study cemented a friendship between the two students, that and *The Columbia Review*, which Giroux co-edited and where Berryman published poems and reviews.

After Columbia, Berryman won a scholarship to Clare College, Cambridge, at which time he heard Eliot and met Yeats and Dylan Thomas. Greatly influenced by the example of Yeats and the behaviour of Thomas, he was there at the latter's death in New York. 'He was my oldest friend still a friend, except Giroux,' he wrote, 'but not personally close for many years.'

He went on to teach at various universities: Wayne State, Harvard, Princeton (where his friend, Saul Bellow, remembered him as 'tallish, slender, nervous, and [giving] many signs that he was inhibiting erratic impulses'), at Washington, Cincinnati, and then at the University of Minnesota from 1955 until his death. Contributing to Berryman's lifelong instability were his parents. Giroux described 'Jill' Berryman as 'a campus mother who haunted him daily, from his undergraduate days at John Jay Hall to his wintertime suicide in Minneapolis in 1972'. Worse had been the impact of his father's suicide: 'The shadow of my father's shaming death / lay over a youth. / Phantoms suckt at my chances.'

Although a keen Shakespeare scholar, Berryman directed his energies principally to poetry and teaching. Demanding and extremely popular as a teacher, he frequently exhausted himself. On one occasion in April 1957 he wrote to Giroux, 'One very fatiguing thing is that my modern course has so jammed with people that every morning at 11:30 I talk to 104 students. My department has never had anything like this before, and I can do it all right, but it is a strain.' Like his friend Lowell, in dark times he might journey from hospital to classroom and back.

On leaving Columbia, Giroux turned first to public relations. He had excelled at school but with the Depression he dropped out to work on a local newspaper, *The Jersey Journal*. With the editor's advocacy he won a scholarship to Columbia, there changing from journalism to literature. After graduation he first joined CBS, before being taken on as a junior editor with *Harcourt Brace & Company*. The famously finicky Edmund Wilson was an early client – and very lightly edited.

Enlisting in the US Navy in 1942, Giroux served as a combat intelligence officer on the USS Essex. In action he witnessed the rescue of a fighter pilot at the Battle of Truk Lagoon in the Pacific and took his account at the war's end to the US Navy Information Office in New York, where Roger Straus worked. Straus sold his story to *Collier's* for a thousand dollars. It was to be a doubly productive meeting since Straus would eventually need exactly the literary talents Giroux had to offer.

Meanwhile the latter returned to *Harcourt Brace*, rising to the position of executive editor, where he published the early work of Lowell, Flannery O'Connor and Bernard Malamud. Eventually frustrations grew with senior colleagues, especially after he was faced with their indifference to his work on Orwell, e.e. Cummings and William Gaddis. Losing *Catcher in the Rye* and *On the Road* further confirmed Giroux's desire to seek more independence. Roger Straus coaxed him to *Farrar, Straus* in 1955.

The story of *F.S.G.* as it was to become – with its famous three fish colophon – is entertainingly told in *Hothouse* (2013), by Boris Kachka. With reluctant family support, the extrovert Straus had bought his way into publishing by taking as a partner the veteran John Farrar. *Farrar, Straus* survived on a catalogue that produced the odd surprise hit (like *Look Younger, Live Longer*, the nation's bestseller in 1950). Straus, however, looked to a niche that would bring them literary respectability in the market. One ploy was to enlist admired, if slow-selling writers (Wilson, Trilling, Van Doren) to serve as decoys for upmarket authors.

Hiring Giroux proved a masterstroke. He possessed excellent taste. He also brought twenty writers over to *F. S.* with him, including T.S. Eliot (now a personal friend) and Lowell and his circle. It was generally conceded that Giroux would go to great lengths to protect his writers, visiting them in distress (Lowell during a manic cycle; working with Jean Stafford's aphasia) and his enthusiasm proved endearing. He prided himself on being an editor in close collaboration with his writers.

In 1964 his reward came in the form of a partnership, with Lowell's *For the Union Dead* as the first collection issued under the new imprint: *Farrar, Straus and Giroux*. The company, braced by Straus's extension of their international list, would eventually include eighteen Nobel Prize winners (among them Brodsky, Miłosz, Heaney and Walcott), becoming the primary mid-size literary publisher in America.

Long before that, John Berryman had re-entered Giroux's life. Their relationship is captured in all its convolutions in the fascinating *John Berryman and Robert Giroux: A Publishing Friendship* by Patrick Samway, S. J. (*University of Notre Dame Press*, 2020). The dramatic kernel in Samway's book relates to the friends' divergent paths after Columbia. The Kellett Fellowship that sent Berryman to Cambridge had been offered first to Giroux – thanks to Van Doren – though without certain details that would prompt him to accept it. He came to resent both Van Doren and Berryman since, according to Samway, he 'had a deep-seated secret desire to surpass the essays written about Shakespeare' by the two of them. Samway, who later knew Giroux well, writes, '"It doesn't matter now," he once told me, "but it mattered a good deal then."' A consummate professional, Giroux kept emotional distance within these intimacies.

In June 1940 Berryman pitched Giroux the idea of a solo collection with *Harcourt Brace*. He explained he was keen to evade a commitment of twenty poems to James Laughlin's *New Directions* anthology *Five Young American Poets*: 'I have never much liked the idea… it took Schwartz, Tate and Van Doren a month to persuade me.' Giroux replied that he would try to publish it, though he had anticipated another book they discussed in New York. Berryman had projected a prose work, a Blitz record of 'the death of our kind of life'. It had been partly a romantic scheme of his to return to England and his 'Beatrice' of 1937.

Now Giroux recommended Berryman pursue the Laughlin offer, knowing that during war time it would be impossible for poets without a reputation to be published. Otherwise he assured the poet, 'I'm ready to battle for you to the bitter end. I'm delighted to; it will be the first occasion since I've been here that I really want to see a book published.' Testament to their friendship: Giroux had been asked to be best man when Berryman married Eileen Mulligan in October 1942. When he could not obtain leave from his naval posting at Norfolk,

Virginia, Van Doren took his place.

Berryman daringly turned down Giroux's offer to publish his first collection, *The Dispossessed* (1948), maintaining a commitment to *William Sloane Associates*. Fortunately, when Giroux later joined Straus he wanted to build up their American list and so approached Berryman about *Homage to Mistress Bradstreet*, his powerful, idiosyncratic take on the colonial American poet: 'I can now sign contracts myself, and there will be none of the Harcourt, Brace ambivalence.' Giroux apparently wanted his next four books, hinting at spring publication for *Bradstreet*.

Ultimately he extracted Berryman from a Viking Press contract for a Shakespeare biography, repaying the advance given, plus offering another thousand to Berryman for the *Bradstreet* collection and the (never-to-appear) Shakespeare. Habitually anxious about publishing, Berryman would soon turn wary in his correspondence with his friend. He ended one letter, 'I take it that the book is thought of now as coming out at once. This is what I very strongly want, for reasons that I'll tell you in a long letter immediately if you'll tell me immediately if this is what you don't plan. But if you do plan it, let me know too.'

In a copy signed to Giroux, Berryman inscribed the sentiment, 'w. admiration & affection', for rescuing the poet when 'dying, not in brain but in heart & spirit'. Unfortunately the response of the literary world to *Bradstreet* proved disappointing, despite Giroux's efforts. By May 1958 things had soured. Berryman wrote complaining of the failure of *Farrar, Straus* to promote his book. He expressed bewilderment that copies of *Bradstreet* were unavailable, citing complaints at various readings and publisher statements recording fewer than a hundred sales in six months. He pointed to a dearth of advertising for the book, repeated the critical fervour for it and questioned, 'what is businesslike and what is not'. The letter occasioned a rift between them.

Giroux, of course, had other clients to devote himself to. Between the winter of 1959 and through the following spring, for instance, he edited sixty-two books. Two years later Berryman attempted to heal the rift with a letter to Giroux's confidante, the editor Catharine Carver: 'Would you or will you make my peace with Robert? I wrote him an angry letter years ago. I shouldn't have done; though I felt even more justified when I saw an ad in some paper later that they were remaindering the Bradstreet poem for a buck – I felt he shd have told me, and moreover I cd have bought some myself. Still I felt very bad abt the letter, not only personally (he is one of my oldest friends and I love him) but professionally.' He felt it had lowered his advance for the Shakespeare biography. He had more to say on the issue, he wrote, but his wife had pointed out, 'I got furious during the Giroux paragraph and I had better shut up' (Straus had in fact remaindered *Bradstreet*.) Carver spoke to Giroux who said all Berryman had to do was drop him a note.

Encouraged at the prospect of reconciliation (and of publishing his Dream Songs), in February 1963 Berryman part-mended fences with Giroux in a characteristically see-sawing manner, 'Let's make an end of the long estrangement. I have felt bad about it a thousand times. I wrote you a letter I should not have sent; but then you did not reply at all, and perhaps that was going too far, too.' He recited again his grievance, before expressing eternal gratitude for Giroux's assistance in bringing his work to the public. There followed the Henry-like confession 'still I feel puzzles and dissatisfactions about all that handling of it back there'. Here his self-pity flared momentarily with the feeling that despite the great merit recognized in his work, it had never had true publisher support. The letter ended with the demand for an offer for his Dream Songs and the accusation that he has never received anything for *Bradstreet*.

Giroux responded placatingly, 'I have never had any but the most affectionate feelings, arising from our most ancient and longstanding friendship' and, despite misunderstandings, 'I was deeply moved by your letter. Let us consider the long estrangement ended, though it never began for me.' 'Oh this is luxurious: thanks,' Berryman replied.

That July he wrote again, feigning uncertainty about what to do with the Songs that continued to pour out. They were, he repeated, much admired by friends and journal editors (Tate, Wilson, Snodgrass, Spender, Alvarez were mentioned): 'I cannot decide… whether to sign with you, and give you 75 or whatever, or as many as 130, or 100 or so, or not to publish any now, I cannot decide.' He assured Giroux that he had signed to no other interested party (citing *Stone Wall Press*), but acknowledged that money worries and other projects pressed on him. 'Maybe the thing to do is stop exacerbating…', he wondered, and simply send them to Giroux, which he did.

Berryman revelled in the massive appreciation that greeted *77 Dream Songs*. At the same time he remained critical of poor readings of them, especially by friends in print. Between the Dream Songs volumes, Giroux decided to publish *Berryman's Sonnets* (1967) – the product of an affair during his first marriage – with a $500 advance and another $500 on publication. Happy with the arrangement, Berryman indicated that the Songs continued to appear, 'some 40 in the last month alone'. When he came to organizing the second book of Songs, *His Toy, His Dream, His Rest* (1968) his editor reckoned, 'the latter two books are longer than they should be'. In response Berryman removed four of six poems mentioned then – continuing to overflow – added two new ones.

Giroux's editorial role grew as Berryman's collapses increased in severity. Aside from tasks like ordering Songs, decoding scrambled letters and overseeing the 'unusually heavy revisions' Berryman would make close to publication, he had to pursue fees for granting permissions, carefully time the appearance of the abundant Songs to avoid overexposure, while finding other outlets ('Don't be surprised if you turn up in McCall's and Playboy.') It was vital to keep the momentum going, to bolster the poet's enthusiasm: ('TOY DREAM REST IS SUPERB. YOUR GREATEST BOOK AND THAT IS SAYING A LOT') and to offer some clear idea of their publishing future, leading when Berryman flagged.

By late 1969 the poet reported a recent royalty cheque had brought him near $8000 (approximately $70,000 today), whereas he had expected a mere £600. The following June he wrote to his mother about his latest venture: 'The book (Giroux thinks it "far & away yr best book" – wh. I don't agree with but am glad to hear) is called *Love & Fame* & it will make a sensation this Fall: though it may also (Mark thinks) be "feared & hated."' Neither proved correct. Without his Henry, the confessional Berryman did not fare as well. But moving on, he reported to Giroux that 'Delusions' (*Delusions, Etc.*) would be the title of a subsequent collection, already containing about fifty poems. In June 1971 he asked for contracts for a novel, *Recovery,* and this collection, 'which is proceeding with slow confidence'. The slowness reflected his state of health; the completed book lacked the vitality of earlier work.

Berryman's last work-in-progress, the novel, would be published the year after his death. Having flown to Minneapolis to act as godfather for Berryman's second daughter in June 1971, Giroux read twenty-five pages of it while Berryman attended his AA meeting. The poet sweated with uncertainty, 'expecting to finally hear I shouldn't go on with it'. Yet Giroux proved encouraging, wrote Berryman: '"It's marvellous, John" & "Let's get a draft" & "What about ten thousand dollars" (advance, that is). Cosmic relief! After he left at 2 a.m., I felt faint & had to take a pain pill.'

Soon Giroux would be writing to a friend about Berryman's suicide, 'Having suffered so much and achieved so much, he had I thought finally reached some kind of balance and acceptance.' At the funeral he delivered a simple eulogy. Death would not be the editorial end, according to Kachka, 'There were [always] a thousand things to do: secure copyrights and permissions for work published and unpublished; amend contracts for the benefit of heirs; work out editing and publishing schedules for manuscripts in various stages of completion.'

In retirement Giroux lived quietly with his partner of fifty years, Charles Reilly. He finally published his book on Shakespeare's sonnets, *The Book Known as Q,* generously dedicated to Van Doren and Berryman (Frank Kermode described it in a 1983 *NYRB* piece as the work of 'a well-informed layman'. A 'condescending phrase' Giroux replied in print.) He died in 2008. At his memorial service, Pat Strachan, once Giroux's assistant, remembered his stoicism, except, 'In the winter of 1972 Bob called me into his office, asking me to shut the door. After I sat down, he said, "John has jumped off the bridge." Tears began streaming down his face. His beloved John Berryman had taken his own life.'

ALFRED KAZIN: AMERICAN OUTSIDER

> 'I love to think about America, to look at portraits, to remember the kind of adventurousness and purity, heroism, and *salt*, that the best Americans have always had for me.
>
> Or is it – most obvious supposition–that I am an outsider; and that only for the first American-born son of so many thousands of mud-flat Jewish-Polish-Russian generations is this need great, this inquiry so urgent?'

February 28, 1942

'It is a horrible book, and the more dangerous, because it sounds (or will sound to so many people) plausible,' Cleanth Brooks complained to Allen Tate in January 1943. Alfred Kazin's *On Native Grounds* had been published the year before. Brooks, a leading exponent of the New Criticism, was complaining of the negative comments on 'The Formalists' in the book. He was correct. *On Native Grounds*, which launched Kazin's career-long study of American literature, is a highly plausible book. More than plausible, it is comprehensive, profound and partisan, a self-confessed attempt at moral history, the summation of a lifetime's reading by a young man of twenty-seven who had barely begun.

It was an astonishing debut, really a series of mini-intellectual biographies relating to the emergent 'struggle for realism' in fiction and criticism from 1890–1940. Although Kazin wrote essay after essay with insight and passion for another sixty years, collecting them in such books as the substantial *Contemporaries* (1963), he could never better it. No wonder it made his name as America's go-to 'literary radical'. It was to be more than forty years before he tried something remotely similar, in *An American Procession* (1984), though time had cooled the radical passion to ingratiating warmth. Even there he could enthral.

Kazin's motivation lay in his sense of literary criticism as an exalted calling. He committed himself fully to it, being 'first astonished by gifts that I do not possess, then excited by the chance to make contact with them through my analysis'. Elsewhere in his self-lacerating *Journals* (2011) he recorded that, 'As a critic, I read and read certain texts, the beloved ones, so as to *possess* them.' The proximity to greatness and the possession of books luminous to the point of sacredness, led him to adopt his subjects: 'the writers as characters in my book were friends and the most encouraging people in the world to write about', he acknowledged in a 1995 preface to *On Native Grounds*.

The impulse was always toward intellectual biography and narrative. 'I was confident that I could read the mind behind a book', Kazin wrote in *New York Jew*. Over a long writing life he pursued – with 'perception to the pitch of passion' in Henry James's phrase – what Melville called in an 1851 letter to Hawthorne 'the inmost leaf", the writer perfectly unfolded within himself (Kazin borrowed the image for a book title). He wrote privately of his mission as the drive to define the 'individual core of talent, "the gift"'. His 'joy' in so doing was in line with Emerson's perception that criticism and commentary, 'if they are not in the service of enthusiasm and ecstasy, are idle at best'.

Kazin's dedication to American literary history, as subject, paralleled his need for it as myth in his life. He was born to Jewish immigrant parents in Brownsville, Brooklyn, in 1915. The difficulties of his early life led to his romanticizing an America in which he always felt something of an outsider:

The past, the past was great: anything American, old, glazed,
touched with dusk at the end of the nineteenth century, still
smoldering with the fires lit by the industrial revolution,
immediately set my mind dancing…in the light from the steerage
ships waiting to discharge my parents onto the final shore, was the
world of dusk, of rust, of iron, of gaslight, where, I thought, I would

> find my way to that fork in the road where all American lives cross.
> *A Walker in the City*

He was, as he declared, 'seeking *sanctions*', finding them in the example of those American writers who lived artistically as well as personally isolated. The fact that Emerson, Thoreau, Whitman and Melville had lived encouraged him. Like them, perhaps, he was a writer 'looking for a place to put his mind'.

Kazin attended City College, became a needy, pushy reviewer in 1934, and then earned an M.A. from Columbia in 1938, the year he married the first of four wives. His biographer, Richard M. Cook, noted evidence in the early reviews of a 'penchant for responding to writers as historical actors and personalities whose moral qualities he closely associates with their literary achievement'. His heroes were the independents, Van Wyck Brooks and especially Edmund Wilson ('the conscience of two intellectual generations'). While the life of the mind became his obsession, he charted the growth of his own in those three atmospheric and lightly fictionalized autobiographies: *A Walker in the City* (1951), *Starting Out in the Thirties* (1965) and *New York Jew* (1978). In the second he described his life as that of a Jewish New York intellectual who avoided the solemnity of the Marxism of his peers: 'I felt myself to be a radical, not an ideologue; I was proud of the revolutionary yet wholly literary tradition in American writing to which I knew that I belonged.'

And so he wrote *On Native Grounds*, in which he set himself the task of describing 'the rise of the modern in American literature, its sensibility, its liveliness, its protest'. In so doing he focused on the realist tradition, feeling himself appealing to 'the spirit of the age'. Vernon Parrington's *Main Currents in American Thought* (1927) had been greatly influential in crystallising the modern liberal tradition. It was to provide Kazin, as Cook explained, 'with a means of selection and a dramatic structure'.

Structurally *On Native Ground* is in three parts, following the ebb and flow of progressivism. This is narrative literary history, concerned always with the movement of the mind, rather than the detailed examination of individual works. 'The Search for Reality' (1890–1917) deals with the emergence of realism, with William Dean Howells, Edith Wharton, Theodore Dreiser, Stephen Crane, Frank Norris and others. The second part, 'The Great Liberation' (1918–1929), offers a more conflicted view where the admired likes of Ellen Glasgow and Willa Cather meet the forces of cynicism (H. L. Mencken) and reaction (Paul Elmer More, Irving Babbitt and other New Humanists).

Kazin wanted to study 'our alienation *on* native grounds – the interwoven story of our need to take up our life on our own grounds, and the irony of our possession'. Progressivism in the figures of Hemingway, Fitzgerald and Dos Passos sailed too close to nihilism. He believed a certain disengagement to be vital ('Who is there to deny that the very fame of American writing in the modern era, the very effort to create a responsible literature in America appropriate to a new age, rests upon a tradition of enmity to the established order, more significantly a profound alienation from it?') The writer's task was to improve America, not dismiss it.

'The Literature of Crises' (1930–1940) describes a period of the social realist novels of Erskine Caldwell, James T. Farrell and John Steinbeck, which Kazin finds both committed and wanting. His greatest antagonism is reserved for the literary critics, the Marxists and the reactionary Formalists, who have marginalised the older liberal tradition. Finally, looking for the optimistic spirit at a time of international turbulence, Kazin turns to the wider, more palatable 'literature of social description' in New Deal America, which includes the Works Progress Administration (WPA), photography, biography and history.

Like a Dickens novel, Kazin's dashingly confident history teems with characters pinned with an image or a touch of novelistic colour: 'Hamlin 'Garland acted as the bandmaster of realism'; 'It was as if [Sherwood Anderson] had been brought up in a backwater, grown quaint and self-willed, a little "queer," a drowsing village mystic, amidst stagnant scenes.' Of Stephen Crane, he writes, 'He baited the universe but never those village citizens who are as benign in his work as small-town fathers in the *Saturday Evening Post*.' There are also many insightful one-liners: 'the symbols Hemingway employed to convey his sense of the world's futility and horror were always more significant than the characters who personified them'. Of Faulkner's characters we learn: 'though the energy that drives them along is torrential, we do not see *them* intensely; we see everything under *conditions* of intensity'.

Kazin joys in extravagant rhetorical flourishes, as in his treatment of the lost generation: 'They had a special charm – the Byronic charm, the charm of the specially damned; they had seized the contemporary moment and made it their own; and as they stood among the ruins, calling the ruins the world, they seemed so authoritative in their dispossession, seemed to bring so much craft to its elucidation, that it was easy to believe that all the roads really had led up to them.' The imagery is always atmospheric, if a little overdone: 'Soon enough, the masters of estheticism and the prophets of languor rose from the ashes of the fin de siècle.' Or, 'No longer did the American realist have to storm the heavens, or in the grimness of creation build his books with massive blocks of stone.' Writing of professional scholars such as Thorstein Veblen, he finds the pompousness of style 'was an article of clothing like the Prince Albert coat, and in many respects resembled it'.

If one stopped to quibble about Kazin's judgements one might have questions. Even Kazin himself admitted to having over-cherished Howells. When he writes of the 'immense distinction' of Carl Sandburg's Lincoln biography, we are more likely to remember Edmund Wilson's quip, 'The cruellest thing that has happened to Lincoln since being shot by Booth was to have fallen into the hands of Carl Sandburg.' Does Crane resemble so much in spirit F. Scott Fitzgerald? Does Eliot's critical style bear 'the overtones of an inexhaustible disillusion', or is it rather the poetry? Is Farrell 'Proustian'?

And what of the New Criticism, which Cleanth Brooks so worried about? The most glaring possibility for disagreement is Kazin's dismissal of it, contrasted here in its inflexibility with the Marxist ideologues (which he knew something about, having matured among the anti-Stalinist left of *Partisan Review*). Marxism he declares has 'something almost too prehensile about it – it lends itself to too many different uses'. The source of Kazin's dislike of the 'Formalists' of New Criticism relates to his simplification of it. In the original preface he writes, 'I have never been able to understand why... those who seek to analyse literary texts should cut off the act of writing from its irreducible sources in the life of men.'

Kazin was not, however – with the honourable exception of a few pieces, on Whitman, Dickinson, Lowell, etc. – a critic of poetry. He creates something of a straw man here. Beneath their surface protest against the partisan sloppiness of other criticism, he finds a loose grouping of academic reactionaries who look for scientifically grounded criticism and prize modern poetry for its distinction, alienation and inaccessibility. This 'group' – Southern-led and therefore a useful counterpoint to Northern (New York) Marxists – also holds a grievance against Northern materialism and egalitarianism. Despite Brooks's fears and Kazin's continuing enmity the New Criticism, as a method of textual analysis, would dominate teaching for many years (In 'The Background of Modern Literature' (1958) Kazin argued that it 'tends to fit too well with the pragmatic temper of Americans'. He compared its practice to the enjoyment of working on a car).

On Native Grounds, as the critic noted in his 1995 preface (with a dig at recent trends), 'was written out of an old-fashioned belief that literature conveys central truths about life, that it is indispensable to our expression of the human condition and our struggle for a better life' – a view with which (perhaps the last part muted) some of us would still agree. Certainly some of his reviewers must have done so. Irwin Edman, Columbia philosophy professor, wrote a front-page review for the *New York*

Herald Tribune (Books), calling its publication 'not only a literary but a moral event'. Orville Prescott in *The New York Times* also referred to 'an effort at moral history'. He concluded his review with a *bona fide* query: 'Alfred Kazin is only 27 years old. With "On Native Grounds" he takes his place in the first rank of American practitioners of the higher literary criticism. How he was able to read in a few years the whole libraries he has and still eat and sleep is a mystery.'

Thirty years later, the 'wunderkind' did not have the same vitality or perspective. Apprehensive about writing another preface to *On Native Grounds* in June 1955 he recognized 'what kills us is the isolation, the lack of dialogue, of growth in ourselves that comes from talking to each other'. In 1982 his complaint was rather, 'Before I came to the end of my book in 1942 the moral bankruptcy of many left-wing writers left me, though still radical, less convinced of the "necessary" connection between literature and social criticism.' He still yearned for the relative purity of the liberal American literary criticism of earlier days as represented by Brooks and Wilson.

There were to be other essay collections. 'The Function of Criticism today', in the wide-ranging *Contemporaries: Essays on Modern Life and Literature*, ends with the thought, 'We must practise criticism on the older writers lest they harden into the only acceptable writers. We must learn to practise criticism on the newer writers, in order to bind them more truly to our own experience.' In *An America Procession: The Major American Writers from 1830 to 1930 – The Crucial Century* (1984.) Kazin turns to his first loves.

An American Procession begins with the founding of a national American literature when the 'God-intoxicated' Emerson left the church to begin his own ministry, ending with the triumph of modernism in the 1920s and the recognition of those modernists *avant la lettre:* Henry Adams, Melville, Whitman and Dickinson. The theme of these modernists of fact and spirit 'was the agony of change, the fear of the masses, the longing for an absolute'. So triumph came twice: in the first part of the nineteenth century (with the transcendental idealists and the great romancers) and then with the modernism of the 1920s, before its free spirit dissipated in the thirties.

According to his biographer, *An American Procession* (1984) is flawed by a number of things: its failure to take the temper of the times in which it was written; it's inability to find a literary-historical structure to wed itself to; its self-indulgence in offering none but his own opinions; and its narrative of decline. Admittedly Kazin does trace decline in the age and in his subjects. Yet one perceived weakness is to me its strength. In keeping his subjects – shaped as always into characters – to himself, Kazin presents a lifetime's album of favourites, a series of monologues that in their atmospheric intimacy give the effect of colloquies. There is a nice balance of historical context and biographical fact and then a turning to the evolution of thought of each of his marquee names.

In his preface, the unnamed Harold Bloom takes criticism in Kazin's reference to a 'debased Freudianism' used to 'exaggerate the natural rivalry' of canonical writers, some of whom were actually friends while others isolates. 'Isolated' is a leitmotif as central to the book as 'insurgency' was to the more radical *On Native Grounds*. Kazin's nineteenth century heroes endured their isolation, both the cause and the cost of their art. He cites Emerson's late recognition 'that the infinite universe cannot be domesticated to man's religious needs. This became the lonely stoic note of America's problem writing in Melville, Dickinson, Mark Twain, Stephen Crane, Wallace Stevens.' He reminds us of D.H. Lawrence's reference to the American as 'hard, stoic, isolate, a killer'. A journal note from January 1957 elaborates: 'such loneliness is an act of criticism, and like all real criticism suffers from an essential formlessness; tends to express itself in fits and starts, in marginal glosses. Hence the lumber of Hawthorne's stories and Emerson's journals and Poe's tales: the profound inner formlessness of Whitman'.

As Howells led *On Native Grounds*, so the dispassionate historian Henry Adams launches *An American Procession*. Kazin's is a wonderful portrait of a man who viewed 'History's mad acceleration into "chaos"', an appropriate choice since Adams was the scion of American presidents and a harbinger of modernism: 'Henry Adams, who despised the masses, despaired of progress, declared himself a failure, and drew the last drop of bitterness from his experience, has turned out to be one of the ruling myth makers of American history.'

You wonder, with Kazin's best portraits here, how he was able to turn his empathy into page after page without over-relying on biographical props and the critical commonplace of constantly entering their books for character and thematic analyses. There is hyperbole and rhetoric perhaps at times, but there is also rare skill in keeping his personalities and the movement of their thoughts before the reader's eye. His method is to surround his subject, darting in with an elegant aphorism here, a subtle metaphor there, a poetic touch, a parallel, a grand statement such as this that springs from his excellent treatment of Melville: 'If ever there was a style that belonged to America's own age of discovery, a style innocently imperialist, romantic, visionary, drunk on symbols, full of the American brag, this is it.'

Kazin is at pains to link his 'history' and so puts his characters in close proximity. Besides he loves counterpointing. So, Adams and Eliot are both sceptics in the prologue 'Old Man in a Dry Month'; Henry James would have found Dickinson's poems embarrassing since 'She was not in the "real" world, society'; 'Nature for Emerson meant everything not himself; for Thoreau it became the other self he walked into.' Faulkner shares Hawthorne's obsession with a locale but is really more like the rhetorically embattled Melville. Crane is teamed with Hemingway ('Style was primary with him, as it was to be with the Hemingway he often anticipates') while Theodore Dreiser, like Whitman, 'disturbed the secularized Protestant elect who had replaced religion with morality and morality with propriety'.

Adams, Twain and Dreiser felt 'mechanistic theories' of the *fin de siècle* sanctioned their disenchantment – *und so weiter*.

Kazin's perceptions are, as always, stylishly expressed and often biographical in nature: 'Emerson owed much of his influence to his private aura; he impressed by seeming inaccessible'; 'It was Lincoln's peculiar honesty… that still makes him unfathomable and endlessly interesting'; Twain 'softened the awful truth [of human nature] by enjoying his own performance so much'; 'The artist in Dreiser was always stronger than the man'; 'At every stage of his life [Hemingway] found himself a frontier appropriate to his fresh needs as a sportsman and his ceremonial needs as a writer.' Then there is the novelistic flair: 'Emerson was an organic writer and instinctive stylist who even on the platform seemed to be waiting for his own voice to astonish him.' Dickinson's 'lifetime investment in the poem as miniature made her see that only the barest lyric could render so much finality, the purest personal fantasy of travelling into death with the mind radiantly poised for novelty'.

The book sparks with literary insights: 'Eliot in America could never have written with such lordliness'; in Hawthorne's unfinishable novels: 'the characters, having this awful symbolic weight to bear, kept turning into each other and getting lost'; 'It is the force of the repressed that Poe made his drawing card, the power not of the past but of the dead, as phantoms preying on unsleeping guilt'; 'Whitman's time sense is one of suspension. There is a longing somehow not to be fulfilled'; Dickinson 'unsettles, most obviously, by not been easily locatable'; 'There was nothing in James's world to conspire about but the secret love to which money is attached'; 'Crane's "lines," as he called his poems, are just that; they breathe an air of satisfaction, they seem too easily satisfied with their contemptuous brevity'; 'Dos Passos sometimes resembles one of those early movie directors resurrected for his "technique" at the Museum of Modern Art'; and Pound, whom Kazin would never forgive for his ardent anti-Semitism: 'was an assimilationist of genius, a ventriloquist able to reproduce alien and ancient voices, cadences, styles – often in wilful ignorance of the actual substance'.

Again we may wonder how astute specific judgments are. And yet we are again swept along in the general passion, as were a number of critics. 'With *An American Procession*, Alfred Kazin confirms a reservation in the front tier of the reviewing stand, next to his eminent predecessors Van Wyck Brooks and Edmund Wilson' – *The New York Times Book Review;* 'A sense of caring intimacy lifts Kazin's survey above the usual inventory of masterworks… *An American Procession* is a refresher in the best sense… It vivaciously refreshes our awareness.' – *The New Yorker;* 'The *Procession* is wonderfully exciting to read… An authentic entrance, as Whitman called the self, to all facts.' – *The New Republic.*

Other reviewers apparently did not share the enthusiasm and the book was politely ignored. One reason his biographer cites is that it did not offer anything new to the critical debate, which is not surprising given Kazin's outsider hostility to academia, with which he was only fitfully engaged (A writer 'can be so exasperated by the intellectual togetherness of critical opinion', he announced in a 1960 review). Another is that these chapters are largely reworkings of earlier published pieces. Sometimes the joins show. His Poe is mostly Pym (a discussion of *The Narrative of Arthur Gordon Pym of Nantucket*), for example. We are told about the eleven chapters dealing with Henry Adams 'scientific' approach to history in the *Education* and then two pages later told it again. He also repeats Eliot's confession that *The Waste Land* was 'just a piece of rhythmical grumbling'.

Such criticism hardly mars the book. Kazin loves his characters and we enjoy his enjoyment and their company. As he confided to his journal in April 1965: 'This is what American writing so often comes down to for me – the familiar pleasure. So one must push the source of this pleasure to the critical limit, in study of the personal, intellectual, and religious sources of the pleasure – one must study this in depth, since to begin with "impersonality" is impossible to me.'

Granted Kazin was of his time and even by 1984 that time was passing as the critical circus moved on to text and meaning. Yet the romantic can admire his commitment to the idea that criticism should show 'almost physical empathy'. His did. In May 1956 he wrote, 'I have always approached all literary and critical questions with the instinctive quick sympathy of the writer, not with the objectivity or heaviness of the critic.' What he gave the reader – and can still give – is the bracing evidence of this, the *salt*. That is what enthrals.

JAMES ATLAS: THE SHADOW AND THE POET

Literary biography is, like criticism, one of the ugly sisters of poetry – and not simply because its sales are better. Behind all the carping – the 'loud chorus of negativity' as James Atlas described it – is the feeling that the written life is not only irrelevant to the art but can marginalize, substitute for, or even extinguish it. On the other hand, one could argue that ephemerality is more the result of changing attitudes and fashions in society. Atlas found that out with his first biography, of the poet Delmore Schwartz, whose reputation is now 'sadly diminished', as John Ashbery observed in 2016.

While not as immersive as Robert Caro, who went to live with Lyndon Johnson's neighbours in an early stage of his research, or as intense as Richard Holmes, for whom biography is 'a kind of pursuit', Atlas was nevertheless highly skilled, imaginative, and indefatigable in his research ('a biographer more scrupulous than Atlas is hard to imagine', according to *The New York Times*). In contrast to Holmes, whom he greatly admired, he acknowledged in an interview, 'I'm a distinctly anti-romantic biographer: brooding, fatalistic, cynical – though not entirely unsympathetic to our human plight.'

Born in Evanston, Illinois, in 1949, Atlas studied at Harvard and Oxford as a Rhodes Scholar, where the influence of his tutor, Richard Ellmann, helped turn him from poetry to biography. In the course of his career he contributed to *The New Yorker*, *The New York Times Magazine*, *The New York Review of Books* and other influential magazines, became an editor, novelist and publisher (of Atlas Books) and founded the biographical series 'Penguin Lives' and later 'Eminent Lives'. He was also the author of two biographies: *Delmore Schwartz: The Life of an American Poet* (1977) and, in 2000, *Bellow: A Biography*. (In a grim irony Atlas was eventually diagnosed with bipolarity. He recognised he had been closer to Schwartz than he had known forty years before, when writing the book.) Before his death in September 2019, Atlas's ruminations on his life with the genre appeared as *The Shadow in the Garden: A Biographer's Tale*.

Two early pieces he published in *PN Review* illustrate his preparation. The substantial essay 'Literary Biography' is both revealing of Atlas's values as a biographer as well as being as an education in the mainsprings of twentieth century biography. He begins with the felt need of other practitioners to venture into theoretical justification of their genre, 'to vindicate themselves not only before the tribunal of the living, but also before their vanquished subjects, whose recriminations are no less effective for being mute'. He turns to a consideration of Leon Edel's method, to which Atlas subscribes. In Edel's conception the writer's role is to explore the subjective as well as the dramatic in a life, while scrupulously avoiding remaking the subject in his image.

This leads to discussion of the complexity brought to biography by the turn to Freudian interpretation, including the need to acknowledge not impersonality but identification. Moving beyond Victorian concealment and innuendo, the biographer is now seen 'interposed, in a version of relativity, between his subject and the reality of his subject's life, which appears before us refracted through the lens of the biographer's own temperament'.

After considering 'that intuitive chronicler of sensibility, Lytton Strachey', most comprehensive in his exploration of the non-dramatic details of a life, Atlas explores in some detail the work of three classic biographers: George Painter (Proust), Edel (Henry James) and Ellmann (James Joyce). These have contributed to 'the peculiarly modern deification of personality', addressing themselves in one way or another to 'the attempt to render consciousness as an event no less important than those external incidents that formerly made up the substance of biography'. All are magnificent in their work and admiring of their subjects, according to Atlas, though Painter (with 'the most remarkable of modern literary biographies') is admittedly reactionary; Edel (the author of 'sprawling, eloquent work') is evasive; and Ellmann ('astonishing and generous') can be condescending.

In a *Poetry Nation* (*PN Review*) review from 1975 of *Pity the Monsters: The Political Vision of Robert Lowell* we find Atlas applauding good critical practice: 'Alan Williamson, while establishing necessary connections between Lowell's poems and what is known of his personal life, does so only to plot the nature and origins of those conflicts which provide a unified motif in the span of Lowell's work.' Implicit in the comment is his belief that the task of the biographer should encompass this.

The celebrated 1938 *Vogue* portrait of Schwartz seen in the mirror boasts the perfect metaphor for biography (if read as the biographer staring at his subject). Correctly viewed, it has the appropriately Freudian association of narcissism and Wildean self-destructiveness. The subtitle (*The Life of an American Poet*) prioritizes the poetry, whereas Schwartz was equally known for his stories and admired for his essays. There was a time in the forties though, when he reigned as the most anthologized of American poets, so much so that he could fantasise posterity would deploy the term 'Delmorean'. It has not.

As we learn from *The Shadow in the Garden*, the biography had its origins in a chance barroom conversation between the son of Schwartz's friend Dwight Macdonald and the owner of a removal company which held the papers of the recently deceased poet. He had died unnoticed. Atlas was offered a contract at the age of twenty-five to write the life. No-one would ever scrutinise Schwartz more exhaustively than James Atlas – except the man himself.

His life might have been expected to absorb future generations – a life with such a dramatically downward spiral and one so well told – yet ironically it is the work itself which marginalized it. Schwartz seems too set in his generation and, as Atlas put it in an article about the New York intellectuals (the *Partisan Review* crowd), 'the passions that animated the 30's and 40's are history'.

Schwartz is too solely preoccupied with Jewish experience, as he once feared ('the Jew in America', Eileen Simpson styled his theme in *Poets in their Youth*). The stories fail to transcend the experience of that Jewish generational bind: the ambitions of immigrant parents versus those of their (literary) children. At the same time – ever the Freudian – Schwartz's obsessive exploration of himself in his poetry, while bordering on the tragic, ultimately slackens and tires.

Atlas's biography, however, still reads as vividly as it did on its first appearance. He had detected behind Ellmann's Joyce the biographer himself. It was a voice like that, 'scholarly but not academic', that he aspired to. He had learnt the lesson, 'If you trust the writer's voice, you'll trust the writer's facts.' From a position close to omniscience Atlas's own voice avoids condescension or a censorious tone, exhibiting discretion in what might easily have offered itself as a subject for sensationalism.

He presents Schwartz as a brilliant student of T. S. Eliot, whose Modernist detachment he adopted; a fine poet and teacher who focused on Literature as appreciation; a first class essayist-critic of the American scene (Hemingway, Tate, Faulkner); and an admirer of Blackmur, Tate and Wilson. He is also depicted as arrogant, obsessed with his Jewishness, impractical, improvident, alienated, dependent on women whom he abused emotionally, capable of self-hatred and remorse as well as great friendships. ('I remember his electrical insight as the young man, / his wit & passion, gift, the whole young man / alive with surplus love', wrote John Berryman in 'Dream Song 155').

Atlas rockets through his narrative giving the drama in the life, while adding a little permissible colouring at times: 'In the fall of 1936, Delmore returned to Harvard in the midst of its tercentenary celebration. More cynical than reverent, he listened to the pompous speeches, observed the grandiose parades festooned with crimson VERITAS banners and noted the celebrities in attendance.' With the bonus of the journals, he is able to convey something of his subject's mental turmoil:

'Delmore had never regarded his birthdays with equanimity, but this December 8 was more ominous than ever, for he was turning thirty "and deceived by inspiration and losing hope & hope's lies." Writing to Berryman that morning he tried to be lighthearted.'

Atlas's characterisation of the poet's style is pithy: 'Delmore's amazing rhetoric, the orotund, passionate expression of grief and rage recited in varied pentameters, owed as much to what he thought to be the high style of nineteenth-century French poetry as it did to his American elders.' He refers to the characteristic voice as 'sonorous, faintly archaic', producing 'uneven blank verse' and to a 'Byronic element in his character, combined with the subtle tonalities of a wry Jewish ironist'.

Atlas also reveals a sound understanding of the context of Schwartz's work, which he expresses in terms of American Modernism and the complex influence of Pound and Eliot, while observing that William Carlos Williams 'was the only poet who carried on the work of Modernism at home'. He also deals with the unsavoury issue of 'the antipathy to Jews that persisted in the English Departments of Ivy League universities well into the forties' (We might note here Richard J. Evans recent comment in a *Times Literary Supplement* review about 'the ingrained antisemitism of many of the [Oxford] dons' a little earlier in the century.)

An entertaining feature of the biography is Atlas's use of humorous anecdotes. On one occasion Schwartz the young student comes to his professor's rescue with 'salt' when the philosopher cannot finish the expression 'take with a pinch of...'. The thankful prof, Alfred North Whitehead, breathes a sigh of relief, 'Yes, yes, I knew it was something mineral!' On another occasion there is an amusing story about Schwartz beginning to enlighten a member of the Hartford Insurance Company about Wallace Stevens's poetic genius, when interrupted by his friend's observation that the old man was a lousy insurance lawyer and would have been fired long before if he had not been a great poet.

Behind Atlas's conception of biography was his belief in the literary tradition. In his contribution to the 'great books' argument in 1990, with *Battle of the Books: The Curriculum Debate in America*, he took a stand in favour of the canon as a defence 'of the claims of society' above those of the individual in the belief – as one of his interviewees expressed it – that the struggle over canonical status was 'a struggle among contending factions for the right to be represented in the picture America draws of itself'. Although his ideas remained conservative (and remain contentious) his position clearly illustrated a commitment to traditional notions of literature and criticism widely adhered to in our generation.

According to a *New York Times* blog interview, the title of Atlas's memoir, *The Shadow in the Garden*, comes from Bellow and its method from Janet Malcolm, whose biographical explorations subvert biography itself. Although a personal memoir of a life in the business, the reader finds reference to a wide number of biographers (including Boswell, Ellmann, Edel, Holmes, Marchand, Strachey), as well as critics (Macdonald, Wilson, Kazin, Rahv, Allan Bloom, Malcolm), writers and academics (Joyce, Isaac Rosenfeld, Edward Shils) and, of course, his own biographical subjects, Schwartz and Bellow.

Considering the purpose of biography as a genre, Atlas offers the following, surely uncontentious, explanation: 'Primarily, I would say, to show what other factors – besides genius – contributed to the making of the writer's life, the genesis of his books, the social and literary influences that formed them.' Where he becomes more personal is in recognizing the impulse that set him off on his career: 'I was beginning to sense that the lives of poets interested me even more than the poetry. I could recite Robert Lowell's "Skunk Hour" in its entirety... but I was also curious about the car crash that nearly killed his first wife, Jean Stafford, while he was driving. I thrilled to the onomatopoetic mutterings of Eliot reading "The Waste Land" on the Caedmon album I owned, but I still wanted to know why he had locked away *his* first wife, Vivienne Haigh-Wood, in a mental institution. Art and life didn't just coexist: they enriched each other.' The higher gossip?

In preparation Atlas read countless biographies, focusing on how they worked, 'with the absorption of a car mechanic' as he puts it in the book. After Schwartz he made a living partly by reviewing biographies, preparing for his subjects by 'speed-reading their books and previous biographies in marathon sessions at the New York Public Library; after a week or so of late nights, I usually knew enough to write a passably well-informed review.'

He learnt also that some sort of empathy with his subject was a prerequisite for the necessary years of work involved. It was largely for reasons of incompatibility that Atlas returned an advance to write on the famous WASP and waspish Edmund Wilson (a work later done excellently by Lewis M. Dabney – despite Atlas's dismissal of this and the Jeffrey Meyers biography as 'adequate'). It may have been an even shrewder move than he knew, since he admits to not being able to finish Wilson's magnum opus, *Patriotic Gore* (an outstanding if flawed work – and a masterpiece of atmosphere). *The Shadow in the Garden* ends with Atlas worrying over the future of books and biography and about whether to dump the 'detritus' of his last research.

While literary biography *is* at best a 'shadow', even a quasi-fiction, it does allow the reader behind the scenes and into the company of not one but two writers. It is unlikely that James Atlas ever seriously regretted being one of them: 'I had devoted my life to an art whose assumptions couldn't be tested,' he wrote. 'Still, its rewards could be great – the challenge of reconstructing someone else's world; the opportunity to educate yourself; the serendipitous encounters and unlikely finds. I found this invigorating.' The evidence is in the books.

RICHARD HUGO & JAMES WRIGHT: 'MAKE IT SCOTCH AND DIRTY RIVER WATER'

They were old friends, driven by insecurities to depression and drink. They had grown up, in Hugo's phrase, in 'poor, often degrading circumstances' during the Depression, with 'loyalty to defeated people' they loved and did not want to be like. They shared 'a feeling of having violated' their lives 'by wanting to be different'. War and education enabled them to escape from home – Hugo's in White Center, Washington State, Wright's in Martins Ferry, Ohio – but memory always brought them back. Their work is marked by a loneliness which seeks identification and acceptance, by a fascination with the rejected (Wright) and the derelict (Hugo) – And yet they wrote with a liveliness of style and a candour that is magnetic.

Wright has the greater reputation. He is the more startling, the more varied, the more technically gifted: *The Branch Will Not Break* (1963); *Shall We Gather at the River* (1967); his *Collected Poems* (1971) which won a Pulitzer Prize. Hugo's best work is to be found in *Death of the Kapowsin Tavern* (1965) and *The Lady in Kicking Horse Reservoir* (1973). His posthumously collected poems, *Making Certain it Goes On*, appeared in 1984.

The two met in Theodore Roethke's class at the University of Montana in the mid-1950s. Roethke, another poet beset by personal difficulties, proved a powerful teacher. In his essay 'Stray Thoughts on Roethke and Teaching' Hugo reckoned Roethke's great strength was that he 'gave students a love of the sound of language': 'He was also playful in class, arrogant, hostile, tender, aggressive, receptive – anything that might work to bring the best out of a student.' Wright 'adopted many of Roethke's methods and modeled his own rapport with students after Roethke's presence in the classroom', according to his biographer, Jonathan Blunk (*James Wright: A Life in Poetry*, 2017). Wright reckoned that 'A course with Roethke was a course in very, very detailed and strenuous critical reading.'

Caroline Kizer – with David Wagoner another alumnus of this group – remembered Roethke's influence in 'rigorous revision'. It should be added that Kizer, while admiring the talents of the men, remained ambivalent about the class, because the opinions of women students were ignored by them. 'I was in a nest of singing chauvinists', she recalled.

Richard Hugo (born 1923) came from a poor Seattle suburb, 'whose reputation for violence and wild behaviour seemed to put it at the edge of civilization', he wrote. He lived with strict, uncommunicative grandparents. Softball and fishing became his 'simple compensations'. During the war he served as a bombardier in the Army Air Corps in the Mediterranean. Subsequently he took two degrees at the University of Washington, and married in 1952. Although employed by the Boeing Company in Seattle as a technical writer, he and his wife lived improvidently and shabbily, by his own account (They also shared a telling fondness for hunting through abandoned houses.)

Hugo always had difficulty in his relationships with the opposite sex and the guilt, which he wrote openly about later, intensified when his first wife left him:

Lawns well trimmed remind you of the train
your wife took one day forever, some far empty town,
the odd name you never recall. The time: 6:23.
The day: October 9. The year remains a blur.
               'What Thou Lovest Well Remains American'

He finally published *A Run of Jacks* with the University of Minnesota Press in 1961, took a year in Italy and became a visiting lecturer at the University of Montana in 1964, the year his wife left him. The title poem of *The Lady in Kicking Horse Reservoir* he disconcertingly described as being 'as close to direct vengeance as I'd come':

> Not my hands but green across you now.
> Green tons hold you down, and ten bass curve
> teasing in your hair.

Hugo's defensive misogyny ended with a stabilizing second marriage in 1974. He was to remain at Montana, later as head of their creative writing programme. Afflicted by health problems in later life, he claimed that he stopped drinking: 'I began to see that a lot of my grief was old and shopworn and only the booze had kept it alive.' However, celebrity made abstinence difficult.

James Wright was born four years later than Hugo, his hometown a rail hub and river port with a population of sixteen thousand, though today failed industry has greatly shrunk it. While he claimed 'a peculiar kind of devotion' to Martins Ferry and the Ohio Valley, he wrote privately of it as an 'unspeakable rat-hole'. His father worked at the Hazel-Atlas Glass Company, his mother in a laundry. The town compounded Wright's personal unhappiness. He saw it as a place of failed dreams:

> In the Shreve High football stadium,
> I think of Polacks nursing long beers in Tiltonsville,
> And gray faces of Negroes in the blast furnace at Benwood,
> And the ruptured night watchman of Wheeling Steel,
> Dreaming of heroes.
>   'Autumn Begins in Martins Ferry, Ohio

After school Wright spent two years in the army, including time in Japan, and then on the G. I. Bill studied at Kenyon College, Ohio, where John Crowe Ransom taught. He learned from Ransom 'the Horatian ideal': a poem with 'a single unifying effect'. In 1952 he married and with a Fulbright Scholarship attended the University of Vienna, where he studied German literature. During this time he decided to teach. Again without knowing the faculty, he matriculated at the University of Washington.

Possessed of a photographic memory, which enabled him to

recite enormous amounts of poetry, Wright went on to teach at the University of Minnesota for six years before being denied tenure because of heavy drinking and missing classes, followed by two years at Macalester College in Saint Paul and then at Hunter College in New York, where he taught courses on the C18th novel, Dickens (the subject of his doctoral dissertation) and Hardy. His reputation well-established by his poems and translations, he and his wife began to spend time in Europe, particularly favouring Italy. He died in 1980 of throat cancer.

Hugo's Italy, unlike Wright's, evoked memories of war service. He published a book of poems, *Good Luck in Cracked Italian* (1969): 'I only came / to see you living and the fountains run'. Though he also wrote a collection on the island of Skye, Hugo is best remembered as a poet of the northwest. He said of his inspiration: 'I often found the sources of poems in the lonely reaches of the world, the ignored, forlorn, and, to me, beautiful districts of cities, like the West Marginal Way area in Seattle, the sad small towns of Washington and Montana, the villages and countryside of Southern Italy, wherever I imagined life being lived as amateurishly as we had once played basketball.' He wrote of his use of the West Marginal Way as a place he could 'melodramatically extend and exploit certain feelings' he had about himself tied to his sense of defeat.

What he repeatedly imagined were the landscape's living things, the lonely and the derelict. He returned regularly to the bars of faded towns, in poems like 'The Milltown Union Bar' and 'Death of the Kapowsin Tavern' :

> Nothing dies as slowly as a scene.
> The dusty jukebox cracking through
> the cackle of a beered-up crone –
> wagered wine – sudden need to dance –
> these remain in the black debris.
> Although I know in time the lake will send
> wind black enough to blow it all away.

Hugo proved consistently critical of his early self ('For many years whenever I did something I was ashamed of, I felt, in addition to the shame itself, a sense of failure.') It is little wonder that he turned at length to psychoanalysis. In *Local Assays: On Contemporary American Poetry* (1985) Dave Smith, who knew him, noted that 'His poems depend upon his own hard self-accusations: he drinks too much, he wastes himself, he lacks courage, he is fat, ugly, uneducated, unsophisticated, inferior, an orphan.' Hugo knew he could work with this. In *The Triggering Town: Lectures and Essays on Poetry and Writing* (1979) he wrote, '*How you feel about yourself* is probably the most important feeling you have.' He knew, he wrote, that 'An act of imagination is an act of self-acceptance', even in the very act of rejection.

In *31 Letters and 13 Dreams* (1977) he published an autobiographical collection, inevitably a talky one. He had been struggling and made no bones about it. His problems with drinking and memories are foregrounded:

> On good days, this
> is just a town and I am just a lonely man, no worse
> than the others in the bar, watching their lives thin down
> to moments they remember in the mirror and those half
> dozen friends you make in life
> 'Letter to Libbey from St. Regis'

What Thou Lovest Well Remains American (1975) is more robust, despite exploiting Hugo's past humiliations ('I think of Dumar sadly because a dancehall burned / and in it burned a hundred early degradations') and depressions ('hours alone in bars with honest mirrors'). It also offers portraits of other casualties and atmospheric description:

That goose died in opaque dream.
I was trolling in fog when the blurred
hunter stood to aim. The chill gray

that blurred him amplified the shot
and the bird scream.
>	'Again, Kapowsin'

In the title poem of *White Center* (1980) Hugo comes home. He had hitherto avoided this because, 'With the strange town… you owe the details nothing emotionally', while his home town, 'seemed blocked by allegiances to memory'. Yet the title poem ends on an optimistic note: on the absence of a feeling of shame. *The Right Madness on Skye* (1980) seemed a gamble, though was partly redeemed by his sense that the landscape twinned with his own ('The sky, water, vegetation and wind are Seattle. / The panoramic bare landscape's Montana.')

In the late poems, the vein seems a little thinner, but Hugo rallies with his Wright poem, with 'Confederate Graves in Little Rock' and 'Making Certain It Goes On'. Finally, in the title poem, he rises again to optimism, a mood he believed always marked his approach, whatever the critics wrote. Here we are at the Big Blackfoot River, where the speaker and his wife imagine a rejuvenated landscape and a thriving community.

Hugo always felt a debt to James Wright, who had been an early champion of his poetry. There are a number of references to it in Wright's selected letters, *A Wild Perfection* (2005). In July 1958 he wrote to Robert Bly (Then editor of *The Fifties* and later a close friend and collaborator on translations) that he thought Hugo's poems shared with Gary Snyder's 'the new imagination' and that he had submitted his friend's manuscript to the University of Minnesota Press from motives of friendship, admiration and guilt 'that a tremendous poet, who is doing something to catch his time and place *alive*' is being ignored. Later he took the manuscript to show Bly.

In a similarly self-deprecating mood Wright wrote in March 1959 to James Dickey, who was still making a name for himself, noting the parallels between Hugo and Dickey (They were the same age, both war veterans and both worked outside academia).

He also stressed Hugo's admiration for Dickey's work, always an incentive to the fiercely competitive Dickey. The two corresponded, which greatly pleased Wright. He was not as successful in impressing Donald Hall (then poetry editor of *The Paris Review*) with his friend's poems, though Hall had responded positively to his push for Carolyn Kizer (whose *The Ungrateful Garden* would appear in 1961).

In another letter Wright mentioned that his 'On Minding One's Own Business', came out of a fishing expedition with Hugo on Lake Kapowsin. Hugo reciprocated in remembering their trips in his 1977 'Letter to Wright from Gooseprairie'. And in a late poem, 'Lament: Fishing with Richard Hugo', Wright returned again to the old days and the private joke about a tavern owner they disliked.

The two poets occasionally exchanged visits, though Wright could be an intolerable guest, as he was in early 1959 when he spent days drinking and playing the same Delius record for hours at a time. He had been obsessed by deadlines, with his wife's recent breakdown and a female student he longed to see. In defence of his friend, Hugo later wrote that with Wright's leaving 'some winning energy, tiresome yet important, had just left our life'.

Aside from *A Run of Jacks*, Wright's most public praise came twelve years later in a piece for *The American Poetry Review* entitled 'Hugo: Secrets of the Inner Landscape'. Writing in an idiosyncratic mood, he celebrates their fishing trips and the poet's talent: 'I believe that Richard Hugo has become one of the best poets alive, in any language I know.' Hugo acknowledged being 'touched and grateful' for the 'glowing' piece from Wright. He hoped it had not been promoted by guilt at his behaviour during the visit in Missoula.

Wright's own poems are generally easy to admire but not always easy to identify with. In 'A Kind of Overview in Appreciation' Miller Williams argued that they: 'are more often than not words out of his own darkness telling us about violence, loss, and death'. It is not so obvious in the formal, early poems of

The Green Wall (1957) where we feel we might lose our bearings: 'Errina to Sapho', 'Eleutheria', 'Elegy in a Firelit Room' ('The window showed a willow in the west, / But windy dry. No folly weeping there.') What holds us are the twentieth century moments: 'A Poem about George Doty in the Death House' and the sly, 'A Gesture by a Lady with an Assumed Name':

> Lovers she left to clutter up the town
> Mourned in the chilly morgue and went away,
> All but the husbands sneaking up and down
> The stairs of that apartment house all day.

In *Saint Judas* (1959) Wright is more demanding, his seriousness more apparent. Here he takes on the lot of the lost and the damned ('A Note Left in Jimmy Leonard's Shack'). We are to share their pain with the poet since it is, arguably, everyman's. Doty reappears in 'At the Executed Murderer's Grave' ('Wrinkles of winter ditch the rotted face / Of Doty, killer, imbecile, and thief: / Dirt of my flesh, defeated, underground.') In the title poem we meet a Samaritan Judas, 'flayed without hope'.

The Branch Will Not Break and *Shall We Gather at the River* (1968) are famous for their epiphanies and blessings, their simple delights and surrealistic touches. Yet the poet also turns candidly to his own depressions in 'Stages on a Journey Westward', 'Inscription for the Tank', and the indelible 'Outside Fargo, North Dakota':

> Along the sprawled body of the derailed
>   Great Northern freight car,
> I strike a match slowly and lift it slowly.
> No wind.

What has been described as another turn in Wright's work came with *Two Citizens* (1973). He could by now, after half a dozen 'crack-ups', write convincingly, 'I have crawled along the edges of plenty / Of scars' ('Son of Judas'). This collection, which Wright claimed he would never reprint, tested his faith in America, as he saw it from abroad. It is a loose collection, a talky one, which only sometimes works ('Ars Poetica: Some Recent Criticism' and 'The Old WPA Swimming Pool in Martins Ferry, Ohio').

His last books, *To a Blossoming Pear Tree* (1977) and the posthumous *The Journey* (1982) are largely concerned with Europe, though when he returns home in memory he finds consolation and community, 'beauty' even, in the hard lives of his working people ('Blood in my body drags me / Down with my brother.') There are still the flashes of grit that fired his earlier work. He attains a kind of acceptance in the meditative poem, 'The Journey', and in the fine 'The Vestal in the Forum', which ends with identification:

> A dissolving
> Stone, she seems to change from stone to something
> Frail, to someone I can know, someone
> I can almost name.

If Hugo could not repay Wright for his decisive early support, he would always recognise their time together and the talent. The late poem to Wright's memory, 'Last Words to James Wright' has the lines: 'You wanted words to sing the suffering on / and every time you asked the words came willing.' His prose celebration appeared in the posthumous, *The Real West Marginal Way: A Poet's Autobiography* (1986): 'No one carried his life more vividly inside him, or simultaneously in plain and in eloquent ways used the pain of his life to better advantage. What maims others often beyond repair maimed him too, but in some miraculous way it also nourished his great talent. It was miraculous too that his obsessive repetitive mind never limited his artistry.'

While they may not have influenced each other's work directly, they shared a great deal beyond their preoccupations and a blue collar perspective: a love for nature, for instance, and a sense of humour. One hears in their comments a similarity of views about the nature of writing and teaching. They were wedded to honesty, plain speaking and occasional sentimentality. They also shared a disarming readiness to confess weakness in their behaviour and error in their pronouncements.

Their differences were clear, too. Hugo found his style early and kept to it (his 'drumming iambics or his stark and alliterative sentences', in Dave Smith's phrase). Wright experimented with formal and free verse, with conventional and deep imagery. For Hugo the wreckage of places is as eloquent of human failure as the portrait of the individuals whom Wright is more prone to seek out.

In the 1970s the two exchanged occasional letters. *A Wild Perfection* reprints one from New York City in September 1975, when Wright is 'off the sauce' and Hugo recently remarried. Wright is asking advice about using prose poems in a book of 'straight poems'. The other is from Italy in April 1979, where Wright, an enthusiast for Naples, asks for news. They last met at a White House reception honouring poets in January 1980, where Hugo is said to have been in tears after meeting his gravely ill friend. Wright would die that March at the age of 52; Hugo two years later from leukaemia, at 58.

Hugo ends his James Wright essay with an account of being in the Greyhound Bus Station in Wheeling, West Virginia in 1963. It was a depressing place, he recalls, and he knew that Martins Ferry lay unseen across the river. He might have been speaking for himself as well as for Wright when he concluded, 'I let that bus station say a lot about where Jim came from and why it was necessary for him to leave, to get away. And why he did get away. And why he didn't.'

ROBERT HASS: A VOICE IN MY EAR

I

In the introduction to his translation of Horace's *Epistles*, David Ferry wrote, 'It's the voice that's the life of these poems.' He characterized it, then added, 'The voice is an invention, of course, or a playing field of inventions, but it gives the illusion of speaking to us as we hear it with a startlingly familiar immediacy.' Although late-Modernist rather than Augustan, the Northern Californian poet Robert Hass also has an endearing immediacy. If I were to characterize his voice – the recognisable personality in his writing – as Ferry does Horace's, I would call it welcoming, conversational, observant, good-humoured and ethical.

Of course with writers who lean toward the autobiographical it is well to remember that the protagonist in a poem is not the poet – even if he almost is. In a famous interview for *The Paris Review*, in 1961, Robert Lowell, spoke of his autobiographical masterpiece *Life Studies* (1959). Lowell reminded his interviewer that in the poems 'There's a good deal of tinkering with fact. You leave out a lot, and emphasize this and not that. Your actual experience is a complete flux.' He added to that common sense by explaining, 'the reader was to believe he was getting the *real* Robert Lowell'. So effective was Lowell that he attracted the label 'confessional' and unintentionally launched a movement.

As a teacher – and that is the stance in Hass's poetry and prose – he avoids trying to sound definitive, omniscient, standing openly with his audience. In an essay 'On Teaching Poetry' he explained, 'teaching poetry for me has been mostly about reflecting on what makes particular poems come alive to me and trying to convey that experience to others'.

In his own interview in *The Paris Review* in 2020, there is a photograph of a younger Hass with the haircut of the time (California 1980) and a wine glass in one hand. He is responding to the photographer with his tongue out. It is a common pose, a humorous 'Get out of here' we are familiar with in our own lives. What struck me (lightly) about it was that in his poetry as in his prose, Hass is the last person to pull a face at his audience. He has a sense of humour, without doubt, but he never deploys it at the reader's expense. 'Which writer does?' you may ask. Well, few, I suppose. But my point is that Hass's voice is unusually trustworthy. Even his anger – and there is anger on humanitarian (read political/ecological) grounds – is leavened with the control of one who wants to discuss it. It is the voice that has kept me reading Hass this past twentysomething years.

And yet I didn't want to begin my appreciation this way. I wanted to write, 'I want to say some things against Robert Hass's poems, which I love.' I wanted to say that, not because it's true – the part about saying things *against* is not true… except if I pointed to occasional moments I find cute, or too laid-back, or ingenuous – but because that is a line he wrote many years ago in a revealing essay on the remarkable James Wright ('I want to say some things against James Wright's poems, which I love'). I wanted to begin this way to illustrate how Hass can put a line in your thoughts for twenty years in prose as well as he can in poems like his well-known 'Meditation at Lagunitas' ('All the new thinking is about loss. / In this it resembles all the old thinking.')

I have puzzled over that poem since I discovered it in my favourite American anthology, J.D. McClatchy's *The Vintage Book of Contemporary American Poetry*, which I bought in Virginia in August 1992 (and from which I also picked-up on Wright, Dave Smith, Donald Justice, Galway Kinnell and others). I have puzzled over Hass as he has puzzled over Wallace Stevens and I have sought no final opinion because, as he said elsewhere in the prose collection that housed his Wright essay (*Twentieth Century Pleasures: Prose on Poetry* (1984)), when poetry gets into the blood it becomes 'difficult to conduct an argument about its value' because 'it becomes autobiography there' (I subsequently took *Poetry in the Blood* as a title for an essay anthology I edited for Shoestring Press in 2014.)

II

I hear the same Hassian voice in both the poetry and the prose, but I begin with the prose to honour the line about Wright. So, what are the features of Hass's voice that have so appealed to me? Firstly it is his enthusiasm. In *The Paris Review* interview he recalled listening to Terry Gross interviewing Philip Roth, and she asked what it takes to be an artist: 'He said there were two things, to his mind. A deep appetite for play, and a moral stake in the world. I thought, That sounds right to me.' Hass's voice has a conversational tone in the American idiom (an idiom about which William Carlos Williams once wrote, 'The future American poetry has to arise from speech–American, not English… from what we *hear* in America.') With that goes a fondness for anecdote and a willingness to involve himself. Here are two examples from *Now & Then: The Poet's Choice Columns, 1997–2000* (2007). This was a nationally syndicated column and so Hass's audience is naturally very wide. The first is on his interest in Wallace Stevens:

'In Hartford this autumn, a friend drove me by the offices of the Hartford Insurance Company and the house where Stevens lived. I had read that he walked to work, and, taking what seemed the shortest way, I tried to walk his walk to work.'

The second is on explaining Plath's role in *The Birthday Letters*, in answer to his local baker's question stimulated by media interest in the book: 'I felt like I was summarizing a soap opera, not sure which details were the relevant ones, the ones that would answer his question. So I found myself tailing off and said, "You know, what you should do first is read her poems," and the next morning I dropped off a copy of Sylvia Plath's *Ariel*.'

Addressing a poetry audience in *Twentieth Century Pleasures*, we find him in similarly relaxed mood. Here is Hass discussing Rilke's 'Sometimes a Man Stands Up During Supper' and its translation by Robert Bly: 'the poem had a feeling of being too neat, too pat, which disappears, I think, in the English translation, which is a marvelous poem, but one made from the unmetered, unrhymed cadences of a poetic revolution that hadn't occurred yet.'

A second feature of the poet's prose voice is that it is critical without being censorious. Of a misfiring poem by Randall Jarrell he writes, 'In this poem, he has found an interesting perception, an important perception, but the stance has thrown him off himself. He has not found for himself the form of being in the idea.'

And finally from that essay collection we have Hass the poetry enthusiast who likes to share his discoveries: 'I was to hear, from someone who had taken a course from [Czesław Miłosz] at Berkeley, that he had said that the best literary model for the twentieth century might be the gospel of Luke, rough, plain, synoptic.'

Here is Hass from *What Light Can Do: Essays on Art, Imagination, and the Natural World* (2012), his second collection of essays. The tone is similarly conversational, the critical insights accessible and illuminating. Quoting Stevens's 'Of Mere Being' ('The palm at the end of the mind, / Beyond the last thought, rises / In the bronze décor') he adds: 'And then he changed "distance" to "décor". It's as if he had, in one stroke, made the philosophical leap from Romanticism to postmodernism, from the idea of the meaning of the world as attainable but just out of reach to the idea of the world as a stage set, a set of fictions.'

One important influence on Hass's calmness (and sensitivity to nature) can be found in the Japanese haiku tradition. In 1994 he published *The Essential Haiku: Versions of Bashō, Buson, and Issa*. He also learnt the profitable use of metaphor to convey the unsayable. Here is an example from his last prose collection to date, *A Little Book on Form: An Exploration into the Formal Imagination of Poetry* (2017) – actually a big book – intended for young poets who were taking a two-year intensive course of poetry reading and writing: 'At the simplest level the blank verse stanza works like a paragraph does in prose. But it can also mime the rivery movement of the mind in quietly spectacular ways, as in "Tintern Abbey," or the pulses of thought as it does in "Frost at Midnight".'

III

If we turn to the poetry, for which Robert Hass is justly celebrated, we see that the voice is remarkably similar, especially when his poetic line lengthened. In 'An Interview with Robert Hass' in 1916 – with Spanish professor Viorica Patea – he described himself as operating 'like many writers of my generation on a kind of cusp between late modernism and postmodernism'. His roots, he acknowledges though, were in the romantic poetry of Whitman and Wordsworth, which might explain his eventual turn to longer lines and his fondness for plain speaking. The last may also be Japanese influenced ('Somebody asked Buson if there was a trick to poetry, maybe to haiku, and he said, Yes, learn how to be simple without being vulgar.')

Hass's first collection, *Field Guide* (1973) revealed the ecological sensitivity in his work, his delight in naming and friendship, and in the activities of hands. He is often engaged with domestic details which provide the serendipities.

In 'Adhesive: For Earlene', a poem for his first wife, Hass describes the simple pleasures of marriage and a cheerful poverty where they skip lunch to buy tickets for 'Les Enfants du Paradis'. In 'Fall' they are uncertainly gathering mushrooms 'which smelled of camphor and the fog-soaked earth'. There is a rich awareness of the gift of living, like discovering trash nocturnal creatures have scattered:

> A thaw turned up
> the lobster shells from Christmas Eve.
> They rotted in the yard
> and standing in the muddy field I caught,
> as if across great distances,
> a faint rank fragrance of the sea.
>   'In Weather'

Simple pleasures are uppermost, but there is a hint of

childhood distress ('House') and recognition of historical and contemporary abuses. In 'Palo Alto: The Marshes', the Dow Chemical Company is manufacturing napalm locally. Hass now reckons, 'In *Field Guide* naming the world more or less committed me to the concrete, which tended to be rendered in staccato and short-breathed language.' These, he says, are the poems of a young man who had learnt from Lowell's early poetry of New England that poems could resonate from the regional.

In *Praise*, his 1979 collection, the approach is more meditative, more metaphysical and the lines become longer. Take the opening poem 'Heroic Simile', which distils Hass's thoughts on the limitations of the imagination and the need to recognise 'the silence of separate fidelities'. Or 'Meditation at Lagunitas', the poem which leads away from talk with all its obstructiveness, toward the simple rituals of loving, making bread, and sounding the language. While these poems suggest the limits of empathy, they also recognise the richness of plurality. His preference in 'Santa Lucia' is in observation not communication, in the uninterrupted deer feeding, not its confrontation with the observer.

Human Wishes appeared in 1989. It is a more inclusive collection, as the title implies. Hass had been experimenting with prose and some of these poems are in paragraph form. 'Vintage' opens with 'They had agreed, walking into the delicatessen on Sixth Avenue, that / their friends' affairs were focused and saddened by massive projections'. Personal histories are the subject of a number of poems and anecdotes.

Being Hass, there are also paeans to the community and to the ecology of the Sierras. In 'Spring Rain' the rain produces larkspurs, whose seeds the gray jays spread, which lead the poet to simulating the process with 'the coffee we drank in Lisa's kitchen'. The rhythms of life and casual beauty flow into 'Late Spring':

> and after swimming, white wine; and the sharing of stories before dinner is prolonged because the relations of the children in the neighborhood have acquired village intensity and the stories take longer telling

Strangers are as comfortably included in Hass's world as friends are. They are observed as is the flora and fauna. The 'Museum' presents a couple with a sleeping baby sharing the newspaper and Hass, observing, having 'fallen in love with this equitable arrangement'. There are couples in 'Quartet' whose inner life he imagines and anecdotes from a friend about himself and the former Vice President, about a duck hunting judge, a composer who had had a double mastectomy (also the subject of a short story by Richard Ford) and in 'On Squaw Peak' a gesture at that inclusiveness: 'It was the abundance / the world gives, the more-than-you-bargained-for / surprise of it.'

David Barber, writing for the *Boston Review,* noted that Hass had 'cultivated a more open, intimately epistolary verse that makes room for everything from strenuous metaphysics, beguiling storytelling, and wry recollections to haiku-like snapshots, flinty epigrams, and tremulous lyricism.'

From 1995 to 1997, Hass served as the United States poet laureate. In that time he published *Sun Under Wood* (1996) a more autobiographical collection, revealing the difficulties rather than the simple pleasures in his own life. For all its problematic subject matter the book, which won the *National Book Critics Circle Award*, begins with 'Happiness':

> It is December, very cold,
> we woke early this morning,
> and lay in bed kissing,
> our eyes squinched up like bats.

There follow poems which deal with painful references to his mother's alcoholism and the diversions with which he and his brother tried to occupy themselves. In 'My Mother's Nipples' he writes, 'In grammar school, whenever she'd start to drink, / she panicked and made amends by baking chocolate cake.' And in 'Regalia for a Black Hat Dancer' she is living the last of her life breathlessly in a hotel room, while Hass's brother is 'in the psych ward / at San Francisco General' coming down from 'crack'.

The same poem has reference to the end of Hass's marriage: to the 'two emptinesses: one made of pain and desire / and one made of vacancy'. But if sadness and cruelty seem 'infinite' and pain hollows out its victim, there is also the possibility of experiencing a revitalising new love (the poet's second wife, Brenda Hillman). Life has taught him the lesson: 'Private pain is easy, in a way. It doesn't go away, / but you can teach yourself to see its size. Invent a ritual.'

To that end, perhaps, the idea of singing first appears in 'Faint Music': 'I had the idea that the world's so full of pain / it must sometimes make a kind of singing.' And despite the pressures and pains in the course of it, 'Interrupted Meditation' ends: 'I'm a little ashamed that I want to end this poem / singing, but I want to end this poem singing.'

Time and Materials: Poems 1997–2005 (2007) won both the National Book Award and the Pulitzer Prize. When I wrote of it on its appearance I stressed the vitality and excellence and I still see that (along with his characteristic references to literature and art. and its focus on the process of the poem). However, on rereading now, the *Weltschmerz* (literally the world-pain) shows more immediately. Hass is not a consolatory writer, or at least one side of him is not. One side is that observer – perhaps again from his training in the Japanese tradition – and this time, rereading the darker poems, it came through most forcefully. In 'Winged and Acid Dark' he writes of abuses: 'We pass these things on, / probably, because we are what we can imagine.' We wonder at what pain teaches us in 'The World as Will and Representation', which ends:

> My mother at the kitchen table gagged and drank,
> Drank and gagged. We get our first moral idea
> About the world – about justice and power,
> Gender and the order of things – from somewhere.

Then there are the grim indictments: 'A Poem' ('The nations of the / world could stop setting an example for suicide bombers'); 'Bush's War' ('It's not just / The violence, it's a taste for power / That amounts to contempt for the body'); and in 'Ezra Pound's Proposition' we follow the economic process by which a girl-child is forced to turn prostitute.

After *The Apple Trees at Olema: New and Selected Poems* (2010), which included a poem on his brother's death and another on leaving his failed marriage, *Summer Snow* appeared in 2020. It is a collection gathered over the past decade in which, in his conversational way, Hass mulls over a lifetime's preoccupations: the ecology of his native Northern California; meditations on love and loss; political and eco-activism; the serendipities of language and the simple life. In his empathy and social activism, Hass follows in the tradition of critical compassion he so admires in Chekhov.

In *Why Poetry Matters* (2008) Jay Parini explored the question of voice, concluding that the High Modernists – Yeats, Frost, Stevens and Eliot – 'all seem to have understood that personality is an invention as much as a discovery'. He quotes Yeats's 'The Mask': 'It was the mask engaged your mind, / And after set your heart to beat, / Not what's behind.' One would put money on Hass's real and poetic selves as being close to identical.

REVIEW: DAVE SMITH, *LOOKING UP: POEMS 2010–2022* (2023)

My friendship with Dave Smith began in admiration of his considerable body of fine work. At eighty he is one of the last of a generation of honoured American poets, while at his back are his mentor, the great twentieth century poet Robert Penn Warren, and the controversial James Dickey, two writers of a Southern sensibility like himself, as well as other admired poets like James Wright and Richard Hugo. Smith's substantial new collection is an event: the accumulated poetry of a decade, love poems, memories, meditations on age and ill health, as well as observations on current American culture. This is the poetry of experience.

Smith's method is direct, unflinching. The veteran critic Helen Vendler once wrote of his early poems, 'His work is that of a man writing dense verse out of hard moments.' One thinks of the advice from Warren in Smith's 'Man Swimming in Home-Dug Pool': 'Go / to the bottom not touched, touch *it*. Look up. Push *it*.' His poetry has kept faith with 'hard moments', yet here there is warmth and accessibility too. He is by turns loving, grateful, regretful, angry and bemused. To me the collection's excellence lies in Smith's ability to sustain the atmosphere around a single voice grappling with events past and present.

To illustrate certain themes, let me begin with love. From the opening poem, 'City Point' ('What can it hurt to feel again, to hear / love's tale of aches on dream's flesh-eating shore?'), through the beauty of the butterfly morning in 'Monarch', to the final, architectonic 'Tomatoes', we are made aware of the poet's sense of gratitude at having the loved life he has led. He is at his most tender in poems that involve his wife, Dee. Moments of their time together reveal her deep and sustaining importance to him, as in 'Flying in Sewanee' and 'A Sunday Story'. These poems are at times comic ('Cow Story' and 'Reading Obituaries'), erotic, or rueful like the title poem where Smith unadvisedly attempts to clear a mould stain from the bedroom's 'cathedral ceiling' via an improvised ladder: 'I flew / ten feet, bounced on bed's gullied heart, old / man hurting, scared, alive.' The poem ends in calm reassurance, as does 'Dead Fish' with its lyrical last verse:

> the moon is
> filling our house with pleasure like seafoam
> silvering the marsh edge. The tide is going,
> wind in the trees makes note of it, lying
> alone we can feel death in all things slink away.

While he transcended his regional perspective – Smith was raised in Portsmouth, Virginia – some of his well-known early poems reached back to the Civil War; others took place among the watermen of the Chesapeake Bay. He observed in attentive detail their hard lives, their skills, their pragmatism. Now he opens that same poem, 'Dead Fish', which is a version of a Horatian ode:

> Sometimes in late afternoon I wonder why
> I go on writing about banged-up boats,
> marshes where east wind drags a sour stink,
> men's sewage sliming the gold-tinted spears
> you'd be hard pressed to imagine as glory,
> a word rank in the mouth as saltwater bilge
> I've swallowed and floated happily on.

Unlike most British poets, then, Smith is closely in tune with nature, attentive to local landscapes, birds, his own loved dogs and horses. The second poem in the collection, 'Audubon's Peewees', has the young artist-ornithologist tying silver thread to the legs of these birds so as to identify individuals. His pictorial skill finds a parallel in the poet's imaginative recreation:

> Then, they return! Ice-morning, on his palm the male,
> his female hovering back, juddering, cocked
> peeps of fear, him squinting his blue eye.
> His hat swallowed both, settling, as if in his brain.
> A silver ribbon, ratty in the end, pennant.
> What far flight! Hadn't they been everywhere together!

Scrutiny and narrative are at the heart of Smith's poetry. He does not sentimentalise Nature. Yet his admiration is clear. Here are hummingbirds, red-winged blackbirds, buzzards ('blacker than doom's dreams'), fated Siamese cats, an amorous, irritating Louisiana tree frog, slinking grey fox, the outcast 'Yellow-Headed Night Heron', all colourful, all fitting comfortably or not into his world and requiring recognition. At one moment he ruminates on their survival and our arrogant destructiveness :

> The wonder is, I suppose, how much we want
> to believe we'll hear and see it all tomorrow.
> And how we are convinced the world here
> stands agreed to perform without regard for
> explanation or whatever abuse we may bring.
> 'Grim Permissions'

The dogs in Smith's poems are family and share human traits. His bird dog is rashly eager to chase down a poisonous garden lizard with 'that muscle that's desire / balling up like an aging hamstring' ('Hopeless Dog'). In 'Armadillo' it 'chewed up the ass of one trying / to transcend our backyard fence', then looked ashamed as those should be who bought into the myths about such 'immigrants'.

This is an upbeat collection – as its title suggests – but unillusioned in the face of time. It has its own hard facts and hard lives ('I wanted to know / why a man I admired was found like a boot / in his yard, and no one seemed to care.') Smith documents failures, regrets and cruelties (physical abuses, the blight of progress, terrorist outrages, the poisoning of his dog). Poems deal with his difficult mother, his father's death in a traffic accident, his own health failing. This last is an issue in the wry 'Prophecy', in the moving 'Quail', and in 'Seizure', where he captures the terror of a diabetic attack while walking the dog before dawn past a flood-destroyed house ('words / in my mouth sloshing like water, tongue like glass / where windows burst, floor buckles'). But I won't dwell on these because the collection doesn't. Rather it poses the question: 'How does a man say what life's gift feels like?' We may be subject to 'just what happens, here, now', but we learn that love, compassion and remorse are what redeem us:

> I must have wanted then what I want now,
> a quiet room's forgiveness for what's been
> done or not done.

Death, as Smith says, is 'the cost of happiness'. Contemplating their Frank Cole painting, 'Emotional Tomatoes' (which adorns the book cover), the poet remembers a young marriage, an old planter neighbour and the thrill of the red-winged blackbirds of his youth:

> In the flickering light of those days, death passed by us.
> We ate, we made love, we laughed. What more
> could we have asked? Taste them, he said,
> his venerable voice at our door, that day, him looking up.

DISCOVERING F.T. PRINCE

One of the great pleasures in reading is of course discovery, though one often needs a little help. Late in my school life I became absorbed in the soliloquies of Shakespeare and their Victorian incarnation (or misrepresentation) in the dramatic monologues of Browning, Tennyson and then in Eliot. In the decades since, one poet has led me to another. To Anthony Rudolf's inspiring *Silent Conversations: A Reader's Life* (2013), I am indebted for an introduction to F. T. Prince's poetry.

Frank Templeton Prince (1912–2003) was a South African born poet with a Jewish and Presbyterian background, who converted to Catholicism in 1937. He studied at Oxford and Princeton before serving in British army intelligence during World War II. Prince taught at Southampton University from 1946 to 1974. A Milton and Shakespeare scholar, his influences included the poetry of fellow countryman Roy Campbell, as well as that of Yeats, Pound, Eliot and Rimbaud. He first came to prominence through *Poems* (1938) published by Eliot at Faber, although subsequent collections appeared with smaller presses, including Rudolf's own Menard Press, which co-published a *Collected Poems* in 1979. Prince is currently best served by Carcanet Press with *Collected Poems 1935–1992* (and two late pamphlets from Perdika Press).

He is a fine poet: exacting, intriguing and technically highly gifted. He shared his friend Geoffrey Hill's attitude to accessibility in poetry, a feeling that poets should not talk down to their readers whatever the difficulty of the work. Difficulty in itself is no great recommendation as far as I am concerned. However, Prince has such a command of style, character and atmospheric detail that his poetry deserves be introduced to a wider audience.

He showed great interest in the dramatic monologue, where he is at his finest producing what Peter Robinson terms 'the psychologized portrait poem'. His subjects are generally trapped in some way by circumstances or time. We catch them mulling over their accomplishments and failures, their frustrated desires and their fates. Except that these are historical figures coerced by the corruptions of power, they are Prince and ourselves in our existential moments, confronted by what he described as 'those two conundrums, faith / and human passion' (*Walks in Rome*). Significantly his shorter poems offer untroubled landscapes that yet reveal man's inner turmoil and love lyrics working through metaphysical conceits, which perhaps suggest something about the hidden life.

One central characteristic of Prince's poetry is its foregrounding of style to an unusual degree. Imagery, prosody, syntax, lineation are together responsible for an overall richness of effect. Another recurrent feature is his use of the past. The idea of a courtly world offered itself as an early preoccupation, allowing Prince to explore subjects and registers sympathetic to his romantic imagination and to his love of semantic possibilities. He was able at the same time to imply contemporary parallels to the dangers of power. The old world offered rich possibilities for allegory.

The *Collected Poems* opens with just such a poem – and my own favourite – 'An Epistle to a Patron', from *Poems* (1938). It begins exquisitely, as a request for preferment might:

> My lord, hearing lately of your opulence in promises and your house
> Busy with parasites, of your hands full of favours, your statues
> Admirable as music, and no fear of your arms not prospering, I have
> Considered how to serve you and breed from my talents
> These few secrets which I shall make plain
> To your intelligent glory.

In these long lines the opulence referred to is mirrored in the fulsome language the architect uses in order to convey his admiration (and his talents). He is bent on obtaining commissions, having 'plotted' to design 'a hundred and fifteen buildings'. Enormous wealth has brought 'a war-like elegance' to his patron's world, which the man offers to enlarge in terms of 'defence and offence'. There is a sensuous splendour in the architect's vision. He writes, for instance, of window mouldings 'as round as a girl's chin', of halls 'that cannot be entered without a sensation as of myrrh' and of his magical craft: 'None better knowing how to gain from the slow pains of a marble / Bruised, breathing strange climates'. All is to be beautified by light ('That to me is breath, food and drink') the effects of which he will manipulate. The whole will be an inventory of delights, he reassures his patron.

There remains a dark contrast in the epistle with the man's own circumstances. Words like 'agony', 'starved' and 'failure' he associates with his present position and a household comprised of 'a pregnant wife, one female and one boy child and an elder bastard'. The architect yearns for the freedom of being bound to his patron and it is his urgency that brings the poem to life. His is an ego that admits to having no patience but hope, wherein he can almost taste his patron's indulgence.

'Words from Edmund Burke' is a second character portrait of a voice crying out to be used, another 'artisan of fire'. Here the eighteenth century Anglo-Irish statesman both bridles in frustration and delights in moral rectitude as he commits himself to 'the odious office of a priest / Among a diseased and desperate people'. It is creative labour, hard but fulfilling, 'To give the truth my voice.'

Prince's diction is again extravagant, the syntax strained from the first to capture the passion of the orator's task and to comment thematically on the creative process as a labour, literary and philosophical. Again the imagery is vividly achieved, as we see in his description of London:

> like a fuscous rose, her door-ways
> Warm with the flux of quality, her shops bundles of muslin sown
>   with rubies,

> Her frigates tilted above the mud at low tide, and the town
> Like a heap of fresh wet stars

The other long monologue of the 1938 collection is 'Chaka', a poem in the voice of the Zulu warrior-king, a self-styled 'bird of prey'. In four sections of the poem Chaka indulges in contemplation of his power, a pleasure flecked with doubt. At first he is the watcher contemplating the judgement of the world of night on his ambition:

> I have wandered out in the thin tang of white stars
> While my friends were asleep below the hills.
> Depending only on rumours of my starry meals,
> It was not for them to know how far my gaze was set.

He dwells on tribal customs, how they 'reverenced the dead' and then, conquering all, added greatly to that number. His awesome power he has expressed through regiments of impis, who 'weep with hurry at my commands'. Chaka turns his thoughts to tribal festivals and how 'I have brought fear to this people, / I have rendered them as rich and smooth as ox-blood.' In part four he deliberates on penitence, but concludes that all are guilty, 'And there is only this, that we are worthy.' 'Chaka' ends with the voices of his people, 'the People of Heaven', celebrating 'the gifts inflicted upon us who trembled / At their brilliance'. The chilling paradox lies in the poem's last line where Chaka's people speak of 'our noons made loud by abolished clans'.

There are a number of shorter, lyric poems in *Poems* (1938) which deal with love's complications. 'Into the Wood' is a Yeatsian love poem in which the speaker wishes to remove even himself in order to admire his lover freed 'of all but being'. 'On a Cold Night' captures our interest from the outset with its curious syntax and question:

> What mind lying open to my mind,
> At a brazier crouching do I watch
> A winter's night?

The shrouded answer is that of a departed lover's, we assume, though possibly departed in two senses of the word. Similarly enigmatic are 'The Intention', with its play on betrayal and reflection and 'The Token', another love poem out of sorts. The idea of betrayal – this time on the part of the speaker – returns in 'The Letter', while 'False Bay' begins 'She I love leaves me, and I leave my friends / in the dusky capital.' There is a restlessness, a resigned sense of loss in these poems, captured in such titles as 'For the Deserted' and 'For Fugitives', which boasts extravagant imagery:

> For you who loved me too
> As the mistress of transparent towns that showed
> Like sea-beasts the embodied ruins
> As their bones

Such poems, temporally unstable and ingenious in expression, really do not necessitate 'decoding' to enjoy. Their meanings are matched by the pleasures of their craft. There are occasional poems, however, which readily offer up their meanings. 'To a Man on his Horse' is one in which Prince figuratively evokes the dance of an Arab stallion for an envious observer, and 'The Babiaantje', in which wild hyacinth cannot summon the youth who has lost his peace of mind. (It was of 'The Babiaantje' that John Ashbery wrote, 'The charm... has nothing to do with its "meaning", which is obvious.')

F. T. Prince's later poetry is of equal interest. Lyrics aside there are absorbing monologues of characters 'Rooted in limitation, strength and weakness / Of fiery piercing mind that wears the waning body.' Among the finest of these are 'Apollo and the Sybil' and 'The Old Age of Michelangelo' from *Soldiers Bathing* (1954), the collection famous for its much anthologised title poem ('Their flesh worn by the trade of war, revives / And my mind towards the meaning of it strives.') Then there are 'Strafford' and 'Gregory Nazianzen' from *The Doors of Stone* (1963).

The oracle in 'Apollo and the Sybil' has been reduced to deathless age for denying the god. She is found ruminating on the sensual joys of a living world she is denied ('White sunlight and the dripping oars!'). She remains caught between the effects of her refusal and her inability to love. Michelangelo is another lost soul, worn out by the reality of self-sacrifice to his art. He sees his work as a perpetually losing battle to wrest beauty from nature ('I finish nothing I begin. / And the dream sleeps in the stone, to be unveiled / Or half-unveiled.') He also broods on the impossibility of realising his other dream, of personal happiness. Returning to Rome for the last time, lost in images of wings and Heaven, he longs to look upon his beloved ('My dream grows drunk within me') but is ultimately aware that he is only an old man in need of indulgence.

Prince's other great portrait is of 'Strafford' (Thomas Wentworth, 1st Earl of Strafford, Lord Deputy of Ireland) who died in defence of the obdurate though vacillating King Charles 1. The rough syntax and imagery of the poem's opening suggests his authoritarian presence:

> Dark steel, the muffled flash
> On iron sleeve and cuff; black storm of armour,
> Half-moons and wedges, scaly wings and hinges,
> Ovals and quadrilaterals and cylinders
> Moulded in nightshade metal.
>   So he stands

In the poem, 'the black-browed Yorkshire magnate' is portrayed in his last days, an ambitious man congenitally unsatisfied, a man with an insatiable desire for power, driven 'Not for the greatness only, but the difficulty' in attaining it. Prince debates a late 'sweetness' that came over the condemned man when betrayed by his monarch. He dies with dignity 'forgiving all the world / From my dislodging soul'.

Two other monologues remind us of the Catholic Prince's interest in the agonies of faith: 'Gregory Nazianzen' and 'Campanella'. In the first the theologian is praying for God's love ('Whose dancing deluges the world with light') to resolve theological in-fighting among his countrymen. The appeal of the poem, as often in Prince, lies in its descriptive power:

> Drenched in the silver of old olive-trees
> The little bay lies empty, in a trance.
> I watch the far sea bathed in pale blue light,
> And on the rough sea-wall the tone of time

'Campanella' concerns the Italian Dominican philosopher, a utopian conspirator, who after so many years of imprisonment urges in his unhappiness the intercession of God ('Transfer my sorrow to eternal gain') for he feels that ultimately he will fail in his fortitude 'And that the time will come when I repent.'

Later in his career Prince added to the monologues and the shorter lyrics sequences on the Hasidic Jews and the poems of Po Chü-i, verse autobiography, and literary ruminations. These last have a biographical fascination. *Afterword on Rupert Brooke* (1976) weighs the life versus the legend. In this poem, written in the prosier form of syllabics in order to distance emotion, Prince captures the social loves, frustrated creativity and honesty of Brooke, with imaginative attention to the period ('We cannot disinter the girls of nineteen-eight / Or nine, ten and eleven, from the faded layers / Of verse, dead leaf on leaf.')

'A Byron–Shelley Conversation' appears in *Later On* (1983), the spirits of the two – rebel and revolutionary – discuss unlicensed erotic joy: passion as innocence. *A Last Attachment* (1979) concerns Laurence Sterne's *amour*. The author languishes in love as his young sweetheart, Eliza Draper, 'a last best pearl', sails to India to return to an unhappy marriage, leaving him, 'a body like old paper / That tears easily – to look, love and work on.'

Is there a downside to F. T. Prince's poetry? T. S. Eliot twice published Prince in 'The Criterion' before Faber produced the woodenly named *Poems* in 1938. He rejected later work as being too painterly, as 'straining after something too grandiose', or lacking 'that feeling of the relation of the ideas to the private passion'. Was he correct? Is there finally something overweening in the ambition of Prince's work? The poet who was able to 'catch at visions, worlds in brief' could be extravagant, perhaps too eclectic, too bookish at times, but he is splendid nevertheless. He offered another facet of modernism while adding to the resources of the dramatic monologue. And the proof is that Prince's poetry is still with us – albeit half in shadow – a discovery in waiting.

THE LOW VISIBILITY OF NORMAN CAMERON

Norman Cameron's posthumous reputation – what Pope called 'our second life' – is hardly secure. Symptomatic of the confusion surrounding his low visibility is Ian Hamilton's claim, in *Against Oblivion* (2003), that Larkin failed to include Cameron, whose voice is thought to be in sympathy with his own, in *The Oxford Book of Twentieth Century English Verse* (1973). Larkin did, however. The anthology included 'In the Queen's Room', 'The Compassionate Fool', 'The Disused Temple' and 'Green, Green is El Aghir'. Hamilton began his short essay: 'Norman Cameron is almost better known for his poetic friendships than he is for his own, often admirable, poems.' The uncertainty of that 'almost' would hardly have surprised this intermittently productive poet.

While his friends have marquee names – Graves, Thomas, Empson – Cameron (1905–1953) has not, nor has the quality of his best poems always been recognised. A. T. Tolley, for one, considered them as 'a rather drab supporting act' (to use an accusation Hamilton feared might be levelled by critics). In *The Poetry of the Thirties* (1975) Tolley describes Cameron's work as Gravesian, though lacking 'the punch or the resonance' of Graves at his more inspired. And in a 1992 review of Scottish poetry (collected in *With the Grain*) Donald Davie wrote of 'the combination in his poems generally of extreme and witty delicacy in expression with paucity of energy, and indeed of subject matter'.

Perhaps not unconnected with that judgment is the fact that Cameron's poetic output (approximately 70 published poems) is modest in the extreme. His *Collected Poems* include the one slim volume, *The Winter House* (1935), plus his contribution to *Work in Hand* (with Robert Graves and Alan Hodge in 1942). By 1936 Cameron had produced almost two thirds of the poems that have formed his flickering reputation and would later describe himself, unsurprisingly, as a poem-a-year man. In the place of his own work came translations, mainly from the French.

Fortunately Cameron has also his supporters. He made a fair showing, for instance, in Robin Skelton's 1964 anthology, *Poetry of the Thirties*, with eight poems, one more than Empson (though his characteristic brevity may also have been an attraction). In Brian Gardner's 1966 war anthology, *The Terrible Rain*, he appeared twice. Christopher Ricks, for *The Oxford Book of English Verse* (1999), took two of his poems: 'Naked Among the Trees' and 'Forgive me, Sire'. And Paul Keegan's *The Penguin Book of English Verse* (2000) found space for 'Green, Green is El Aghir'.

Also, it must be acknowledged that Cameron's reputation has been bolstered by Warren Hope. He has contributed substantially to what we understand of both poet and man, firstly with his edition of the *Collected Poems and Selected Translations* (1990) – edited with Jonathan Barker – and then through his 2000 biography, *Norman Cameron: His Life, Work and Letters* (on which I have largely relied here for my narrative). While Cameron's admittedly short life seems crowded with incident, and these formally controlled and cleverly ironic poems merit greater visibility, the protagonist of the life, like the voice in the work, seems somewhat detached. As far as the life is concerned, beyond what we know of the events, there is little texture and much is conjecture, since Cameron's opinions and feelings have gone largely unrecorded.

He was born in Bombay (Mumbai) on April 18 1905 to Scottish parents, the eldest of four children of a military chaplain, a Presbyterian Minister who died in 1913. Sent for schooling to Edinburgh, Cameron is said to have been a precocious child with a bluntness which led to his expulsion from his grandmother's house. He then boarded with a family friend before being sent on scholarship to Fettes College, Edinburgh, at the age of eleven, and at length to Oriel College, Oxford. If the Old Testament, classical literature and chess interested him, sport did not and Cameron was to remain physically awkward into maturity. He would grow 'tall, pale, never very strong, with a stutter in his voice, gentle, witty, clumsy, shrewd, over-generous and utterly reliable', according to Robert Graves. Others would find the adult Cameron highly sociable, generally charming and enthusiastic (though at times depressive), well-dressed (with a bohemian touch) and well-read in politics, history and current affairs.

Graves met him in 1927. Cameron, then president of the Oxford English Club, had invited Graves's partner, Laura Riding, to give a talk on Edgar Allan Poe. The poets interested the undergraduate Cameron, whose own verse appeared in *Oxford Poetry* that year (six poems including the 'The Thespians at Thermopylae' and 'Pretty Maids All in a Row') along with work by Auden, MacNeice and Day-Lewis. A student interest in psychoanalysis may have made him receptive to Graves's *On English Poetry* (1922) which, according to the latter's biographer, Jean Moorcroft Wilson, was 'the first book of its time to take a truly psychological approach to poetry using modern psychological methods'. In the year they met Cameron, Graves and Riding published *A Survey of Modernist Poetry*, with its very personal slant on the poetry scene (A sixteen-page treatment of the potential meanings in Shakespeare's Sonnet 129, 'Th' expense of spirit in a waste of shame', became an acknowledged inspiration to Empson's *Seven Types of Ambiguity*).

Cameron's left-leaning sympathies had led him to accompany his friend A.J.P. Taylor to Preston, to engage in support of the labour movement during the General Strike of 1926, where Taylor drove strike leaders to meetings while his friend wrote strike sheets. Unfortunately somewhere along the line Cameron's academic focus slipped and he graduated with a fourth class degree in philosophy and classical ancient history. A timely inheritance saved him from making immediate career plans. Instead he rented a flat in London to which he invited a friend, the artist John Aldridge. They became part of the Riding-Graves circle, devoted to literature, international improvement, their small Seizin press and high spirits – their endeavours being underwritten by Graves's successful 1927 biography *Lawrence and the Arabs* and by Cameron's legacy.

In April 1929 Riding, in emotional turmoil, attempted suicide and on recovery moved with Graves to Deià, a coastal village in Mallorca. Cameron had contributed £100 to her hospital bill, then took employment as an education officer in Nigeria, having found himself to be unproductive in London. Within two years the Riding-Graves circle drew him to Mallorca and their intellectual, creative and romantic ménage. Cameron's fascination seemed primarily with Riding (who dubbed him 'Zero the Companionable') – as of course was Graves's, for whom she was Muse and, at the time, possessed of his White Goddess's powers. With characteristic generosity and impulsiveness, Cameron decided to have a house built near theirs, while reputedly intending to invest £4000 (approximately a quarter of a million pounds today) in their greater building ambitions.

To meet the Riding-Graves household – at least in Miranda Seymour's page-turning biography (*Robert Graves: Life on the Edge*, 1995) – is to be in the presence of what might be highly intelligent and downright odd children. The reader quickly becomes irritated by Graves's worship of his self-centred, authoritarian lover. In *The Long Week-End* (1940) he wrote of Riding: 'In England she was assailed as a "leg-puller", "crossword puzzle setter", "Futurist", "tiresome intellectualist", and so on: none of her books sold more than few dozen copies.' Her worth to Graves, however, was inestimable. As Michael Schmidt explained in his *Lives of the Poets* (1998), 'To a rudderless Graves she preached craft as a servant of truth, an instrument of revelation. The poet was not a witty entertainer, a word-player, but a truth-teller, or he was nothing.' Riding's intentions were never anything but serious. Charismatic and certainly uncompromising, her views on saving the world from war (their group became the 'Covenant of Literal Morality') gradually took her away from poetry.

Cameron initially settled again into their bohemian

atmosphere. This was not to last. He had gone 'slightly mad' (according to his subsequent recognition) in determining to invest in their Mallorcan enterprises. In March 1932 he left the island, after generously turning his house over to Riding. Their relationship had soured, while his with Elfriede Faust, now a less-popular member of the circle, had developed. Cameron did not sever ties with them. He resumed publishing poetry – in Geoffrey Grigson's 'New Verse' – poems less self-advertising than theirs, though his commitment looked flagging against that of the indefatigable Graves.

Back in London Cameron resumed socialising, He met Dylan Thomas, probably in 1934 when the latter was almost twenty. Cameron tried to mentor the younger poet (as his friend Grigson also did), though Thomas could be highly undependable. 'The Dirty Little Accuser' is said to be a sort of commentary on Cameron's fated friendship with the *enfant terrible*, for whom he became 'Nagging Norman':

> Who invited him in? What was he doing here,
> That insolent little ruffian, that crapulous lout?
> When he quitted a sofa, he left behind him a smear.
> My wife says he even tried to paw her about.

Thomas quickly become part of the Cameron drinking group on his forays into London. In a 1935 letter he wrote of 'Celebrities I meet often and too often, they being a lousy set on the whole, or off it', though he acknowledged Cameron (soon to be 'Normal Cameron') and Grigson to be among the best. This does not mean he was above slandering them, perhaps taking exception to their conventional lifestyle and better education. He once wrote to a friend a scathing 'lecture' on Cameron, judging: 'Norman is good, but too much of him is made personally interesting and interestingly eccentric through financial invulnerability.'

Cameron's marriage to Faust was effectively over by the time

The Winter House and Other Poems appeared from Dent in 1935. By now he had begun working as an advertising copywriter in London at J. Walter Thompson (one of his successes being that nonsensical campaign pitting Horlicks against 'night starvation'). In 1938 he married again, to another protégé of Riding and Graves. They had returned from Mallorca at the advent of the Spanish Civil War. The Russian-born Catherine de la Roche worked in the scenario department of Alexander Korda's film studio. Although their return seems to have reconciled Cameron and Riding, Catherine grew to feel that Riding's presence had a negative effect on her husband, as would his constant socialising. Cameron's relationship with Riding soured only after her breakup with Graves during their disastrous American enterprise the following year.

The fall-out from the Riding-Graves years (1926–39) would be evident time and again into the 1980s and 90s, as may be witnessed in the pages of *The New York Review of Books*. The question of who had stolen what intellectual capital from whom seems to have been the crux of the matter. For instance, countering Graves's biographer Martin Seymour-Smith's 'maniacal animus' towards her (She 'could never have existed as a serious entity'), in the letters pages Riding referred to 'discoveries I made and appropriations and untruths perpetrated against me by Graves'. And so it went on.

During the war Cameron turned his advertising skills to propaganda for Political Intelligence, devising a radio programme with art historian Bruno Adler. Their scripts for 'Kurt and Willy' subverted Nazi propaganda. Cameron's wiki entry offers one glimpse of drama: 'At some time,' it is reckoned that, 'he was parachuted into Yugoslavia as a translator in dealings with Tito, probably with the 1943 mission led by Fitzroy Maclean.' The war certainly took Cameron to Algeria and in January 1946 he was awarded an MBE for his services to allied intelligence.

His second marriage effectively ended in 1942. At the war's end he stayed abroad, working as a journalist with the British

Delegation of the Allied Commission for Austria based in Vienna, until his paper was shut down at the end of 1945. He returned the following year. 'Life here is all right. I've started writing a series of political articles for the local newspapers printed in English for the Austrians', he wrote shortly after arrival, adding that the Austrians, many of whom could read English, believed in the reliability of information in English. 'I'm also a kind of copy-writer-of-all-work for the outfit', he added.

In Vienna Cameron met the woman who became his third wife: Austrian journalist Dr Gretl Bajardi. During this period he published poems and translations, reviewing and working for the BBC, until an illness which required brain surgery undermined his always uncertain health. The patchwork career interrupted, he did publish a translation of Rimbaud's *A Season in Hell* in 1949, the year his brother died and his own health worsened further. Cameron died of a brain haemorrhage at the age of forty-seven on April 20, 1953.

Although it may be fanciful to pursue his reticent self through the poems in search of a portrait of the artist, it is certainly a temptation. One starting point could be Robert Graves's observation that his friend was fundamentally divided: 'alternately a Presbyterian precisian and moralist; and a pagan poet and boon-companion.' One way lies through his mythic, historic and biblical narratives, where Cameron tells pithy, tautly controlled tales of temples, leviathans, sorcerers and strange lands, producing what Geoffrey Grigson described as 'peculiar and isolated' poems. It is worth pointing out that, while Cameron's diction is always accessible, his meaning is at times evasive.

Firstly though there are the 'contemporary' poems which at first glance *do* seem to invite the reader in. While these deal openly with the idea of a divided self, they are not to be taken too seriously – 'Public-House Confidence', for example, or 'Meeting My Former Self', and the satirically Freudian 'Nostalgia for Death'. 'Punishment Enough' is another. We might seize on its reference to 'scorecards', which flags up Cameron's interest in golf.

Yet this would read against the evidence of the 'you' addressed in the poem, unless of course the pronoun is self-referential (I think of Robert Lowell's off the cuff remark on the advantage of writing in an ambiguous style.)

Admittedly the majority of the poems seem to illustrate the ironies of human nature, rather than simply his own, many in Cameronian costume: moral fables like 'The Thespians at Thermopylae', 'The Voyage to Secrecy', 'The Disused Temple', 'By Leave of Luck', 'Naked Among Trees', 'Lucifer'. They illustrate Kant's now-worn plank, "Out of the crooked timber of humanity, no straight thing was ever made", while frequently piercing the hypocrisy of lapsed (pre-) Christian ways.

Still, we cannot shake the feeling that *sometimes* Cameron may be confessing his true divided self, perhaps more obliquely, more metaphorically so. With no real knowledge of his emotional life, we are tempted to see a hint of the frustrations of reticence in poems like 'Let Him Loose' ('Should the hot, aching man of blood within / Ever attain the surface as he wishes'), 'No Remedy' ('Smite the devil underground: / It blooms with danger all around') and in the emotional turbulence of 'The Winter House'. There is, too, subterranean passion in the excellent 'Dwellers in the Sea' ('My soul is some leviathan in vague distress.') He failed to include this poem, which seems to deny ambition (and ends 'And who would give his life up for a story?') in *The Winter House*. Was that significant?

Perhaps we may sense Cameron's awareness of the perils of his often remarked-on generosity in 'The Compassionate Fool' ('My enemy had bidden me as guest. / His table all set out with wine and cake'), or his mild self-loathing in 'The Dirty Little Accuser', where he is left to ponder on the accusation, 'You and I are all in the same galère.' Perhaps even 'The Shack' and 'Via Maestranza' may evoke a sense of guilt:

> The cornice of my room
> Is decked with grinning faces in relief;

> The tiled floor bears a large masonic sign.
> And in this room a whisper down the street,
> 'Let me in, Pietro! Quickly, the patrol!'
> Sounds loudly as though uttered by my bed.

Then, given Cameron's three marriages, we might read for evidence of his feelings about love and conclude that in his experience it is a state freighted with fear and sexual disgust (to read the following poems straight). That would be the evidence of 'Nunc Scio Quid Sit Amor' ('Now I know what love is') where the protagonist is seized by a 'fierce outlander': 'I fear you and I fear you, barbarous Love. / 'You are no citizen of my country.'

In 'Pretty Maids All in a Row' the details are literally earthy and crude, while 'The Downward Pulse' explores the tempestuous, compulsive nature of desire. Even with the more sexually temperate 'Three Love Poems' the moods are threatening ('Love as you please – I owe you nothing back.') One wonders about the fate of the dallying shepherd – or his seduction technique:

> Now it is late. The tracks leading home are steep,
> The stars and landmarks in your country are strange.
> How can I take my sheep back over the range?
> Shepherdess, show me where I may sleep.

It seems we are on slightly safer ground when ascribing poems – as his biographer and others have – to Cameron's relationships with friends. Aside from 'The Dirty Little Accuser' there is 'A Visit to the Dead', which could well be an oblique commentary on the Riding-Graves group. 'Forgive Me, Sire' would be apt perhaps for Robert Graves, as 'The Wanton's Death' ('His new-adapted element more kindly / Than the fair promiser who brought him thither') might be read as a rather wild rejection of Riding's influence.

'A Visit to the Dead' could be read as a rather jaundiced

memory of his time with the two of them, though more likely the experience simply offered Cameron the potential for myth spinning. After all, their influence on him had been formative:

> I bought (I was too wealthy for my age)
> A passage to the dead ones' habitat,
> And learnt, under their tutelage,
> To twitter like a bat
>
> In imitation of their dialect.

In the poem the laughter that is said by 'Marco Polo' to have 'supervened' to save him ('like sunlight in the cucumber, / The innermost resource, that does not fail') suggests his exuberance in recognising their absurdity, which dispels the cynicism we might have read in the poem. 'Forgive Me, Sire', said to be addressed to the militaristic Graves, is more a humorous credo on Cameron's part:

> Forgive me, Sire, for cheating your intent,
> That I, who should command a regiment,
> Do amble amiably here, O God,
> One of the neat ones in your awkward squad.

Neither poem suggests that Cameron can be co-opted for long in the service of others.

Unsurprisingly his time abroad produced several poems, including 'Liberation in Vienna' which is built on a metaphor of winter seen as an occupying power. 'Steep Stone Steps' comes from his Italian time, as does 'The Verdict', and 'Wörther See' dates from his Austrian service. But it is from North Africa, in 'Green, Green is El Aghir', that Cameron produced his most indispensable poem. In *Second World War Poetry in English* (2013) John Lucas reads an inner contentment into the last verse, when the desert truck finally reaches water:

> Green, green is El Aghir. It has a railway-station,
> And the wealth of its soil has borne many another fruit,
> A mairie, a school and an elegant Salle de Fêtes.
> Such blessings, as I remarked, in effect, to the waiter,
> Are added unto them that have plenty of water.

To Lucas the material benefits listed (the school and so on) 'are worth celebrating. Cameron doesn't say this, but the tone of the lines, gleaming with inner laughter, pleasure, a discreet relish (the waiter has presumably served hm food and drink) imply as much'. This imaginative approach to reading 'Green, Green is El Aghir' works well it seems to me, though even in this poem Cameron focuses on describing the event, as Jonathan Barker observed, 'at last free from introspection'. Anything about the speaker must be gleaned from the telling, his punctiliousness ('I said, in a kind of French'; 'as I remarked, in effect'), his informality and thoughtfulness, for example. Here to me at least, if not a portrait, is a glimpse of Cameron at his most visible.

II: The Age of Arnold

MATTHEW ARNOLD'S LETTERS: A BICENTENARY PORTRAIT

> [Having read the 2,750 pages of the six volumes of *The Letters of Matthew Arnold* over five months of 2021 (during the Covid lockdown), I offer the following as a celebratory, bicentenary portrait of the great poet-critic, who lived from 1822 to 1888.]

One has to sympathise with G.W.E. Russell who, in 1895, was persuaded to edit a two-volume edition of Matthew Arnold's letters. Although the response proved welcoming, one admiring American reviewer suggested that 'a gleam of humor' remained a rarity in the volumes. Russell had not set out to be dour.

In his 1904 *Matthew Arnold*, written for the 'Literary Lives' series, he acknowledged this unsatisfactory edition, explaining that it had been compromised by the interference of the estate, so that 'in reality my functions were little more than those of the collector and the annotator'. Gone were decent instances of 'Arnold's most characteristic traits – such, for example, as his overflowing gaiety, and his love of what our fathers called Raillery.' The culprits, he wrote in a 1918 letter to Arnold's niece, Mary Augusta Ward (the novelist, Mrs. Humphry Ward), were Arnold's wife and daughter: 'Mrs. A. wished me to edit them; and I wished to make them as much of a biography & a portrait as might be. But hardly anyone except Mrs. A. & Miss A. supplied me with any material; Mrs. A. deleted every admiring reference to herself, & Miss A. every trace of humour. This was done deliberately – she said, "Everyone knew my brother's lighter side; but few his serious & domestic side."'

It took Cecil Y. Lang and considerable help – including that from Arnold's grandson, Arnold Whitridge – to produce a fully-rounded portrait of the man. Eighty years earlier another family member, Arnold's niece, had reacted with disfavour at even 'Mr. Russell's indiscriminate volumes', arguing that Arnold would have disliked seeing them all in print. Rather he would have favoured 'a small volume' of the best letters such as that he had wished to do with George Sand's. Undeterred, between 1996 and 2001 Lang collected all the letters that could be found into a six-volume edition for The University Press of Virginia. His efforts have been abundantly repaid by the quality of the letters. As Arnold wrote to his mother, Mary Penrose Arnold, while groaning at the amount of incoming correspondence, 'I like to say what I mean in a letter just as much as in an Essay and to say what one means often costs thought.'

This proved problematic, since more than most literary men of his energetic generation Arnold lived under the pressure of time constraints. Fortunately, unlike many of his peers – James Anthony Froude, Arthur Hugh Clough or his brother, Tom, for instance – he experienced no crippling intellectual or religious crises. As an indulgent father and attentive husband, hard-worked government inspector of schools, poet, literary, social and cultural critic and theologian, what pockets of time he found he devoted to socialising, botanising, angling and travelling. For our benefit his variousness makes him – as he once wrote of Wordsworth – an 'inexhaustible subject'.

A dutifully regular correspondent home, Arnold showed himself quite cavalier about correspondence he received from others ('Of all the letters I send [on], Fan may keep what she likes for autographs and destroy the rest'). After his mother's death in 1873 his sister became his home correspondent and, as collector of autographs, received this light-hearted instruction: 'I send you Jowett's letter which turned up in a sorting of letters and papers today. You may burn it when you have read it. I send you also Mr Farr; he too may burn. And I send you Mr Anderson, an East End incumbent; he may share the general fate.'

Despite the considerable distances that came to separate male members of the family (William to India, Tom to Tasmania), the Arnolds remained close. Their father, Thomas Arnold, had famously transformed Rugby School by force of personality. His democratic impulse and inclusive Anglicanism had greatly impressed the family, though he died suddenly in June 1842. As Arnold wrote to his mother, 'I constantly feel, even while treading ground he did not tread, how much he influences me, and how much I owe him'. In remembering his father, Arnold offered what was for him the highest praise: 'the characteristic thing about Papa is the loftiness and fine ardour of his spirit and life, as in the great men of antiquity and Plutarch's heroes'.

There are nearly four hundred 'weekly' letters to his mother, whom Arnold thanked in a birthday greeting of 1852 'for the bringing up we had: so unworldly, so sound, and so pure'. There are also ninety to his youngest sister, Frances ('Fan'). These letters were addressed to 'Fox How', Ambleside, which Thomas Arnold had built as a holiday home (Wordsworth being a neighbour and soon a friend). Arnold's mother and the unmarried Frances continued to live there, the latter into the twentieth century as something of a celebrity.

Arnold married Frances Lucy Wightman ('Flu'), daughter of Judge Wightman, on Jun10, 1851. They had met at a party given by her father. Although the relationship flourished, they had been separated because of Arnold's lack of prospects until he gained employment as a government inspector of schools, on the recommendation of Lord Lansdowne for whom he had acted as private secretary. As an inspector, Arnold's lack of experience, even his lack of interest in this area proved no bar since, as Kate Campbell explained in *Matthew Arnold* (2007), 'A classical education was widely thought to qualify men for this civil service employment by giving them the necessary detachment for their work, especially for factual analysis.'

Arnold's journal entry for Sunday March 30, 1851 reads: 'at ¼ past 1 to Hampton. to church with Flu, all the afternoon with her. after dinner talked to the Judge. He consented to the engagement. talk with dear Flu. back to town.' Arnold wrote to his sister Jane on May 10: 'she is so loveable: I am more inclined sometimes to cry over her than anything else: it is almost impossible to be soft & kind enough with her.' Small and Belgravian, according to Clough, Frances Lucy had more intelligence, determination and health than may have been supposed from Arnold's remark and from her privileged upbringing. More than seventy letters to Flu over their thirty-seven years of marriage also survive. In the early days they sometimes deal with the rigours of travel and inspecting, for the couple were often apart, although gradually family matters and social activities take precedence.

Eighty-two letters exist to Jane (addressed by the family diminutive 'K') with whom Arnold possessed an intellectual and emotional closeness, particularly prior to her marriage to the Liberal politician William Edward Forster (of the 1870 Education Act). After all, as the two oldest children they had shared early experiences in Laleham, when Arnold was physically dependent. As a very young child he wore leg braces – a consequence, according to his father, 'of a bad habit of crawling before he could walk… which has greatly bent one of his legs' (rickets, it has been suggested since). As Jane mentioned to their brother Tom in May 1855, 'the dear boy's great affectionateness is always both touching & refreshing to me – and I believe he never sees me without going back in thought to the old times'.

As for Arnold, he wrote to a convalescing Jane shortly after her marriage and before his own, 'Seldom as I write to her and cold as my tone often is I never think of my K in weakness or suffering without remembering that she has been to me what no one else ever was, what no one else ever will exactly be again; unless indeed we were both to lose what we have dearest, and then we should be drawn together again, I think, as in old times.' It is well to remember, as Arnold's biographer Park Honen reminded us, that 'The Victorian ethos exalted the family, and outside the family it tended to keep the sexes apart before marriage, almost ensuring that middle-class brothers and sisters – of about the same ages – might depend excessively upon one another.'

Jane described family moments which reveal the bachelor

Arnold relaxing. Such vignettes provide absorbing glimpses of Victorian leisure. On Monday January 17th, 1848, she wrote, 'Matt and Edward & Willy have been amusing themselves since dinner by dancing the Polka, & Mary is probably reading Manning's Sermons, which Matt has given her… Susy is sitting by my side copying out Walter's last letters, and Mamma & Fan are sitting over the fire reading. Outside the world does not look very cheerful.'

And two years later she offered a teasing description: 'In the drawingroom we are a quiet party – Mother writing at her little table and I at the great one (littered as usual with books & newspapers); close to me Master Edward reclines at ease in an arm chair (with his pocket-handkerchief over his head to defend him from the smoke – a luxury of these late degenerate days since I left home) reading [Mme De Staël's] Corinne. Matt is stretched at full length on one sofa, reading a Christmas tale of Mrs. Gaskell's which moves him to tears, & the tears to complacent admiration of his own sensibility – and on the other sofa, also exceedingly at his ease, is stretched my respected spouse reading a newspaper.'

Mrs. Humphry Ward wrote her own romantic vignette in *A Writer's Recollections* (1918), which reflected on Arnold's status within the family and implicitly on that of his sisters: 'In these early days, "Matt" often figures in the family letters as the worldling of the group – the dear one who is making way in surroundings quite unknown to the Fox How circle, where under the shadow of the mountains, the sisters, idealists all of them, looking out a little austerely, for all their tenderness, on the human scene, are watching with a certain anxiety lest Matt should be "spoiled".'

Arnold's own family letters, largely undramatic but vividly observed and sometimes affecting, constitute a comprehensive account of a successful, literary, middle-class Victorian life. They report on an active social calendar of visiting, dinners and theatres, where friendship among the famous and titled is given a regular airing ('I think both he and & Fanny Lucy are quite enough inclined to value the externals & proprieties of life,' Jane observed). They describe holidays at home and abroad; money concerns; the taking of houses and servants. Arnold liked to include news of the activities and sayings of their six children. Somewhat less pleasurable, often, were reports on the boys' school performance and the costs. There are records of medical attention (doctors for the children; dentists for the adults). Arnold writes of the health or spirits of Frances Lucy, especially during her pregnancies and following the death of three of their four boys.

The heartbreak that the Arnolds felt at the death of their young sons is communicated with eloquent sadness or stunned silence. Exhaustion, a sense of general helplessness and, inevitably, gloom are the immediate consequences. Infant mortality, the bane of family life, necessitated stoicism, as did much else in the uncertainty of Victorian times. When their infant, Basil, died on January 4th, 1868, Arnold appeared bereft of hope. He wrote to Jane on the day, 'And so this loss comes to me just after my 45th birthday, with so much other "suffering in the flesh," – the departure of youth, cares of many kinds, an almost painful anxiety about public matters, – to remind me that *the time past of our life may suffice us*! – words which have haunted me for the last year or two.'

Of the three lost lives, the one that most shocked him, being the most unexpected, was that of Budge (Trevenen) who died of meningitis ('I cannot write his name without stopping to look at it in stupefaction at his not being alive.') Once, attempting to give consolation to another bereaved parent on the evidence of his continuing grief, Arnold wrote what he could hardly have felt himself except in rare moods: 'There is nothing to say in the way of comfort, except what you cannot possibly feel or admit at present: that to lose young those whom one loves is really not so dreadful after all – the memory of them is so beautiful, so secure.'

Occasionally the letters reveal opinions on the activities of his siblings and invariably they offer news of his own nature ramblings ('It is an east wind and a grey sky, but I had meant to go to Horsley and see the daffodils.') Arnold could be transported by what he witnessed in nature. He once told Jane, 'You do not know what you lose by living out of the hearing of nightingales.' In excitement he once wrote, 'I must not begin about the trees, or I shall fill my letter with them,' and in September 1887: 'I don't know whether I like fishing because I so much like rivers, or like rivers because I so much like fishing, but I rather think the former; hardly anything gives me so much pleasure as to see a new and beautiful river.'

One early critic wrote that the letters 'contained all his books in solution', since we learn of Arnold's ideas, his poetry, the essays and the controversies they frequently excited. We hear his thoughts on English dullness and complacency as against the ferment of ideas on the Continent; his negative view of politics, of Dissenters, of the English class system; of the democratic spirit abroad; of his fervent commitment to education and culture; the fortunes of his reputation; his beloved Oxford; his ambitions and the news of the day – all these against the background grind of inspecting.

***

Arnold's student days at Balliol lived with him forever. He loved to reminisce about 'the *freest* and most delightful part, perhaps of my life – when with you [Tom] and Clough and Walrond I shook off all the bonds and formalities of the place, and enjoyed the spring of life and that unforgotten Oxfordshire and Berkshire country... I am hardly ever at Oxford now, but the sentiment of the place is overpowering to me when I have leisure to feel it.' While a student there, foppish and affecting languor, he bantered with friends like Arthur Hugh Clough, 'Todo' Walrond, John Duke Coleridge (eventually Lord Chief Justice of England) and M. E. Grant Duff, later a politician and author. At times he lent himself to misrepresentation among his friends ('I laugh too much, and they make one's laughter mean too much.')

When Arnold fell under the spell of the French actress, Rachel, Clough gave an amusing pen portrait of him: 'Matt is full of Parisianism; theatres in general, and Rachel in special: he enters the room with a chanson of Beranger's on his lips – for the sake of French words almost conscious of tune; his carriage shows him in fancy parading the rue de Rivoli – and his hair is guiltless of English scissors; he breakfasts at twelve, and never dines in Hall, and in the week or 8 days rather... he has been to Chapel *once.*'

At this critical stage in Arnold's creative life, with and against Clough he forged his poetic values. To him he would write most seriously, most critically and most frequently on the subject of poetry. In a letter of February 12th, 1853, while 'past thirty, and three parts iced over', he would spell out his debt: first, 'your company and mode of being always had a charm and a salutary effect for me', and more importantly: 'I am and always shall be, whatever I do or say, powerfully attracted towards you, and vitally connected with you: this I am sure of: the period of my development... coincides with that of my friendship with you so exactly that I am for ever linked with you by intellectual bonds – the strongest of all.' These bonds they shared were firmer from Arnold's perspective, 'for your development was really over before you knew me, and you had properly speaking come to you *assiette* for life'.

Where Clough was going wrong, he felt, was in losing infinite time to a scrupulousness of thought, which rendered him indecisive. In reviewing Lionel Trilling's intellectual biography *Matthew Arnold* (1939), Edmund Wilson noted this difference between the two men: 'The figure of Clough... contrasts with the figure of Arnold and throws it into relief – since Clough, with perplexities similar to Arnold's, lacks the principle of life which Arnold always possessed.'

Clough had been born in Liverpool and educated at Rugby School under Dr. Arnold, for whom he bore real reverence. There he became almost a member of the Arnold family. Hence these well-known letters from Arnold to Clough generally betray the easy banter of student days. In one from March 1845, for instance, Arnold played on his listlessness to veil criticism: 'But my dear Clough, have you a great Force of Character? That is the true Question. For me, I am a reed, a very whoreson Bullrush: yet such as I am, I give satisfaction.' We see the clever undergraduate irreverence and allusiveness frequently in their twenties, often laced with the ever-exploited Shakespeare tags.

Persiflage aside, Arnold could be a difficult friend. This emerges in his criticism of Clough's innovatory poetry, fundamentally because it is different to his own – more driven by ideas at the expense of beauty to Arnold's taste, more modern to ours. His negative attitude fits his thesis about the state of poetry in England at the time ('how deeply *unpoetical* the age & all one's surroundings are. Not unprofound, not ungrand, not unmoving: – but un*poetical*'). It also presumably addresses his uncertainties regarding his own work. According to Lionel Trilling, 'What Arnold feared in all his friends, and especially in Clough as the most intimate, was a thing that he feared in himself. He perceived in his friends the driving restless movement of the critical intellect trying to solve the problems of the nineteenth century.' Intellect alone was not enough in these 'damned times' when 'everything is against one', as Arnold wrote. He warned Clough. whom he felt relied too much on his intellect, 'I often think that even a slight gift of poetical expression which in a common person might have developed itself easily and naturally, is overlaid and crushed in a profound thinker, so as to be of no use to him to help him to express himself.'

Consequently he was frequently severe. Of the latter's 'The Mystery of the Fall', for instance, Arnold supported his feeling that the poem is 'not suited to me at present' with an allusion to Goethe's feeling that one's tastes changed with the *zeitgeist*. He acknowledged a certain talent ('The good feature in all your poems is the sincerity that is evident in them.') And yet this was the time of Clough's *The Bothie of Toper-na-fuosich* (subtitled 'A Long-Vacation Pastoral', but in its main title, apparently, unintentionally obscene – 'the hut of the bearded well'). It was also close to that of Clough's justly famous, epistolary *Amours de Voyage*. In February 1849 Arnold asked his friend to 'consider whether you attain the *beautiful*, & whether your product gives *pleasure*, not excites curiosity & reflexion. Forgive me all this: but I am always prepared myself to give up the attempt, on conviction: & so, I know, are you: & I only urge you to reflect whether you are advancing.'

Granted the 'sincerity', but if beauty and pleasure were missing? To Clough he wrote, 'there are two offices of Poetry – one to add to one's store of thoughts & feelings – another to compose & elevate the mind by a sustained tone, numerous allusions, and a grand style'. He cited on style Milton, Keats ('a style & form-seeker') and Sophocles ('the grand moral effects produced by *style*'). For Arnold 'the style is the expression of the nobility of the poet's character, as the matter is the expression of the richness of his mind: but on men character produces as great an effect as mind'. In his landmark biography Trilling concluded bluntly, 'In short, so far as Arnold can see, Clough is simply not a poet. However admirably sincere, devotional, rhetorical, metaphysical, Clough's poems may be, they are, says Arnold, never "natural".'

This is all an early instance of a tendency on Arnold's part to miss or undervalue instances of the excellence he discussed endlessly in prose. It is also why even Arnoldians, as Timothy Peltason suggested, tend to read his prose 'for the companionship of a distinctive and vividly rendered personality' rather than for his judgments. The root cause of his underestimation of Clough's poetry lies in their divergent view of what poetry should be and how it should sound.

Yet they were friends and he offered the needy Clough advice in 'place-hunting' at the Education Office ('I think an Inspectorship would be better suited to you though than an Examinership, beside the pay being better.') Clough had lectured before working in educational administration and also gave substantial secretarial assistance to his wife's cousin, Florence Nightingale. He died in 1861. Eventually Arnold came to realise he had undervalued his friend's work. Apropos of reading his poems in manuscript, he wrote to Francis Turner Palgrave in 1871, 'Some of Clough's best things I was not just to, which, if I had read them in print, I should have seen with the same eyes as now.' And yet in the end he and his family felt that Clough had never realized his potential. Arnold said as much to one correspondent in the last year of his life: 'I was glad to find you quoting Clough; some very little thing more in him, and he would have had all the public quoting him.'

He had spelt this out to his mother on reading Clough's letters and journals in December 1865: 'The loose screw that was in his whole organization is, however, much more evident to me in reading this book than it was in consorting with him in life: and then the rigid overtaxed religiousness of his early life was a surprise to me – of his whole Rugby time, I mean. I first knew him, really knew him, some five years later.' He suggests that his father's influence on Clough proved too strong, that 'certainly Clough appears to have felt him *too much*'.

***

The mature Arnold habitually bared his opinions, while also developing an entertainingly informal relationship with his publisher, George Murray Smith ('My dear G. S. On the 6th, with the greatest pleasure. On the 7th I have to dine at the Garrick, so on the 8th I shall probably be very ill; but as that will be after your dinner, not before, you will not care. Ever yours affectionately. M. A.'). He also began – always deferentially – to share ideas and news with Lady Louisa de Rothschild, the philanthropist, whom he met in 1858. His literary connections included Browning, Swinburne and Gosse, while Arnold remained reverent of his early influences: Goethe, George Sand, Sainte-Beuve, their Ambleside neighbour, Wordsworth, and his father's old adversary, John Henry Newman.

Since he had known him and his poetry at an impressionable age, Wordworth (d. 1850) had been formative for Arnold. In the last decade of his life, reporting the imminent appearance of his selection from *The Poems of Wordsworth* (1882) to his oldest friend, John Duke Coleridge, Arnold explained, 'well as I knew him, I am really amazed at his greatness when I see all his best things put together and his flatter things left out'. He hoped to do the old poet justice, he wrote to his sister Frances, since 'He can show a body of work superior to what any other English poet, except Shakespeare and Milton, can show; and his body of work is more interesting than Milton's, though not so great. This seems to me to be the simple truth.' He hoped his selection would 'help Wordsworth's fame', he wrote elsewhere. Later he felt it *had* helped to promote it, reporting to Coleridge his delight at the *Saturday Review* comments: 'I thought the Saturday article important, because it is the first time, so far as I know, that an accredited literary organ of the highest authority has fairly given Wordsworth his place as the greatest English poet of the last two centuries.' Arnold went on in that letter to offer a list of eight English poets: Wordsworth, Milton, Shakespeare, Chaucer, Burns, Spenser, Gray and Keats. 'Where is it to be matched outside of the Greeks?' he asked. He would tell a French colleague that Wordsworth was 'one of the best and deepest spiritual influences of our century'.

Arnold and Sainte-Beuve had corresponded and met, each appreciative of the other's work. At Sainte-Beuve's death in October 1869, Arnold declared himself not immediately inclined to write a piece adding, 'But I have learnt a great deal from him, and the news of his death struck me as if it had been that of some one very near to me. When George Sand and Newman go, there will be no writers left living from whom I have received a strong influence.' Then in June 1876 at the death of Sand, Arnold wrote, 'Her death has been much in my mind; she was the greatest spirit in our European world from the time that Goethe departed.' He cherished a remark Renan had passed on: that Sand had been given the impression of Arnold, after his brief pilgrimage to her Nohant home, as a young Milton.

Scattered through his letters are comments on other great contemporaries. He wrote of Ruskin that he liked him better in middle age than in youth. Ruskin had told Arnold that 'he had always been under the impression I thought him rather a fool! But he has done much good in his time, besides pouring out a great deal of questionable stuff.' On the other hand, he had 'never much liked Carlyle. He seemed to me to be "carrying coals to Newcastle," as our proverb says; preaching earnestness to a nation which had plenty of it by nature, but was less abundantly supplied with several other useful things.' A 'moral desperado' he called Carlyle in a letter to Clough. He conceded some gifts to Victor Hugo: 'he has power, pathos, life, all sorts of things; only just the very charm and accent of a poet are what I miss in him'.

To Ralph Waldo Emerson Arnold wrote on July 30, 1867, as a preface to the gift of a copy of his poems, 'Your writings have given me and continue to give me so much pleasure and stimulus, that I consider myself almost bound to make an offering to you of any production at all considerable which comes from me; since you are sure to have had some part in it.' From his last home, at Pains Hill Cottage, Cobham, he wrote to an American correspondent, 'A large photograph of [Emerson] hangs already in the little drawing room of my cottage here, close to one of Cardinal Newman; they are men, both of them, to whom I have many obligations.' In America Arnold opened his lecture on Emerson 'with a bit about the three interesting men to me in my undergraduate days – Newman, Carlyle, Emerson'. He acknowledged having 'a very very deep feeling for him'.

In his *The Dons* (1999) Noel Annan wrote, 'No don has ever captivated Oxford as John Henry Newman.' He had certainly been a powerful, inescapable influence on Arnold almost at the time the elder Arnold's Anglicanism had clashed with Newman's High Church elitism. Newman did not change Matthew Arnold's views, but the later cardinal's sermonizing style meant a great deal to him.

Malcolm Woodfield, in his *R.H. Hutton: Critic and Theologian* (1986), makes the point that, 'In retrospect we can see Arnold as having secularized some of the important elements of Newman's thought.' Arnold would have contested this. In November 1871 he wrote to 'Revd Dr John Henry Newman': 'I cannot forbear adding, what I have often wished to tell you, that no words can be too strong to express the interest with which I used to hear you at Oxford, and the pleasure with which I continue to read your writings now. We are all of us carried in ways not to our own making or choosing, but nothing can ever do away the effect you have produced upon me, for it consists in a general disposition of mind rather than in a particular set of ideas.'

In May 1880 Arnold gave an account, first to his friend and his father's biographer Arthur Penrhyn Stanley and then to his sister Frances, of his presentation to Cardinal Newman at a party of the Duchess of Norfolk's. He had been pleased to be offered the opportunity 'to tell him how much I owed him… nothing of any interest passed, but I am glad to have spoken to him and shaken hands with him'. He told his sister that he 'wanted to have spoken once in my life to Newman'.

***

According to John Henry Raleigh, in his stimulating *Matthew Arnold and American Culture* (1957) the letters, with their 'consistent humility, punctuated only briefly by a disarmingly genuine delight in local triumphs and successes, laid forever the ghost of snobbery'. This was by no means the case with the man himself; one had to look more closely. In 1850 Charlotte Brontë, meeting Arnold in Ambleside with Harriet Martineau (no favourite of the Arnold family), noted: 'Striking and prepossessing in appearance, his manner displeases from its seeming foppery… Ere long a real modesty appeared under his assumed conceit, and some genuine intellectual aspirations as well as high educational acquirements, displaced superficial affectations.'

Frances Power Cobbe, who met him at a dinner at Walter Bagehot's in the sixties, described Arnold then as 'gently looking down on the follies of mortality from the superior attitudes of Olympus, or perhaps of Parnassus'. Some reacted unfavourably to this posture of Olympian detachment, although Eleanor Mary Sellar recorded in her *Recollections and Impressions* (1907),'I had met him once before at Balliol, so had, in a way, got accustomed to the "grand manner" which was characteristic of him, and which – though it savoured of affectation – was really natural to him, and, unlike most seeming affectation, was neither repellent nor did it put you off your ease.... He was quite aware of the effect his manner had on many, and was often very humorous about it, as when he said to an old Oxford friend shortly after his marriage, "You'll like my Lucy; she has all my sweetness and none of my airs!"'

We may add to the last an admittedly partial description from Arnold's niece, Mrs. Ward: 'He stood four-square – a courteous, competent man of affairs, an admirable inspector of schools, a delightful companion, a guest whom everybody wanted, and no one could bind for long; one of the sanest, most independent, most cheerful and loveable of mortals.'

Good humour, often self-deprecating, and even gaiety, run through the correspondence: 'Palgrave's verses always seem to me to want any real reason for existing: but so too, I daresay, to a great many people do mine.' To George Smith he quips, 'for Paris is a place where it is well that one's family should think one ruined and irremediably without credit at one's bankers'. A note of February 1877 to Richard Monckton Milnes (Lord Houghton) reads: 'I am sorry to say mornings are impossible to me. A wretched school-inspector, in full work, with managers and teachers gaping for their grants, going out to breakfast at 10 like a gentleman! I am sorry to say it is quite impossible.' Arnold's vanity reflected his essential cheerfulness. He dressed well, taking pride in his mutton chops, his centre-parted, wavy dark hair and youthful appearance (His early biographer, Russell, noted that in those days the centre parting was considered 'the sign of a fop'). Leslie Stephen, who forgave such vanity which he distinguished from conceit, remembered an 'obvious sweetness of nature, which it is impossible not to recognize and not to love'.

Arnold's probity reflected his concern to maintain a good reputation. He showed qualms about taking a foundational benefit for the Harrow education of his sons and later over accepting a literary pension for himself. When suffering neuralgia from a fall at the ill-lit Cannon Street Railway Station, in which he broke two teeth, he reported to his mother, 'Pleasant as it would be to mulct the Philistinism which administers our railroads, I shall be satisfied if they pay my dentist's bill, and undertake either to close their court at night or to keep the portico lighted.' He would offer no criticism of fellow poets – in print – either to avoid seeming envious or to protect his relationship with them – or in solidarity because, 'Few of us can be satisfied with the judgments passed upon what we write by those who propose to direct the public mind.' Privately, he found Tennyson 'deficient in intellectual power', while Browning 'a quite remarkably agreeable converser' and 'a real man of genius', but woefully unclear. He privately advised others to read the literature of the previous century and not that of his contemporaries.

***

Poetry dominated only into the early years of Arnold's marriage. Its melancholic cast and classical inspiration produced *The Strayed Reveller* (1849) and *Empedocles on Etna* (1852). Given his belief in the modernity of the ancients, he remained unimpressed by mere originality. He once dismissed Walt Whitman's practice with the words, 'no one can afford, in literature, to trade merely on his own bottom and to take no account of what other ages and nations have acquired: a great original literature America will never get in this way'.

While proud of his achievements in verse, he could see his limitation. To Clough he had admitted in December 1852, 'As for my poems they have weight, I think, but little or no charm.' Charm or not, five years on Arnold won election as Professor of Poetry at Oxford for the first of two, five-year terms, lecturing in English (against the Latin tradition) – and somewhat dogmatically, according to Jane. His classical tragedy *Merope* largely failed; his poetic inspiration slowly diminished. When he famously wrote to his mother on June 5, 1869, of his place in the canon, his characteristically confident tone betrayed a sense of work completed: 'My poems represent, on the whole, the main movement of mind of the last quarter of a century, and thus they will probably have their day as people become conscious to themselves of what that movement of mind is, and interested in the literary productions which reflect it.' He felt himself to be more in touch with the *zeitgeist* than either Tennyson or Browning.

Although to Arnold the world of his poetry might later be repossessed, in reality his poetic gift revived only fitfully. His 1873 collection, *New Poems*, would contain his greatest poem, 'Dover Beach', though it was hardly new. Recently written poems did exist among standard selections in the new editions. The chief difference seemed rather to be in the public's reception to them. Critics and readers began to value rather what they had earlier overlooked or dismissed. In an 1869 review of his two-volume *Poems*, *The Guardian* finally included the observation, 'we must admire in Mr. Arnold the equable culture of his thought, and the exquisite taste of his trained and modulated emotions'.

Further support came from among prominent literary peers: 'George Eliot says, a lady tells me, that of all modern poetry mine is that which keeps constantly growing upon her', he confided in February 1876. Eleven years later he reported to Jane his having seen the politician and former journalist John Morley, who told him 'He was going to dine alone with his wife and to read my poetry afterwards, as he constantly did.' 'The poems are having a better fortune now', he reckoned, 'in their old age than they ever had in their youth.' One instance came in October 1877 when he reported that the *Saturday Review* 'devoted three or four columns to praising my poems with a solemnity which is generally reserved for the dead and divinised. It was, however, very proper and very beautiful.'

As with most poets, Arnold could not help worrying over details of the promotion of his poems. In a letter to his publisher Alexander Macmillan in early May 1869, he wrote at 9 p.m. from a school in the market town of Saffron Walden, while still engaged in examining pupil teachers in a dismal classroom: 'it occurs to me there is no mention of a *new edition* on my title-pages. Perhaps this is better so; but consider whether in advertising you would not say something about its being a new edition – or the first collected edition, or something of that sort.' By the end of his life he had learnt not to meddle in such details. He wrote of Macmillan's niche promotion of his work, for instance: 'I think he is of the opinion that the sort of people who want my poems are people who do not mind a high price if they get a handsome book; and I leave the matter very much to him. I never have been broadly popular, and I cannot exactly bring myself to believe I shall ever become so.'

Like all but the most successful of poets, Arnold had given limited attention to the remuneration he received in the early years. As his reputation grew he began to see the possibilities. On May 30, 1877, for example, he wrote to Macmillan that he had been given the terms for a new edition of the poems, but 'I was disappointed, for I had expected, judging from the last edition, £350.' And in April 1885, when the prospect of retirement put him more in a mood to bargain, he became forthright: 'As it is better to settle these things beforehand, I should like to know what you propose to give for this new edition of the Poems.'

The poetic aspiration died hard. As late as July 1882 he wrote to Swinburne, 'If my daily grind at school inspecting ever ceases, I mean to try my hand at a project of mine more than thirty years old, a Roman play with Lucretius for its centre… But I daresay I shall die in harness, and do no more poetry.' Alternatively, he confided to his sister Frances the following year – five years before his death – 'I must, before I die, get another volumeful of things done if I can; they are all in my head, but when am I to collect myself for accomplishing them? Meanwhile I must perform my promises in prose; but I make no more of them, and hope to get most of what I have already made performed this year. Then I shall be free. But after sixty it seems presumptuous to be looking forward and planning in this way.'

***

The truth was that Arnold's preoccupations had some years before effectively turned from self to society, influenced by two roles which would direct his fortunes almost to the end of his life: that of paterfamilias and schools' inspector. As a family man Arnold approached his days with cautious optimism, joying in his children's company. Once, from Vienna, he wrote home to his mother, 'I miss them all more than I can say, and Dicky and Nelly particularly have so good an effect on my spirits that it is almost impossible for me to be depressed when they are with me.' In October 1885 he wrote to Lucy, 'We all agree that Mr Woodhouse in *Emma* is rather like *me*; in particular, so far as his sayings to and of his daughters are concerned.' He also told her that he always cried when her letters were read to him by his wife, 'but it was a happy cry'.

The children were, of course, at the heart of the Arnolds' frequent money concerns. In April 1866, and not for the first time, he worried over school costs: 'I find Rugby will be £150 a year, Westminster (where Tom is going as a day boy) £30 a year; the little girls must soon have a governess – some £50 more; and how am I to find another £150 for Dick's public school.' School fees required commitment on the part of the boys, also. 'For me, Rugby is an expense which is only justified by the boy's making use of his advantages.' Of the Rugby experience, Howard Foster Lowry (*The Letters of Matthew Arnold to Arthur Hugh Clough*) wrote in 1932, 'Rugby did not teach boys to worry about their souls and the souls of those about them.' Budge's failure there – later to be reversed somewhat – almost confirmed this. Arnold considered at one time sending this floundering son abroad for a cheaper education in Bonn, especially given his doubts about the value of the old English public school system, 'with it almost unlimited freedom and leaving the boy to himself'.

Improvidence generally ruled. Arnold once cautioned his mother that the family could not visit her in Ambleside, 'because it is incompatible with the strict economy our straitened condition compels us to practise'. In February 1867 he wrote of hoping to reduce their dining out to two or three occasions a week. Moving to Harrow for the boys' education – a good thirteen miles from London – required a change in their social life. On the eve of moving there, he declared, 'I feel more than most people the distracting influence, on which Byron in one of his letters insists so strongly, of London society, and am sure I can do most when I am away from it – though I like it well enough.'

And yet the sociable Arnold rarely dimmed. Always susceptible to the flattery of knowing the right company, in May 1869 he reported in a Pepysian manner of attending a dinner with the Literary Club: 'yesterday week – my first appearance amongst them; Walpole, the President, put me on his right hand, and on the other side of me was Lord Lytton'. Opposite sat Lord Stratford de Redclyffe, while the Archbishop of Dublin, the Bishop of Oxford, and Lord Dufferin also attended, 'and all very civil'.

***

At the same time, Arnold had chosen a difficult career. The problem lay largely in the exhausting travel required to oversee educational provision across the breadth of southern England and Wales. He was responsible for assessing and for compiling reports on the non-established church schools (such as those run by Methodists or Quakers) with children to the age of fourteen. To Flu he wrote hopefully in October 1851: 'I think I shall get interested in the schools after a little time; their effects on the children are so immense, and their future effects in civilising the next generation of the lower classes, who, as things are going, will have most of the political power of the country in their hands, may be so important.'

He expected to 'like it well enough', though enthusiasm was hard to sustain. From Battersea he wrote only a year later: 'This certainly has been one of the most uncomfortable weeks I ever spent. Battersea is so far off, the roads so execrable, and the rain so incessant. I cannot bear to take my cab from London over Battersea Bridge, as it seems so absurd to pay eightpence for the sake of the half-mile on this side; but that half-mile is one continued slough, as there is not a yard of flagging, I believe, in all Battersea.'

Arnold's working pace seemed to have accelerated over the early years and sometimes he shared the impossibility of his vocation. In a letter to his mother of May 7, 1864, he described an intense day: 'Up at 6, writing and working till breakfast at 8 ½. In the Saffron Walden school at ¼ to 10, and from then till ½ past 12, at which hour a carriage came to the door for me and I got into it, leaving my assistant at work to finish for me; drove to Great Bardfield, through the heart of Essex, 12 miles in the rain; reached the school at 2, there till ¼ past 5 – then up to Great Bardfield Hall, belonging to a half farmer, half gentleman, a Quaker, to dinner; at ½ past 6 the carriage at the door again, and at 8 I was put down at the school door in Saffron Walden again, where the scholars of a night school kept me till nearly 10.'

Arnold turned out to be a frequently popular school visitor, supportive of teachers and keen to celebrate the successes of pupils. On a professional level, in the words of Park Honan, 'He began as a naïve H.M.I. and became, in time, a mediocre one, if one considers his work quite apart from his foreign reports… Arnold was known to be ebullient, too careless, too frank and sympathetic in classrooms. Later he had a reputation for being distractable.' That *may* have been the case. It was reported by one of his school's managers that he did little more than chat with administrative heads, pass through the ranks of children at their desks, looking over shoulders, and then leave, but this is a snapshot from one perspective.

His determination to be positive can be seen as both morally and practically necessary in the face of the government's penny-pinching educational philosophy and a financial squeezed department. Also, on a personal level, he valued fairness, appreciated the difficulties involved in the work of teachers and pupils from poor homes – and, admittedly, enjoyed having a good reputation. As he told his mother, 'I like what it says in the Schoolmasters' newspaper, because it shews that I am reputed among the teachers, as I wish to be, kind and considerate.'

Eventually Arnold learned to adapt to the rhythms of the job, building time for creative work into his commitments. Eleven years into his career, he wrote, 'All this is a busy life, but I am very well, and enjoy it – inspecting is a *little* too much, as the business half of one's life in contradistinction to the inward and spiritual half of it, or I should be quite satisfied.'

Promotion only came near the end of his career, given his principled stand on some educational issues. When the Liberals came into office in November 1868, Arnold wisely did not assume preferment, though he did indicate his state of mind regarding the balance of work and creativity: 'unless the post, if it comes, is one in which I think I can do real service, I shall not leave my present post which I have so thoroughly mastered and which gives me much independence and time for my own work.' Six months later, before the rumour of a possible advancement again came to nothing, he wrote, 'I can truly say that the power of doing something in literature which my present post leaves me, and the prospect of losing this power if I passed to another and more anxious post, makes me not discontented to remain where I am.'

In refusing a public speaking engagement in November 1877, he acknowledged: 'The Department which I serve has always left me perfect freedom in my literary publications. In return, I consider myself bound to abstain from all appearance on the stage of public life.' This slyly avoided the truth that he had taken adversarial public stand by pamphlet, essay and letter on the Revised Code of 1862 and other government follies.

In January 1864 he wrote to Richard Cobden explaining, 'All I have seen abroad, all I have seen in this country, convinces me how ruinous a policy for themselves the middle classes pursue in helping the aristocratic and governing class to prevent any real public establishment off education.' By now his ambition encompassed the extension of its provision in England. 'I firmly believe the establishment of secondary instruction is a more urgent matter than even that of primary.' He sensed, as he told Cobden on a later occasion, 'a ferment in the spirit of the middle class', that the time for opening its mind had come. But not quite, for in 1867 he could still talk of its obstructive 'zeal against centralization' and 'fondness for private pottering'. And he explained to William Forster in May 1879, 'it is no use for a politician to contend for public secondary schools in England at present, because he cannot possibly hope to carry his body of citizens with him.'

Arnold's views on the higher education curriculum echoed his lifelong commitment to the classics. Late in life he wrote to a colleague: 'I have no difficulty in saying that I should be glad to see at the Universities, not a new School established for Modern Literature or Modern Languages, but the great works of English Literature taken in conjunction with those of Greek and Latin Literature in the final Examination for honours in *Literae*

Humaniores.' He would add no literature except that of England's to the classical literature taken for the degree. Nor would he countenance a separate school with degrees and honours for the modern languages, though he believed that teachers needed 'certificates of fitness to teach'.

As a realist, Arnold expected egalitarian educational reforms to take time. He was not overly ambitious personally, either. His occasional attempts at promotion, encouraged by Flu, proved unsuccessful and unsettling. In December 1869 he confessed, 'I more and more wish to turn my thoughts from all notion of advancement in official and public life, and to go on quietly and soberly as I am.' He might not gain promotion, but neither was he censored for his views. Unsurprisingly, given the various positions he took, promotion to Chief Inspector of Schools came to Arnold only in 1884, two years from retirement and four before his death. At least his district had been reduced in 1871 to the London area (Westminster and three Middlesex parishes, 'as good as it can possibly be') and by then he had been given an assistant.

***

Arnold also enjoyed secondments on two occasions, the first in 1859 reporting on schools in France, Holland, Belgium and Switzerland for the Newcastle Commission. Though he professed no deep interest in the subject, he loved to spend time in travel and found the experience eye-opening (and useful in terms of developing contacts abroad). France especially had long interested him.

To Harriet Martineau he offered his thoughts on it in July 1864: 'What gives France its power is, it seems to me, that the nation is *alive*, alive in mind and spirit I mean, down so much further into the body of the community than here. This they get from their Revolution and the electric shock it gave... There are the highly cultivated and intelligent people here as there – but, besides these, the middle and lower class there seem to have been touched by an electric current of mind and soul which prepares them for modern society and its new conditions – and this current seems not yet to have reached the middle and lower classes here.'

The French Revolution and the Napoleonic era had thrown into relief the differences between France and England, destabilising both countries to dramatically different degrees. Recommending Burke as a man like Wordsworth, to his friend Ernest Fontanès in January 1880, he wrote, 'The old order of things had not the virtue which Burke supposed. The Revolution had not the banefulness which he supposed. But neither was the Revolution the commencement, as its friends supposed, of a reign of justice and virtue.' To Arnold, as to his correspondent Edmond Schérer, the French theologian and critic, it was both confused in its instincts and yet necessary for renewal.

French morals were another thing entirely. During the Franco-Prussian War of 1870 he wrote privately, 'The French provoke one by their incorrigibility, by their persisting in regarding themselves and Paris as something to which another measure is to be meted than is meted to the rest of the world, and by their utter failure to see that in their own fatal want of morality and seriousness is the source of all their disasters.' He reckoned that 'what has been their destruction has been their *sensuality*, which Prince Albert 20 years ago pointed out'. He had little time for the victors, however. In a letter to his friend Wyndham Slade five years before the war he claimed: 'the Germans, with their hideousness and commonness, are no relief to one's spirit but rather depress it. Never surely was there seen a people of so many millions so unattractive.'

In January 1871, after France's defeat, Arnold mused on the role it had lost and was perhaps not to recover for some time: 'The qualities of the French genius, their lucidity, directness of intellect and social charm must always make themselves felt, as the far higher qualities of the Greeks did and do: but it is quite a question whether the practical military and political career of France may not be now ending, not again to revive, as that of Greece did after the Macedonian Conquest.'

Nor was the government of France safe from its own people. In March he warned, 'One thing is certain, that miserable as it is for herself, there is no way by which France can make the rest of Europe so alarmed and uneasy as by a socialist and red republic. It is a perpetual flag to the proletaire class everywhere – the class which makes all governments uneasy.' Yet Arnold did 'not think well enough' of Adolphe Thiers and the French upper class: 'what is certain is that all the seriousness, clearmindedness, and settled purpose is thitherto on the side of the Reds'. He believed the Paris Commune would triumph.

It did not. On May 31st, two days after the government won, Arnold waved a more democratic flag than he had at England's own agitation in the Hyde Park Riots: 'The Paris convulsion is an explosion of that fixed resolve of the working class to count for something and *live*, which is destined to make itself so much felt in the coming time, and to disturb so much which dreamed it would last for ever. It is the French working man's clearly putting his resolve before himself and acting upon it, while the working man elsewhere is in a haze about it, that makes France such a focus for the revolutionists of all Europe.'

When the Arnolds passed through Paris that August, they noted the surprising extent of the ruins, 'but the natural tendency of Paris to gaiety and splendour is indestructible and the place is fast on the way to have all its old fascinations over again'.

***

Longman's had published his report for the Commission as *The Popular Education of France* in 1861; it would cost Arnold £80 in unrealized sales. Its introduction survived to be collected as an essay, 'Democracy', which appeared in *Mixed Essays* (1879). Nicholas Murray, in *A Life of Matthew Arnold* (1996), explained its importance: 'Just as the 1853 Preface launched some primary critical ideas that were later to be expanded and developed into something like a body of critical doctrine, the essay on democracy contains the first outlines of his cultural criticism.' In this introduction Arnold recognized the growing need and desirability of democracy and made a plea for the State to involve itself and to foster a national culture.

His reputation has been made to suffer under a charge of elitism from the misrepresentation of what he meant by this, but to Arnold 'culture' should be accessible to all. He was glad, he wrote to his mother, of contributing 'to the cause of popular education' with the book. For Arnold – as he had written to Flu in the year of his appointment – the education of boys of the working class offered 'a civilizing agent' as much as an 'instructing agent', 'almost the only great civilizing agency directly at work'. In the words of Kate Campbell, 'The cultivation of emotional, moral and intellectual capacities was supposed to overcome class conflict by inducing a sense of shared human identity: as pupils became "humanized" through such cultivation, they would tend to discount the material differences between social classes.'

And furthermore, Arnold believed, it would dramatically change the future. 'If there is one thing more certain than another', he wrote, 'it is that popular education will bring the question of the right distribution of wealth, and of the wrongness of the present distribution, into prominence.' On the subject of the education of English girls in girls' schools, he remained circumspect, never having had professional experience of them. He worried that they would lack the status conferred by the clergy in boys' schools.

His essay 'A French Eton', also looked to the State (1864) to involve itself in education. It had become a pressing need. The seriousness with which he focused on it may be gleaned from a comment in a November 1863 letter in which he mentions, 'I am anxious about this second part [of the essay], as the prejudices are strong, and I want to prevail against them – this cannot be done without prodigies of persuasion and insinuation.' It was as if he stood in need of constantly reminding himself that 'one must convey the true doctrine with studied moderation'.

The Revised Code of 1862 – 'a fatal educational blunder' – introduced a system under which support for schools depended on attendance and examinations in reading, writing and arithmetic. This led to a narrowing of the curriculum to meet the iniquity of payment by results. Having taken soundings from MPs and 'county gentlemen' on the code, while on the circuit marshalling for his father-in-law, the judge, Arnold wrote a pamphlet against it. Attempting to mollify Flu in March 1862 about its effects on his employer he wrote: 'I don't think, however, they can eject me, though they can, and perhaps will, make my place uncomfortable. If thrown on the world I daresay we should be on our legs again before very long. Any way, I think I owed as much as this to a cause in which I have now a deep interest, and shall always have, even if I cease to serve officially.'

One pernicious aspect of the Code continued to annoy him. In June 1870 Arnold replied to a paper by George Harris, '*Teaching by rote* is the bane of the system introduced by the Revised Code; if you look at the forthcoming blue book of the Committee of Council you will see that this is my opinion as strongly as it is yours. And it is most true that what education our school children get, they do not follow up: parish libraries would do something to cure this, and it would be well to institute them; but the horrible pell mell, over-crowding and utter misery of our social state at the bottom of society, is what in truth pulls people down, and to deal with this is an immense matter.'

The increased administrative work, including marking, weighed on Arnold but, while he complained in a letter to his mother that Council Office rules were becoming 'more rigidly mechanical', he hoped to help change them: 'Meanwhile I find the increasing routine of the office work a good balance to my own increasing literary work – but unless I throw myself into the latter, the irrationality of the former would worry me to death.' Irrationality was always the way of Education.

Arnold might complain of the pressures of the job, as he did in declining membership of the Wordsworth Society, as he had the Shakespeare Society ('Life is too short for these things – at least *my* life, as school-inspecting has made it, is.') On the other hand, he possessed a keen awareness of the benefit of employment. In June 1881 he informed a correspondent, 'I am a school-inspector myself, and know well what it is to feel oneself tied and bound, and unable to do what one would most like to do; but I am sure that the precariousness and anxiety of living by one's pen (if one is not a popular novelist) is worse for one than the taskwork of a profession or an office.' And yet he would not die in harness: 'I have no wish to execute the Dance of Death in an elementary school.'

***

Arnold's reasons for effectively moving from poetry to prose were various: time constraints and potential earnings; the feeling that he had accomplished all he could with his poetry; the question, perhaps, of failing inspiration; his only modest success with readers and critics; the general failure to appreciate the importance of Greek verse to the present day. Beyond these, Arnold felt the need to speak out on matters larger than himself and his own personal concerns. Here his experience of education, the uncertain times, and the influence of his father became decisive. (He greatly admired Thomas Arnold's historic sense: 'he was so wonderfully, for his nation time and profession, *European*, and thus so got himself out of the narrow medium in which after all, his English friends lived').

As Daniel Brown has noted, the periodical essay had by now come 'to supersede the book as the main means of directly communicating new ideas to the public'. The essays reflected, then, a more robust engagement with the greater world of pressing concerns. Though Arnold remained ambitious into the 1860s to 'give the next 10 years earnestly to poetry', he could not.

He had emerged as a critic with his preface to the 1853 poems and went on in this spirit to publish essays for monthly magazines, such as Smith's *The Cornhill*, which had taken on the critical role of the earlier prestigious quarterlies like the *Edinburgh Review*. These essays he later collected in books, an increasingly popular publishing initiative: *On Translating Homer* (1861), *Essays in Criticism* (1865) and *Culture and Anarchy* (1869). With *Literature and Dogma* (1873) he turned to modernising theology. These books came to shape modern criticism.

Arnold could seem as 'Olympian' in his criticism as in his personal manner. Yet one letter reveals a curious naivety regarding his tone. After insulting the Homer translation by Francis W. Newman – albeit amusingly – the response from *The Spectator* caused him to complain in July 1861 that they questioned his amiability when 'my sweetness of disposition is my most distinguishing characteristic'. He regretted Newman 'should be so deeply annoyed by what I intended far more as an illustration of the want of *justice d'esprit* to which the English are prone, than as an attack upon him.' He learnt from this, if somewhat slowly. So, in July 1875 he asked Macmillan to send a copy of the third edition of *Essays in Criticism*: 'I should like to look through them – there may be one or two personalities to strike out; – as I draw nearer to my latter end, the desire increases in me to die at peace with all men.'

Despite such criticisms, Arnold's success as a polemicist made him well-known, earned him his sons' school fees, entrée into high society (notwithstanding his attacks on 'Barbarians') – and sometimes amused him. In November 1863 he wrote of 'seeing myself placarded all over London as having written on Marcus Aurelius – and having walked up Regent Street behind a man with a board on his back announcing the same interesting piece of news.'

His style relied largely on a light and bantering tone, charm – and irony. He explained to author and editor James S. Spedding, his need for the last: 'If in continuing my essay I seem to you to proceed in a somewhat roundabout and indirect manner, pray remember that I have to deal with a public which requires the most delicate management if one is to make an impression upon it. This is why I use irony so much; because the ordinary Englishman is so hard, strong, and pugnacious, that he will contend with you, instead of weighing your words, if you appear to expostulate with him directly.'

In December 1867 Arnold boasted to his mother of its success: 'I see more and more what an effective weapon, in a confused, loud-talking, clap-trappy country like this, where every writer and speaker to the public tends to say rather more than he means, is *irony*, or according to the strict meaning of the original Greek word, the saying rather less than one means. The main effect I have had on the mass of noisy claptrap and inert prejudice which chokes us has been, I can see, by the use of this weapon; and now, when people's minds are getting widely disturbed and they are beginning to ask themselves whether they have not a great deal that is new to learn, to increase this feeling in them irony is more useful than ever.'

He had earlier attempted to impress upon her the value of charm: 'It is very animating to think that one at last has a chance of *getting at* the English public – such a public as it is, and such a work as one wants to do with it: partly nature, partly time & study have also by this time taught me thoroughly the precious truth that everything turns upon one's exercising the power of *persuasion, of charm*; that without this all fury, energy, reasoning power, acquirement, – are thrown away and only render their owner more miserable. Even in one's ridicule one must preserve a sweetness and good-humour.'

In these he failed to secure her confidence. However encouraging the Arnold family might otherwise be to the eldest son, his essays did not altogether satisfy what he once called their 'Puritan streaks'. Of the preface to the *Essays in Criticism* Arnold wrote home in February 1865, 'I was sure that my own family, from their training and their habits of thinking and feeling, would not find this preface to their taste.' To Tom he added shortly after 'there is a vein of *strictness* in our family which makes them a little averse to that sort of style – but one must think of the world, and with that it seems, so far as I can see at present, to be having very much the effect I intended'. Four years later he began a different approach. He explained to his mother and sister, Frances, that he ascribed the main idea of his essay 'On the Modern Element in Literature' to his father, as he did ideas in the preface to *Culture and Anarchy*. Then he conceded, 'but the treatment has much of that persiflage which I find necessary to use, but which I know you do not like' and therefore he had told them the previous month that he would not send it.

Nevertheless Arnold felt perfectly justified in the style he adopted: 'my sinuous, easy, unpolemical mode of proceeding has been adopted by me first, because I really think it is the best way of proceeding if one wants to get at, and keep with, truth'. His commitment to influencing change would be unflagging, despite the handicap of such demanding employment. It is among his most impressive quality. To Fan, he confessed in a letter of late 1870, 'As one's years increase and the desire to fulfil certain projects while one has yet time becomes keener and more pressing, the interruption caused by the continual travelling about which inspection requires, becomes trying…. The times are wonderful and will be still more so – and one would not willingly lose by negligence, self mismanagement, and want of patience, what power one has of working in them and having influence on them.'

The British public, like his family, appeared only slowly won over. Arnold's writing would not make him wealthy, since his book sales were mostly modest, yet he avoided that other profitable source of income: lecturing. Showing the spirit of Wordsworth, who described Coleridge's public lectures as 'a most odious way of picking up money', he would charge only travel expenses on the occasions he lectured. While he took pride in paying school bills with the industry of his pen, on more than one occasion he found it necessary to borrow from his publisher (and his mother). In March 1867, for example, after working on his foreign school report for much of the previous ten months, he requested from Smith a loan against future writing which would be all for the *Cornhill* until the debt was repaid, since 'I made literature put my boys to school, and literature failing me, I want £200.'

Although he readily acknowledged his modest sales, he took pride in knowing he had some influence. In June 1868, after dining with a group of Liberals, he declared himself 'struck to find what hold among these younger men what I write has taken. I should think I heard the word *Philistines* used at least 100 times during dinner and *Barbarians* very often.' In one choice anecdote he tells of being interviewed by Income Tax Commissioners who assessed his profits at £1000 a year. In his defence he declared himself 'an unpopular author' and the amount was reduced to £200, at which he said he would have to write more articles in order not to lose out. This drew the response, 'Then the public will have reason to be much obliged to us.'

His supposed unpopularity became an article of faith with Arnold and offered lighter moments of reflection, such as this from October 1874: 'I am amused to see Strahan's handbill stuck in all the magazines and bookstalls, announcing Gladstone and me as his two attractions this month [in the *Contemporary Review*]. But no one knows better than I do how little of a popular author I am' – this observation was instantly qualified with – 'but the thing is, I gradually produce a real effect, and the public acquires a kind of obscure interest in me as this gets to be perceived.' Arnold could never entirely decide about his status. His unpopularity, from another angle, looked like a kind of popularity.

In point of fact he shared Bulwer-Lytton's shrewd assessment, 'that it is no inconsiderable advantage to me, that all the writing world have a kind of weakness for me, even at the time they are attacking me'. His literary peers might grumble and remonstrate with him, but they were his chief audience, even when they frustrated and misrepresented him. Of letters he wrote to *The Pall Mall* he declared in March 1866, 'I was glad to have an opportunity to disclaim that positive admiration of things foreign, and that indifference to English freedom, which have often been imputed to me – and to explain that I do not disparage freedom, but take it for granted as our condition, and go on to consider other things.' And again in February 1868 he complained to his mother, 'Then too the Spectator does me a very bad service by talking of my contempt for un-intellectual people; it is not at all true, and it sets people against one. You will laugh, but fiery hatred and malice are what I detest and would always allay or avoid, if I could.' Leslie Stephen later said much the same thing: 'Though in controversy he took and gave many shrewd blows, he always received them with a courtesy, indicative not only of mere policy or literary tact, but of dislike to inflicting pain.'

Arnold's success could be partly attributed to his willingness to listen to reasonable criticism of his work, which he would learn from and play off. Responding to it became a way of writing. In early July 1867, for example, he wrote to George Smith, 'I see, or hear, that there are many murmurers against Culture & its Enemies. Would it not be better to let Anarchy and Authority wait a little, so as to be able to gather up all the murmurings into one and see what they come to?'

Otherwise he maintained a healthy attitude to the pain of criticism: 'If one expects any real light or satisfaction from reviews, one is sure to be disappointed. I never do; but I always look at them in the hope of picking up a hint here and there, and I can truly say that I read them with as equanimity as if they were about another man. But this does not come all at once.' So, he adopted a pragmatic strategy: 'I do not read a purely personal article till it has been out at least a week. Then one cannot be excited by it, for one says to oneself: "It has already passed out of people's minds with the appearance of the new number, why trouble yourself about it?'

In July 1861 he described another strategy for absorbing negative criticism – in this case from the *Saturday Review*: 'When first I read a thing of this kind I am annoyed: then I think how certainly in two or three days the effect of it upon me will have wholly passed off – then I begin to think of the openings it gives for observations in answer, and from that moment – when a free activity of the spirit is restored – my gaiety and good spirits return, and the article is simply an object of interest to me.' He then cautioned, 'To be able to feel thus, one must… be on ground where one feels at home and secure – that is the great secret of good humour.'

His industry appears staggering at times. He listed his work for the early months of 1863: the Guérin and Colenso articles in January (for *Fraser's Magazine*); February: Marcus Aurelius (*Fraser's*); March: A French Eaton (*McMillan*); April: on Academies (*Fraser's*); May: Eugénie de Guérin (*Macmillan*). They bolstered the family finances. He wrote regarding school fees the following year: 'Bagehot has sent me £22 for Joubert, and I think of sending my Oxford lecture to the Cornhill, which will be £21 more. These two last parts of the French Eton make £23 more, so there is Budge's half year paid for, and £20 over.'

Aside from taking gratification in such work, Arnold could show a little humility. In such a mood, he told his mother, 'To the last day I live I shall never get over a sense of gratitude and surprise at finding my productions acceptable, when I see so many people all around me so hard put to it to find a market.' He also remained insightful of the pitfall of success. 'I would far rather have it said how delightful and interesting a man was Joubert,' he wrote, 'than how brilliant my article is. In the long run one makes enemies by having one's brilliancy and ability praised; one can only get oneself readily accepted by men by making oneself forgotten in the people and doctrines one recommends.'

Of his French Eton article he continues, 'I really want to *persuade* on this subject, and I have felt how necessary it was to keep down many and many sharp and telling things that rise to one's lips, and which one would gladly utter if one's object was to show one's own abilities.' He now thought of his ideas as 'more and more matters of my deepest belief and parts of my nature – not the triumph of myself'. Rehearsing his seriousness before his family, he wrote 'one cannot change English ideas so much as, if I live, I hope to change them, without saying imperturbably what one thinks and making a good many people uncomfortable. The great thing is to speak without a particle of vice, malice, or rancour.'

***

Unlike Leslie Stephen and many of his peers, Arnold was never – as Noel Annan phrased it – 'subtly tainted with the English contempt for culture and the world of ideas'. As a patriot, his despair at the state of England accounted for his proselytizing zeal: 'I have a conviction that there is a real, an almost imminent danger of England losing immeasurably in all ways, declining into a sort of greater Holland, for want of what I must still call ideas, for want of perceiving how the world is going and must go, and preparing herself accordingly. This conviction haunts me, and at times even overwhelms me with depression; I would rather not live to see the changes come to pass, for we shall all deteriorate under it.'

Ultimately he attributed England's decline to the class system. Writing in admiration of the effect on the Welsh of the Eisteddfods, he made clear his views: 'We in England have come to that point when the continued advance and greatness of our nation is threatened by one cause, and one cause above all. Far more than by the helplessness of an aristocracy whose day is fast coming to an end, far more than the rawness of a lower class whose day is only just beginning, we are imperilled by what I call the "Philistinism" of our middle class; on the side of beauty and taste, vulgarity; on the side of morals and feeling, coarseness; on the side of the mind and spirit, unintelligence, – this is Philistinism.'

In *Culture and Anarchy* (1869) he elaborated on this. The aristocracy became 'the Barbarians', individualistic, moneyed, backward looking; the middle class; the Philistines, pragmatic when it came to industrialization and commerce, yet impervious to ideas otherwise. The working class, 'the Populace', constituted the exploited, coming into political consciousness and agitating for democracy. In the course of publishing the papers which would make up *Culture and Anarchy* he reported, 'I think *Barbarian* will stick; but as a very charming Barbarianess, Lady Portsmouth, expresses a great desire to make my acquaintance, I daresay the race will bear no malice. In fact, the one arm they feel and respect is irony, as I have often said; whereas the Puritan middle class, at whom I have launched so much, are partly too good, partly too gross, to feel it. I shall tell upon them, however, somehow before I have done.'

Culture and Anarchy popularized this and other Arnold's sloganizing notions: 'sweetness and light'; 'seeing things as they really are'; anarchy versus culture; and Hebraism and Hellenism. Encouraged by Swinburne's public admiration for his 'criticisms', he wrote home, 'This reputation for seeing and saying the thing as it really is, is one which is a very useful one to have just now, and it is beginning to attach itself to me.' The phrase 'seeing things as they really are' made more sense than it might today appear, since Arnold meant by it not only the obvious clarity of thought, but also seeing without a distorting ideology or political bias, as had been the case with earlier periodicals like the *Edinburgh Review*.

Another of those coinages also seemed to be hitting home: Hellenism & Hebraism. A combination of Hebraism (determined action and 'strictness of conscience') and Hellenism (clarity of thought and 'spontaneity of consciousness') would be much to be desired, though in England the Bible-fed middle class, prided itself too much on action, on Hebraism, and barely knew about the Greeks and Hellenism (with its spirit of 'Sweetness and Light'). As David Morse explained Arnold's position in *High Victorian Culture* (1993), 'Hebraism was right in the infancy of the human race; now as humanity reaches towards a fuller and more harmonious conception of spiritual development, it is the example of Greece that can lead it there.' Arnold felt the chapters on these two 'so true that they will form a kind of centre for English thought and speculation on the matters treated in them'. He cited his artist friend Frederick Leighton who told him that he was 'always trying to Hellenise' and remarked delightedly that 'the Princess Alice is quite fascinated with my Culture & Anarchy, uses all its phrases, & knows long bits by heart. The Crown Princess is now reading the book.'

He knew exactly what he was doing: 'the merit of terms of this sort is that they fix in people's minds the *things* to which they refer'. He knew to play the long game with subtlety, influence being the goal rather than glory. Defending a weak expression in *Culture and Anarchy* ('strictness of conscience') to a senior judge of his acquaintance in April 1869, he opted to take the altruistic view, 'Many of the notions in these Essays are notions for which our time is so ripe that they lodge in people's minds even while they are controverting them, and will produce their effect sooner or later, when nobody will care to ask who uttered them.'

Arnold had much to say about the middle-class Dissenters. In a letter to Gladstone of June 10, 1864 – accompanying his gift of a copy of 'A French Eton' – he explained: 'I may add that in a now twelve years' acquaintance with British schools all over the country and with their promoters, I have perhaps had more than common opportunities for studying the English middle class – and particularly one of its strongest and most characteristic parts, – the Protestant Dissenters.' While his relationships with those he met visiting their schools were generally good, these people needed 'more sense of public responsibility'. He told Harriet Martineau, in July 1860, 'The Nonconformists, it seems to me, have in their day done good service by maintaining the cause of individual freedom and independence: but at the present day, in England, freedom and independence are pretty well secured, and our great want is intelligence, which Nonconformity rather obstructs than advances.'

***

In November 1869 – the year of *Culture and Anarchy* – he wrote to Charles Kegan Paul, '[I]am convinced that their stolid assurance that they clearly possess the undoubted unadulterated Gospel in the theology which passes current among them, is an absolute stoppage to all real progress and mental activity in them – and if in them, in a good large part of the nation and one of the strongest parts. Ideas which are still absolutely dominant among them about the interpretation and inspiration of Scripture are no longer possible among the more educated clergy of the Establishment. I do not profess to be bringing anything new or instructive to them; but what I have written for, is the untouched mass of Protestant Dissent, and into this I hope to have found my way.'

This was partly the reason Arnold turned his critical attention to theology (this and the deaths of his boys). As Coleridge wrote after Arnold's death, he had 'a religious nature'. He attended church but did not attend to much of the 'claptrap' he heard on matters of any faith. To his friend Arthur Penrhyn Stanley he suggested, 'The *profound natural truth* which lies in Christianity, independent of all glosses which churches and theologians have put upon it, it is the thing to insist on.'

Biblical references are very common in the letters home, as are theological concerns on occasions, as in August 1867: 'But something of what Papa did as against the Evangelicals – an enlarging of the idea of religion and a bringing into it of a number of other things which the old narrow religionists thought had nothing to do with it – is the great want of our spiritual intellectual life in England at the present.' He was engaged on work he felt his father 'would have approved and seen to be indispensable'.

Despite his intention to be a 'populariser' on religious issues though, Arnold would prove to be highly controversial – which had the positive consequence of increasing his book sales. In one decade he published *St Paul and Protestantism* (1870); most notably *Literature and Dogma* (1873); *God and the Bible* (1875) and *Last Essays on Church and Religion* (1877). Personally, he reckoned *Literature and Dogma* to be 'really one of the most religious books of our Century'.

He believed, he declared, they would 'see in our time a change in religion as great as that which happened at the Reformation'. He also knew that organised religion would need reorganizing to meet the changing times. Writing to Ernest Fontanès, Arnold expressed the view that 'man feels himself to be a more various and richly-endowed animal than the old religious theory of human life allowed… I think it is like all inevitable revolutions, a salutary one, but it greatly requires watching and guiding. The growing desire, throughout the community, for amusement and pleasure… have their good side… The awakening demand for beauty, a demand so little made in this country for the last century and more, is another sign of the revolution, and a clearly favourable sign of it. Religious disputes have for so long a time touched the inmost fibre of our nation's being, that they still attract great attention, and create passions and parties; but certainly they have not the significance which they once had.

Arnold's interest was in 'the movement of men's minds at present'. He felt that progress would occasion 'blunder and misconception'. In his view, the central blunder concerned the supernatural and religion. Consequently he took exception to his friend Frederick William Farrar's defence of miracles in his *Life of Christ*, 'I regard the belief in miracles as on a par, in respect of its inevitable disappearance from the minds of reasonable men, with the belief in witches and hobgoblins.' Religion as myth, as literal truth, would eventually fail, the sea of faith withdraw.

The second blunder would be in baldly dismantling these metaphorical accretions of belief. Much subtlety would be required. In April 1875 he wrote frankly to the theological critic Walter Richard Cassels, 'I look upon the Bible as the only means by which our people, naturally hard and brutal, get any exercise of its soul and imagination, and I look therefore with disquietude on all merely negative criticism of the Bible, which must certainly at first dispose them to throw the book aside.' To his brother Tom he wrote of dispensing with the supernatural, 'The whole end and aim of L. & D. [*Literature and Dogma*] is to edify the many by giving them a ground for loving the Bible when their old grounds fail them'. He sought to convince others, when the great change inevitably came that 'it need not be in terror and despair, that everything essential to its progress stands firm and unchanged'.

Unfortunately, it remained beyond his powers to persuade adherents of miracles and the resurrection. To James Thomas Knowles, his editor at the *Contemporary Review*, he accepted that the first part of his 'Review of Objections to Literature and Dogma' had angered many 'but really the question is between not having the Bible studied and prized at all, in some ten years' time, or having it studied and prized with new ideas and on new grounds'. On the other hand he remembered to keep his feelings in check, never forgetting that 'vicious attacks on the orthodox position do nothing but harm in every direction'.

Neither was he censorious of other faiths. As he wrote to John Henry Newman in January 1876, 'I would gladly, for my own part, see a Catholic University established in Ireland with the same kind of independence which the English Universities have.' And elsewhere, 'were I born in a Roman Catholic country I should most certainly never leave the Catholic Church for a Protestant; but neither then or now could I imagine that the Catholic Church possessed "the truth," or anything like it, or that it *could* possess it'. Newman credited Arnold views in return: 'It is that sympathy you have for what you do not believe, which so affects me about your future.' He prayed Arnold might convert to Catholicism as he had.

When he declined to participate in the election for the Poetry Chair at Oxford for a second time, it was because he knew his writings on the Bible were controversial. He explained in February 1877 that 'I refrain because a religious row over a literary election is an odious thing – and I think there would be one.' To Stanley he confided after his next article, 'I shall quit the subject of theology – at any rate the direct treatment of the subject; I shall have said what I specially wanted to say, and a layman may well go on too long at these subjects and do more harm than good by his persistence.'

It is important, though, to remember that with religion, as with other institutions, Arnold argued as an insider. He believed essentially in those systems against which he would take a stance on specific issues, and the positions he took were never too radical. Corroboration of a kind that he was treated as an insider came when he noted, 'We dine on the 3rd of June with the Archbishop of Canterbury, which I always think a gratifying marvel, considering what things I have published.'

***

Although nominally a Liberal ('a Liberal tempered by experience, reflection, and renouncement' as he wrote in the introduction to *Culture & Anarchy*), he felt himself above politics as both parties lacked vision. As a consequence of this myopia England stood unsteadily at times. When put to the test, as in the Hyde Park Riot of July 23, 1866 for political reform, Arnold's reactionary response illustrated his essential fear of violence and political agitation. In a letter to his mother after the event, he blamed everyone including the Home Secretary, Spencer H. Walpole: 'whereas in France, since the Revolution, a man feels that the power which represses him is the *State*, is *himself*, here a man feels that the power which represses him is the Tories, the upper class, the aristocracy, and so on; and with this feeling he can of course never without loss of self-respect accept a formal beating, and so things go on smouldering. If ever there comes a more equal state of society in England, the power of the State for repression will be a thousand times stronger.'

When Disraeli's Tories defeated the Liberals in February 1874, Arnold wrote to Lady de Rothschild, 'What a beating it is! You know that Liberalism did not seem to me quite the beautiful and admirable thing it does to the liberal party in general, and I am not sorry a new stage in its growth should commence, and that the party should be driven to examine itself and see how much real stuff it has in its mind and how much claptrap.' And to Jane, 'the Liberal party, it seemed to me, had no body of just, clear, well ordered thought upon politics, and were only superior to the conservative in not having for their rule of conduct merely the negative instinct against change'. Three years of the Tories was enough, however. At the reorganisation of the Liberal party at the time of the Russo-Turkish War (May 1877) he wrote, 'I cannot say I much regret to see the Liberal party in a state of chaos, but I am sincerely sorry that a charlatan like Dizzy should be Premier just now.'

He repeated his ideas to his sister Jane in April 1880 in a 'congratulatory' note on her husband William Forster's return to Parliament with Gladstone. 'Lord B. [Disraeli]was demoralising for our people, and the Tories show their bad side more and more the longer they stay in.' He was characteristically unexcited by the Liberals though: 'at best, they are in a very crude state, and with little light or help in them at present. But through their failing, and succeeding, and gradual improving lies our way, our only way.'

He believed in a strong State, a legacy from his father: 'In my notions about the State I am quite Papa's son, and his continuator... I inherit from him a deep sense of what, in the

Greek and Roman world, was sound and rational.' To Fontanès, Arnold contrasted the 'over-meddling' of the French government to England's situation where, 'The State has not enough shown a spirit of initiative, and individuals have too much thought that it sufficed if they acted with entire liberty and if nobody had any business to control, them.' To Arnold the State should be 'the organ of the best self and highest reason of the community'. He disapproved of reducing the state to insignificance, he said, which would be cultivating 'the American ideal'.

***

For many years he had strong reservations about America, even though it lacked an aristocracy. Arnold felt under-enthusiastic about the middle class there, having little faith in its 'nobility of nature'. He showed no inordinate interest in the Civil War – at least in his existing correspondence – despite being an avid reader of the newspapers. Americans – 'that *rara avis*, a really well-bred and trained American' aside – seemed alien at the time to his sensibilities: 'I don't imagine the feeling of kinship with them exists at all among the higher classes,' he wrote, 'after immediate blood-relationship, the relationship of the soul is the only important thing: and this one has far more with the French, Italians, or Germans than with the Americans.'

He did recognize, however, that America enlarged his reading public. He wrote to Frances of the positive reception to his poems there, and also acknowledged the 'intellectual liveliness and ardour' he has seen in those Americans he had met on the continent, which he understood 'as one of the good results of their democratic régime's emancipating from the blinking and hushing-up system induced by our circumstances here'. Years later his attention was more readily engaged. Citing the New York *Nation* as an example, he commented in a letter of May 1876, 'To read the more serious criticism that comes from America interests me always extremely.'

Money finally lured him there. He might write, 'I don't like going. I don't like lecturing. I don't like living in public – and I wish it were all over.' But he needed 'a certain sum of money, to enable me to take my small pension and retire'. Besides he also wanted money to pay off the considerable debts of his son, Dick, who had been 'idle at Oxford'. Dick had been packed off to Melbourne to work in a bank, 'that he might learn what regular work was'. These expenses required Arnold to reverse his decision on lecturing. Given the American refusal to grant copyright, he felt 'we may fairly try to make by Lectures the money we may not make by our books'.

He described the prospective trip 'a formidable prospect', though he had socially eminent contacts and natural curiosity to attract him, not to mention the fact that he had every reason to expect receptive audiences, given his popularity there as a literary critic. Arnold's literary writings offered a positive vision and more than a whiff of tradition to influence America's own nascent critical tradition. In the end he decided on three lectures which he would alternate: on 'Literature and Science', 'Numbers" and 'Emerson', the last largely written on the voyage. He sailed on the 'Servia', and since his wife worried about his going alone, she accompanied him, which required their elder daughter along to take care of her.

The American lecture tour began in October of 1883 and continued until March 1884. Despite difficulties consequent on his lecturing style, which he overcame to some extent, the tour proved a modest success. Things looked a little different from his perspective. Arnold was reluctant to acknowledge, especially to his family, the idea that his New York performance and his lectures generally were inaudible or at least at times undecipherable. He wrote to Frances on November 27, 1883, to assure her 'the desire to hear me was not at all quenched by it, and I had no doubt at all about being able to make myself heard'. He pointed out that it was unnatural for him to speak so slowly and then there was the English intonation. He did concede that when he read his poetry he was apt to forget his audience 'and to repeat for my own delectation'; again he could overcome the difficulty. Arnold defended his performance once again to Frances in a letter from Chicago near the end of January: 'the fact is that the lectures are going as well as possible and far better than anyone who knew this people on the one hand and my style of dealing on the other, could have anticipated'.

At the end of February and from New York City he announced to Jane, 'I have succeeded in a very difficult task – I have brought the Americans to my lectures and interested them in them, without putting into the lectures anything catchpenny, or anything to offend those at home whose good opinion I value.' In fact, except on a social level, he felt he had never courted popularity – a view supported by a number of hostile critics.

A little grudgingly the Arnolds' opinion of Americans, if not their press ('They are the worst feature in the life of the United States') began to change. In a letter to Jane from Hartford, Connecticut, in November, Arnold had praised 'that buoyancy, enjoyment, and freedom from constraint, which are everywhere in America, and which confirmed in all I have said about the way in which the aristocratic class acts as an *incubus* upon the middle class at home. This universal enjoyment and good nature are what strike me most here. On the other hand, some of the best English qualities are clean gone; the love of quiet and dislike of a crowd is gone out of the American entirely.'

Approval might be regularly shadowed by criticism, but circumstances had their lighter side. He told John Hay, diplomat and editor, in January 1884, 'I consider myself now as an actor, for my managers take me about with theatrical tickets, at reduced rates, over the railways, and the tickets have *Matthew Arnold troupe* printed on them.' The newspapers on occasion provided amusement to him, generally regarding his manner or appearance. Arnold told the description against himself: 'He has harsh features, supercilious manners, a single eye-glass, hair parted down the middle, and ill-fitting clothes.' He told Hay,

'The papers get more and more amusing as we get west. A Detroit newspaper compared me, as I stooped now and then to look at my manuscript on a music stool, to "an elderly bird pecking at grapes on a trellis" – that is the style of the thing.' From one local paper he quoted, amused: 'Mr Arnold, author of the Light of Asia and son of Tom Brown of Rugby'.

Eventually, inevitably, he wearied of the travel and yearned for home. Virginia had impressed him while Canada appealed most, especially Quebec. When the Arnolds returned it was with some satisfaction both with the visit and with the money it realised, though he knew he might have made substantially more if he had done without his agent, D'Oyly Carte. When back in Cobham in March he wrote to John Duke Coleridge, 'As to profits, there was a certain sum of £1000 which I had borrowed to pay Dick's Oxford debts and to send him to Australia; this I have enabled myself to clear off, and I have also paid all expenses of our journey. I have not done much more, but I have learnt how to make £3000 or £4000 if I go again, with a better system of management.'

As a public speaker, Arnold had improved from the experience. In reply to Jane's comment after the tour, he conceded on October 18, 1884, 'How right you were about what you called my too "solemn" and poor Mrs Carnegie my "ministerial" manner in speaking. Since I have spoken so much, I have perceived that it is my great defect, inasmuch as it strikes every one.' He had also learned 'to hold up my head and talk my lecture, instead of reading it with my eyes in the manuscript – and this is everything'. Furthermore, he had extended his influence and established a number of Americans friendships. Being Arnold, he would continue to write critically of the country where he felt it let itself down, while the marriage of his elder daughter there created another bond with the country.

***

He had not ignored British affairs during his American time, having written home to *The Times* presenting his views on Irish Home Rule. He thought England's treatment of Ireland 'cruel and unjust', as he believed his father had, but like him he would go no substantial way further. Arnold accepted that the Irish 'have cause to hate us', since we have been' irresolute and feeble' which he ascribes to 'signs of the real hollowness and insufficiency of the whole system of our public life'.

He recognized, too, the urgency of 'the Irish question', while at the same time reacting negatively to Irish nationalism. He was no friend to agitation for civil rights. In December 1867, for instance, he had argued against a double standard in response to rioting from Fenians: 'what the State has to do, is to put down *all* rioting with a strong hand, or it is sure to drift into troubles'.

The Times letters presented his views on Irish Home Rule, on the 'desperate Irish policy'. All men shared, he felt, 'Mr Gladstone's declaration that his principle is "to give Ireland an effective government by Irishmen"'. Gladstone, however, wanted a national Irish Parliament, which Arnold and others felt had dangerous potential, given the loquacity and commitment of those Irishman bent on an independent nation. He drew a parallel here between Ireland and the American South. There must be limits; local government he felt to be the answer ('legislative machinery by which the localities can manage their own affairs'). Then, having reasserted his belief in self-government, in a letter of the following year he added, 'But I would also break down the present state of refractoriness and defiance issuing in what is really a revolutionary condition.'

While the news from around the globe interested Arnold greatly, he responded to it as a patriotic Englishman, as an imperialist, one whose experience brought a degree of cynicism. After Isandlwana and Rorke's Drift in the shameful Anglo-Zulu War in January of 1879 he wrote, 'The news from Africa is absorbingly interesting for the moment. You see the 17th Lancers are going out, in which young Starling Benson is. Good will come, I suppose, of this disaster, because it will lead to a more thorough subjugation of the Zulus, and to a more speedy extension of the Englishry as far as the climate will let them extend... And unattractive as the raw Englishry is, it is good stuff, and – always supposing it not to deteriorate but to improve – its spread is the spread of future civilisation.'

***

In his last years Arnold's view of the efficacy of his self-appointed mission to bring culture to the native 'Englishry' remained only fitfully positive, depending on his mood and audience. In answering a birthday letter from his sister Susanna, in December 1879, he mused on the little he had accomplished in trying to influence the public, as opposed to fellow writers on whom he felt he had had some effect. It would have required an unprincipled and probably profitless commitment on his part to be more popular: 'I think I could manage to hit the great public, if I gave myself to it; but then I must give myself to it entirely, recoil from no strife and no invective, pass my life in abusing and being abused, abandon a number of things I sincerely like and which I do manage to keep in contact with, however imperfectly, now; and very likely do no real good after all.'

Looking more positively toward his peers he could argue, 'I produce little effect upon the general public, but I have some excellent readers nevertheless.' And in reply to a note of admiration accompanying Oscar Wilde's newly published *Poems* (1881) Arnold wrote, 'I have not much to thank the *public* for; but from my fellow-workers, both in poetry and prose, I have met with kindness and recognition such as might satisfy any man.' The great public, he told Edmund Gosse, 'never did like me much and never will'.

Then again, responding to the writer of a review of his *Mixed Essays* in March 1879, Arnold had this to say: 'It is worth while to have passed all one's youth "out in the cold," so far as the public is concerned, to be so kindly brought in and treated in one's old age.' And when a new edition of *Culture and Anarchy* was wanted by his publisher, Macmillan: 'I do think my works are at last taking hold, or have even taken hold, of this precious public of ours.'

As with the poetry, Arnold had not hitherto been attentive to remuneration for his essays but had been prompted to be so by friends. Now he had begun to 'reflect that I am growing old and must attend a little more to my literary profits'. Stung at the thought of being given unsatisfactory reimbursement for his essays, he complained to Alexander Macmillan in March 1875. He also fell out briefly at the beginning of the following year with George Smith on similar grounds. Each felt betrayed in turn, and Arnold even suggested they part company but early the following year he wrote to 'end all difference between us'. He decided henceforth to get all his prose books into Smith's hands, 'or I shall have the look of playing you and Macmillan off against one another, which would be odious'.

He had had his books, his honours, his discriminating readers, a full pension after thirty-five years of inspecting and in August 1883 a Civil List pension of £250 a year 'as a public recognition of the high place you have taken in the poetry and literature of England'. He initially explained his misgivings: 'Mr Gladstone had obstinately refused to promote me in the public service, so I suppose he hit upon the pension as a consolation; I hesitated about accepting, because, being a salaried official already I feared invidious remarks; and indeed the Echo has already said that I am "a very Bonaparte for rapacity" – or so I hear.' His income approached £1000 'from the public purse' and he would be taking the pension 'from the small public fund available for pensions to letters, science, and art'. However, "by the advice of friends" he accepted. Not unsurprisingly his literary work could not always be relied upon to make up spending deficits, if only for the reason that other commitments caused him throughout his career to defer the submission of essays.

A glimpse into his creative preparation in these late days may be gleaned from a March 1885 letter to his daughter Lucy: 'I am pressed by an article which I am now preparing for the Contemporary – you know how these things worry and upset me, and I am more pressed than usual; but somehow I am not quite so much worried, as I know pretty well what I want to say and feel as if it would come easily within the limits proposed.' Late that year he was immersed in Sainte-Beuve's letters for the *Encyclopaedia Britannica* and declared, 'I am getting into work at my Ste Beuve, and shall soon be feeling happy and interested; the beginning is what always worries and upsets me.'

The pleasure in writing hardly ever failed him. A year before his death Arnold wrote from to Lucy, 'I have Dowden's Life of Shelley to read through for the first time and all the Poems to read again, before I begin to write. Still it is a great thing to have this occupation, living so quietly as we do; it makes the days seem as full and busy as if we were living in the high pressure of London.'

This proved fortunate since money remained a constant need, given the lifestyle the Arnolds assumed. As late as his final January he wrote candidly to her, 'Both she [Nelly] and Mamma are excellent about not going to London, but we really cannot afford it.' A typical sentence from the letters of this time might read: 'I do not like to undertake anything as to contributing, for I have promised as much as I can well perform for this year. But…'. Even so, his reputation harried him: 'My leisure is delightful, but I can as yet hardly turn round, I have so many letters to answer and promises to fulfil.'

***

He had lived with the awareness of his own mortality since his father's death from inherited heart disease in 1842, when Arnold was twenty. He had not really expected to live as long as he had because of 'the faulty valve of my heart' and was quite frank about this. For many years he had casually used expressions like 'if I live' in his letters. The deaths of his three sons had confirmed his fatalistic attitude. Now in the 1880s he knew his last decade was here, especially since his heart had begun to make difficulties and to impinge upon his healthy exercise. Ironically, perhaps the travelling for all the years had lengthened his life.

He wrote later of plans for a return to America 'if the blind Fury permits me' and referred to avoiding lawn tennis or 'going fast or going up hill', though a doctor thought it might be indigestion, this 'sense of having a mountain on my chest'. It was, as he reported to his daughter, 'a mortifying change. But so one draws to one's end.' He had, he decided, been prescribed too much digitalis or for too long, 'so that I have been reduced beyond what is expedient'.

To Andrew Carnegie he explained his decision not to return to give a second lecturing tour of America, firstly because his daughter was coming home to visit, and because he did not want to try the patience of his American audiences so soon again. 'Add to this,' he wrote, 'that I have been having a horrid pain in my chest when I walk fast or go up hill; and as my family is full of heart complaint, my father and grandfather having both of them died of it long before reaching my age, the doctors insist on my taking care of myself.' Because 'this climate makes me feel too sensibly my mortality', he told Charles Eliot Norton on his last visit to Lucy, he would not return to America.

Back in England there were moments of relief. At Fox How, he reported being free of pain (though with lumbago) and even of slipping off alone to Loughrigg Fell. In a contented mood he could claim, 'to be of use is more and more my aim in what I write; my name is quite as much "up" as I can expect or wish it to be, and I no longer want any place or preferment'. As it was, he died in Liverpool on April 15th, 1888, while waiting with Flu for the arrival of Lucy from America. When Robert Louis Stevenson heard of Arnold's death he is said to have exclaimed, 'Poor Matthew! Heaven won't please him'. Exiting the life, Matthew Arnold entered the canon, with all the on-going controversy into which he would have pitched with relish.

THE SOUL OF CHRISTMAS: JOHN FORSTER'S CHARLES DICKENS

Reviewing John Forster's *Life of Landor*, in an issue of *All the Year Round* in 1869, Charles Dickens offered the opinion that, 'The life of almost any man possessing great gifts, would be a sad book to himself.' Doubtless then, John Forster's three-volume *The Life of Charles Dickens* (1872–74) would be a sad read for Dickens: the story of a restless genius – the self-styled 'Inimitable' – for whom great triumph is later marred by marital unhappiness, underappreciation, unachieved ambitions and, finally, dwindling energy.

Yet Forster's is a fine biography – even by the standards of today – loving and intimately in touch with its ebullient subject throughout. As a friend of 'three-and-thirty years', Forster judiciously balanced his book on the recognition that what buoyed Dickens was his relentless inventiveness and incandescent sociability, while what ultimately destroyed him was protracted physical exhaustion and a lack – as Forster described it (with a nod to Byron) – of 'a city of the mind' in which to escape the pressures of fame and family, world and wife.

Being also highly readable, the book sits comfortably with the insightful, reader-friendly biography by Claire Tomalin (*Charles Dickens: A Life*, 2011) and the fine, scholarly thoroughness of Michael Slater's *Charles Dickens* (2009). Sins of omission and, very occasionally, of commission hardly mar it. Granted we are fortunate in having the twentieth century's steely corrective to measure its claims by. If Forster is given to a little self-aggrandizement, posterity has (mostly) pardoned it. If Dickens was not as virtuous a man as Forster presents – and the biography's great omission is of Dickens's behaviour with his wife and family – he is certainly an even greater writer than some of his peers believed, as time has born witness.

John Forster (1812–1876) performed many roles in his life:

journalist, editor, biographer, historian, literary and dramatic critic, lawyer and playwright. Dubbed the 'Great Mogul' of literature by Dickens, his most memorable role was that of business manager and literary adviser to many important writers, whom he befriended. According to biographer Fred Kaplan, 'His creative talents, though, were more managerial than histrionic.'

After a modest upbringing in a Unitarian household in Newcastle upon Tyne, his family cattle buyers, he developed a keen interest in the theatre. He briefly attended Cambridge, studied for the bar in London and left to work as a journalist, writing for *The True Sun*, *The Morning Chronicle* and *The Examiner*, editing the last from 1847 to 1855. As an author he first contributed to *Lardner's Cabinet Cyclopaedia*. Forster also served as secretary and a salaried commissioner (from 1861) for the Lunacy Commission. His success stemmed from his obvious talents, his confidence, his passion for literature and sociability – and partly through a moneyed marriage. Edgar Johnson, an eminent Dickens scholar, described him as follows: 'Voluble, opinionated, overbearing, and quarrelsome, Forster was also sincere, deeply interested in literature, and selflessly faithful to his friends.'

Reminiscing about their meeting at novelist William Harrison Ainsworth's Kensal Lodge, Forster wrote of Dickens in his biography: 'A look of youthfulness first attracted you, and then a candour and openness of expression which made you sure of the qualities within. The features were very good. He had a capital forehead, a firm nose with full wide nostril, eyes wonderfully beaming with intellect and running over with humour and cheerfulness, and a rather prominent mouth strongly marked with sensibility. The head was altogether well formed and symmetrical, and the air and carriage of it were extremely spirited.' By now the well-established Forster had befriended enough writers (including Leigh Hunt, Charles Lamb and recently Browning and Landor) not to be too easily impressed. Yet Dickens struck him in his energy as more like 'a man of action and business in the world'.

Forster's unique qualification for writing the authorised *Life* lies in the pair's intimacy. The two showed an instant rapport, and this he establishes from the first ('He has often told me'; 'I perfectly recollect that, on our being at Portsmouth together'; 'I was his companion oftener than I could well afford the time for'). He makes such remarks throughout. An early footnote reads, 'The reader will forgive my quoting from a letter of the date of 22 April, 1848. "I desire no better for my fame, when my personal dustiness shall be passed the control of my love of order, than such a biographer and such a critic."' 'You know me better,' he maintains, resuming the same subject on the July 6, 1862, 'than any other man does, or ever will.' On the eve of his first American lecture tour, Dickens writes to Forster, 'How I am to get on without you for seven or eight months, I cannot, upon my soul, conceive. I dread to think of breaking up all our old happy habits for so long a time.' And, at the death of Forster's brother, Dickens assures him that 'you have a brother left. One bound to you by ties as strong as ever Nature forged.'

Forster became intimate, also, with Dickens's creations, frequently attending them as an editor or the author's companion. Typical is the following, from a Dickens letter regarding *Nicholas Nickleby*: 'I am very anxious that you should see this conclusion before it leaves my hands, and I plainly see therefore that I must come to town myself on Saturday if I would not endanger the appearance of the number. So I have written to Hicks to send proofs to your chambers as soon as he can that evening; and, if you don't object, I will dine with you any time after five, and we will devote the night to a careful reading.' At another time we read, 'I altered the verbal error, and substituted for the action you didn't like some words expressive of the hurry of the scene.' And on one occasion, with a bad cold and a deadline, the author writes to Forster, 'So do you come, and sit here, and read, or work, or do something, while I write the LAST chapter of *Oliver,* which will be arter a lamb chop'.

As Forster himself puts it, 'There was nothing written by him after this date which I did not see before the world did, either in manuscript or proof; and in connection with the latter I shortly began to give him the help which he publicly mentioned twenty years later in dedicating his collected writings to me.' It is Forster's argument that Dickens's inner self lay in his books, and so they feature heavily throughout his letters: 'Though Dickens bore outwardly so little of the impress of his writings, they formed the whole of that inner life which essentially constituted the man... The story of his books, therefore at all stages of their progress, and of the hopes or designs connected with them, was my first care.'

Forster's 'general plan' is to rely on Dickens's personal writings, but especially on the relaxed conversational letters written to him: 'The purpose here was to make Dickens the sole central figure in the scenes revived, narrator as well as principal actor; and only by the means employed could consistency or unity be given to the self-revelation, and the picture made definite and clear.' In using his own correspondence with the novelist – 'covering all the important incidents in the life' – rather than ferreting out other sources, Forster incorporates autobiography, underlining his own role at the heart of Dickens's enterprise.

Although he reveals this plan rather late in the biography, he has followed it from the beginning, reorganizing and editing on his reader's behalf: 'I limit myself to those [letters] only with allusions that are characteristic or illustrative.' We hear him at work throughout: 'reserving the mention of these for a while, that I may speak of the leading incidents of 1843'; 'reserving what is to be said of *Domby* to a later chapter'; confining 'the mention of such things [publishing disagreements] to what was strictly necessary to explain its narrative'. Forster even explains his need for ellipses: 'What else his letters of these years enable me to recall, that could possess any interest now, may be told in a dozen sentences.' A cardinal 'rule' – scrupulously intended – is to avoid any repetition of already published work.

This is all skilfully done and at times the 'Great Mogul'

becomes the 'Great Borrower', giving us pure Dickens. So, Forster begins the chapter on the second American tour of 1867 with the following: 'It is the intention of this and the following chapter to narrate the incidents of the visit to America in Dickens's own language, and in that only. They will consist almost exclusively of extracts from his letters written home, to members of his family and to myself.'

The American letters covering both tours are among the most interesting in their correspondence, as Forster himself was well aware. He writes of the first, more impressionable visit of 1842: 'It would not be possible that a more vivid or exact impression than that which is derivable from these letters could be given of either the genius or the character of the writer. The whole man is here in the supreme hour of his life, and in all the enjoyment of its highest sensations. Inexpressibly sad to me has been the task of going over them, but the surprise has equalled the sadness.'

Since 'the whole man' is to be found in the letters, we are fortunate to have innumerable instances of the author on form. When Dickens's pet raven – instrumental in the writing of *Barnaby Rudge* – fell ill, both Forster and Dickens responded. Forster waxed heroically: 'Topping had reported of him, as Shakespeare of Hamlet, that he had lost his mirth and forgone all customary exercises' and Dickens brings to the end more than a whiff of theatrical bathos: 'On the clock striking twelve he appeared slightly agitated, but he soon recovered, walked twice or thrice along the coach-house, stopped to bark, staggered, exclaimed *Halloa old girl!* (his favourite expression) and died.'

Another amusing sample comes with Dickens's introduction to American manners, here the phenomenon of ladies smoking: 'When I lighted my cigar, Daughter lighted hers, at mine; leaned against the mantlepiece, in conversation with me; put out her stomach, folded her arms, and with her pretty face cocked up sideways and her cigarette smoking away like a Manchester cotton mill, laughed, and talked, and smoked, in the most gentlemanly manner I ever beheld. Mother immediately lighted her cigar; American lady immediately lighted hers; and in five minutes the room was a cloud of smoke, with us four in the centre pulling away bravely.'

What Forster also achieved by this plan of his was to produce a biography which reads as vividly and effortlessly as a Dickens novel might. Particularly early in the life, he tries to imagine the author's feelings, as well as describe his circumstances. For this period he has access to Dickens's 'durable early impressions' of being 'a very small and not-over-particularly-taken-care-of boy'. Some were recounted to him ('I can repeat it in the exact words employed by him'); others find their way into *Pickwick* or *David Copperfield*. There are brief reminiscences addressed to Forster by schoolfriends. Other moments come from Dickens's numerous published papers. Writing of a solitary stage-coach journey, for instance, he recalls the smell of the damp straw in which he was packed and forwarded like game, carriage-paid ('I consumed my sandwiches in solitude and dreariness, and it rained hard all the way, and I thought life sloppier than I expected to find it.') With such a relentlessly creative mind, it is certain that Dickens enhanced as he remembered – as with the town hall that in his imagination had been 'as a model on which the genie of the lamp built the palace for Aladdin'.

So powerfully vivid are these childhood memories that Forster editorializes as he recounts them: 'I have the picture of him here, very strongly in my mind, as a sensitive, thoughtful, feeble-bodied little boy, with an unusual sort of knowledge and fancy for such a child, and with a dangerous kind of wondering intelligence that a teacher might turn to good or evil, happiness or misery, as he directed it.'

Other memories scarred Dickens for life. It had been obvious to all that he identified with the young, abused Copperfield, as he did with all his persecuted child characters and indeed with all the downtrodden. It had not been apparent to the reading public that he had actually once suffered himself, for he was a man of proven courage. The revelation of Dickens's year in the blacking-warehouse at old Hungerford Stairs at the age of eleven became the great revelation of the first volume of the biography. Forster first prepares for the disclosure by linking the author with his popular creation: 'it will very shortly be seen that the identity went deeper than any had supposed, and covered experiences not less startling in the reality than they appear to be in the fiction'. He then leaves the chapter with a Dickensian cliff-hanger: 'All this is but the prelude to what remains to be described.'

Subsequent to the disclosure of the blacking factory, we are left in no doubt as to its effect on Dickens's mental health. In his own words, 'It is wonderful to me that, even after my descent into to the poor little drudge I had been since we came to London, no one had compassion enough on me – a child of singular abilities, quick, eager, delicate, and soon hurt, bodily or mentally – to suggest that something might have been spared, as certainly it might have been, to place me at any common school.' Slightly later in this autobiographical fragment we read, 'even now, famous and caressed and happy, I often forget in my dreams that I have a dear wife and children; even that I am a man; and wander desolately back to that time of my life'.

Without ascribing blame, Forster allows it to settle on the guilty by declaring that he must give Dickens's own character sketch of his father as 'the best preface I can make to what I feel that I have no alternative but to tell'. Despite his father's kind heart, 'in the ease of his temper, and the straightness of his means, he appeared to have utterly lost at this time the idea of educating me at all'. When finally withdrawn from the 'shame' of the factory, we learn that Dickens remembered bitterly how his mother had been for sending him back there.

This biography, which Forster wrote in very poor health, shines in admiration of the Dickens that emerged from such humiliation. He writes, for example, of being swayed by Dickens's passion for literature and his unselfconsciousness: 'His fine genius and his handsome person, of neither of which at any time he seemed himself to be in the slightest degree conscious, completed the charm.' Such a charm held a social charge: 'To the most trivial talk he gave the attraction of his own character... This, and his unwearying animal spirits, made him the most delightful of companions; no claim on good-fellowship ever found him wanting; and no one so constantly recalled to his friends the description Johnson gave of Garrick, as the cheerfulest man of his age.'

He did not discuss books, we learn: 'I suppose so remarkable an author as Dickens hardly ever lived who carried so little of authorship into ordinary social intercourse.' He possessed however a strong sense of being *sui generis*. Forster is always anxious to place Dickens in the context of the greats, particularly Fielding and Sterne, while still promoting his uniqueness: 'undoubtedly one of the impressions left by the letters is that of the intensity and tenacity with which he recognized, realized, contemplated, cultivated, and thoroughly enjoyed, his own individuality in even its most trivial manifestations'.

Still, the biographer is careful to suggest that there was no 'self-conceit' in it: 'It was part of the intense individuality by which he effected so much, to set the high value which in general he did upon what he was striving to accomplish; he could not otherwise have mastered one-half of what he designed.' In what he 'designed' lies the engine behind Dickens's incredible commitment. Beneath the comedy lay the passionate compassion and the desire to preach improvement in the lot of the poor. Forster, for one, recognized 'in the very thick of the extravaganza of adventure and fun set before us, that here were real people' and all victims. As he observes of *Oliver Twist*, crime 'is also most wretched and most unhappy'.

We are given many instances of Dickens's human sympathy ('it is very much harder for the poor to be virtuous than it is for the rich; and the good that is in them, shines the brighter for it'). His generosity was proverbial and examples of it – to his friends, family, to strangers and particularly to the destitute – are given throughout. On one occasion recounted here, summoned to the inquest of a baby alleged to have been murdered by its mother, Dickens acts on the woman's behalf, having her situation ameliorated while also providing her with a defence counsel. This enlightened approach proved more than a momentary emotional impulse. According to Forster, it conformed with Dickens's belief that education (or religion) could not guarantee social improvement, 'until the way had been paved for their ministrations by cleanliness and decency'.

The public quickly gained an insight into this through *The Old Curiosity Shop*, which Forster reckons first forged 'the bond between himself and his readers [as] one of personal attachment'. Soon Dickens could not control the growing enthusiasm for his work, nor the exploitation of it, especially the unlicensed dramatizations. It did not go unnoticed: 'Of what he suffered from these adaptations of his books, multiplied remorselessly at every theatre, I have foreborne to speak, but it was the subject of complaint with him incessantly.' He suffered also at the mercy of constant begging-letter writers, both at home and abroad. In Paris, absurdly, 'their distinguishing peculiarity [was] that they were nearly all of them "Chevaliers de la Garde Impériale de sa Majesté Napoleon le Grand," and that their letters bore immense seals with coats of arms as large as five shilling pieces'.

Fame, though ever welcome, proved exhausting as the years passed. Dickens's first American tour provided an extreme but perfect example. Here, though he had embroiled himself in controversy regarding his championing of international copyright (which he described as 'war to the knife'), it failed to dampen the passion of the Americans to see him. He captures the ludicrous situation in a letter Forster quotes: 'If I turn into the street, I am followed by a multitude. If I stay at home, the house becomes, with callers, like a fair... I go to a party in the evening, and am so inclosed and hemmed about by people, stand where I will, that I am exhausted for want of air. I dine out, and have to talk about everything, to everybody. I go to church for quiet, and there is a violent rush to the neighbourhood of the pew I sit in, and the clergyman preaches *at* me.'

Bathed in admiration from the populace and his biographer, Dickens is nevertheless presented as a real human being. Forster knew Dickens's foibles, offering glimpses into the psychology of the man, such as his need to contextualise decisions with respect to his past ('the desire... was always strangely urgent in him, associating his [latest] resolve in life with those earliest scenes of his youthful time'). Or, paradoxically for one of Victoria's most famous subjects, 'he believed himself to be entitled to higher tribute than he was always in the habit of receiving'. Forster tells us that Dickens had so worked on his education that others could never see that it had 'been so rambling or hap-hazard'. And not unconnected with this, perhaps, 'He was sensitive in a passionate degree to praise and blame, which yet he made it for the most part a point of pride to assume indifference to.'

Forster was also privy to Dickens's need for London. Although bouts of foreign travel proved essential for rest, the author found difficulty working abroad because of the absence of streets and crowds: 'I can't express how much I want these. It seems as if they supplied something to my brain, which it cannot bear, when busy, to lose.'

His biographer knew, too, the price Dickens paid for his exuberant commitment to his work. He might write, after *Chuzzlewit*, that 'I feel my power now, more than I ever did', and yet he confessed the aftermath: that it 'leaves a horrible despondency behind', one 'which must be prejudicial to the mind, so soon renewed and so seldom let alone'. This did not check him, as Forster noted: 'Unhappily he never thought of husbanding his strength except for the purpose of making fresh demands upon it.' And with illness in later life – manifest first as a lameness in one foot – his priority became making money; ill health could be rationalised. With regard to the spasms in his side, the colds, the faints, failing health, like the fear of dwindling popularity they served only as a spur.

While Forster regrets being inattentive in this one area of

Dickens's life, in all others he took his habitual interest. And on his part, although we know that Dickens might on occasion have reacted to Forster's solid conventionality, and even disparaged certain manners and traits of his through the character of Pecksniff (about which Forster seems or pretends to be oblivious), he frequently relied on his friend's judgment. 'Advise me on the following point' is a characteristic line in Dickens's notes to him. According to Forster, it was he who had suggested Dickens must kill off Little Nell in *The Old Curiosity Shop*. And with Mr. Dick, in *Copperfield*, he persuaded Dicken to change his 'bull and china-shop delusion', as being more farcical than affecting. Also, on Forster's advice the introductory chapter to *American Notes* had been suppressed because of its critical tone (It appears for the first time in the biography).

As his friend's business manager, Forster proved dependable concerning contracts and sales and yet he frankly admits his advice was ignored at times. Dickens's unquestioned generosity to the poor and mistreated co-existed with his financial ambitiousness and an expensive lifestyle. We learn of certain rash decisions made as his wealth increased.

Forster failed also to dissuade Dickens from launching his amateur theatricals on the general public ('The mere effect of the strolling wandering ways into which this acting led him could not be other than unfavourable. But remonstrance as yet was unavailing.') Dickens inevitably threw himself into such work regardless. Of course he excelled at it, as actor, director and stage manager. Even here Forster concedes of one production: 'He was the life and soul of the entire affair. I never seemed till then to have known his business capabilities. He took everything on himself, and did the whole of it without an effort.'

As to the highly lucrative public readings from his works: Forster's opposition similarly failed to stop 'that which he had set his heart upon too strongly to abandon'. It had not been in terms of Dickens's health that Forster initially counselled against them, but for supposedly ethical and aesthetic reasons: 'It was a substitution of lower for higher aims; a change to commonplace from more elevated pursuits; and it had so much of the character of public exhibition for money as to raise, in the question of respect for his calling as a writer, a question also of respect for himself as a gentleman.'

In this, the solidly middle class Forster seems curiously myopic concerning his friend's character. For Dickens the readings clearly fulfilled an entertainer's need. As he wrote with evident satisfaction, 'everywhere I have found that peculiar personal relation between my audience and myself on which I counted most when I entered on this enterprise'. This note from Glasgow attests to the thrill of such evenings: 'Such a pouring of hundreds into a place already full to the throat, such indescribable confusion, such a rending and tearing of dresses, and yet such a scene of good humour on the whole, I never saw the faintest approach to.'

This said, Dickens weighed Forster's advice carefully before making decisions, given his friend's proven expertise on literary and business matters. He had in fact first become aware of Forster's existence in the role of critic. Reviewing the comic opera, *The Village Coquette*, for which Dickens contributed the libretto early in his career, Forster had written: 'Bad as the opera is... we feel assured that if Mr Braham [the producer] will make arrangements to parade the real living Boz every night after that opera, he will insure for it a certain attraction.' Dickens had been both amused and flattered.

Although Forster stated his intention in the biography not to be 'so much critical as biographical', literary comments inevitably emerge and he proves for the most part a reliable, if fond, critic of Dickens's work. Samples of his criticism tend to be summative. He recognizes that, after the caricatures in his early fiction, the 'delightful oddity' of Pickwick's character led the author to an important recognition: 'the art was seen which can combine traits vividly true to particular men or women with propensities common to all mankind'. Forster finds this realised in *Nickleby*:

'He had scrutinised as truly and satirised as keenly; but had never shown the imaginative insight with which he now sent his humour and his art into the core of the vices of the time.'

Character and scene particularly engage the biographer's interest: 'By the exuberance of comic invention which he gives his distinction to Mr Pecksniff, Mrs Gamp profits quite as much… but over and above this, by the additional invention of Mrs Harris, it is all reproduced, acted over with renewed spirit, and doubled and quadrupled in her favour. This on the whole is the happiest stroke of humorous art in all the writings of Dickens.' Or, 'Mr. Micawber's presence must not prevent my saying that [*Copperfield*] does not take the lead of the other novels in humorous creation; but in the use of humour to bring out prominently the ludicrous in any object or incident without excluding or weakening its most enchanting sentiment, it stands decidedly first.' And, the discovery of Pip's real benefactor causes him to conclude, 'If any one doubts Dickens's power of so drawing a character as to get to the heart of it, seeing beyond surface peculiarities into the moving springs of the human being himself, let him narrowly examine these scenes.'

We are used to thinking that in his energy, Dickens's satirical denunciations are intended to nudge the authorities into the betterment of institutions. Forster stresses also the importance of the Christmas stories as affecting individual human conduct: 'Nor is it to be doubted, I think, that, in that largest sense of benefit, great public and private service was done; positive, earnest, practical good.' It may, he believes, 'by a single fortunate thought [have] revised the whole manner of a life. Literary criticism here is a second-rate thing.'

Forster as critic is not without reservations. One can be found in his comments on *A Tale of Two Cities*: 'To rely less upon character than upon incident, and to resolve that his actors should be expressed by the story more than they should express themselves by dialogue, was for him a hazardous, and can hardly be called an entirely successful, experiment.' He notes also the relative failure of design in *Barnaby Rudge*: 'The interest with which the tale begins has ceased to be its interest before the close.' He is certainly critical of Dickens's heroines. In *Bleak House* he finds a contradiction in Esther as storyteller, since she is so vividly observant and yet so 'artlessly unconscious' and 'entirely ignorant' of her virtues (Yet Esther has been told she is damned by her illegitimacy). With *Little Dorrit*, while her siblings 'are perfectly real people in what makes them unattractive… what is meant for attractiveness in the heroine becomes often tiresome by want of reality'.

On the subject of the man himself, Forster also periodically registers reservations. One is of a headlong determination born of self-belief: 'A too great confidence in himself, a sense that everything was possible to the will that would make it so, laid occasionally upon him self-imposed burdens greater than might be borne by any one with safety. In that direction there was in him, at such times, something even hard and aggressive; in his determinations a something that had almost the tone of fierceness.'

Another failing is shown to be Dickens's thoughtlessness in giving the traits of friends to his dubious creations. Caricaturing Leigh Hunt as Harold Skimpole is described as 'a radical wrong': 'The pleasant sparkling airy talk, which could not be mistaken, identified with odious qualities a friend only known to the writer by attractive ones; and for this there was no excuse.'

The two most grievous faults that Forster has to ascribe and yet negotiate are Dickens's relations with his publishers and – more importantly – with Catherine and his family. From neither of these does his friend emerge with credit. The first apparently proved an embarrassment to Forster on a number of occasions. The author lacked patience in his dealings with publishers: 'This did not belong to the strong side of his character, and advantage was frequently taken of the fact.' Dickens came to bridle under adverse contracts he had signed. Having admitted as much, Forster hints at his failure to honour some, then becomes evasive:

'No opinion need be offered as to where most of the blame lay, and it would be useless now to apportion the share that might possibly have belonged to himself.'

On this issue (as on the next), modern biographers can offer clarity. Claire Tomalin explains how knotted Dickens's writing life could be. In late 1836 he found himself committed to continuing *Pickwick* in monthly instalments for another year; to seeing two works through the press; to providing more Boz Sketches; to producing a children's book for Christmas, while 'he had to start preparing for editorship of *Bentley's Miscellany*, which began in January and for which he must commission articles and also contribute a sixteen-page piece of his own every month; Chapman & Hall were hoping for a sequel to Pickwick; Macrone still wanted 'Gabriel Vardon'; and Bentley was expecting two novels'.

This matter of conflicting promises partly stemmed from a recognition that publishers were making all the money and Dickens's own funds were 'inadequate' for his plans and ambitions. Forster is finally sympathetic here, noting the situation 'made a change necessary to so upright a nature' as Dickens's. Consequently the wranglings 'though not immediately, ultimately justified him'.

But the more damning of Dickens's actions is rightly seen in the treatment of his wife, Catherine, and its impact on the family. The quiet, supportive and neglected Catherine, who had borne ten children, was dismissed from the family home in 1858 (the year after Dickens had met the eighteen year old actress, Ellen Ternan). Forster acknowledges that her husband had had for some years, an 'unsettled feeling' with respect to home, which he initially kept to himself. When it worsened, Forster concedes that, 'What was highest in his nature had ceased for the time to be highest in his life, and he had put himself at the mercy of lower accidents and conditions.' He himself had not understood the severity of Dickens's feelings, he explains: 'I attributed it to other causes, and gave little attention to it.'

Finally Dickens expressed his marital discontent forcefully in the words, 'Why is it, that, as with poor David [*Copperfield*], a sense comes always crushing on me now, when I fall into low spirits, as of one happiness I have missed in life, and one friend and companion I have never made?' He told Forster that he and Catherine 'were not made for each other' and that they failed to bring each other happiness. Forster urged him to reconsider his separation, but then Dickens would have expected such advice from a friend with conventional priorities.

Devastating as the rejection was for Catherine and their children, it also put Dickens in a bind. Firstly, as the admired novelist of family harmony he could not be seen publicly to destroy his own and secondly, more unforgivably, he felt the need to appear the wronged party. Forster mentions his failed attempt to stop Dickens from publishing a statement in *Household Words* in response to rumours soon circulating against his conduct: 'All he would concede to my strenuous resistance would be to suppress it, if another friend agreed, which he did not.' Forster does not deal with Dickens's attempt to blacken Catherine's character as wife and mother. Instead he concludes the matter by repeating that he has already established his rules of privacy and discretion in the book.

Modern criticism has been directed at Dickens and at Forster's biography in not making the situation clearer, nor in bringing to attention the existence of Ellen Ternan, the author's 'magic circle of one'. However Forster is not completely silent on the issue. As has been pointed out since, at the end of the book he publishes without comment Dickens's will, the first beneficiary of which (for £1000) is 'Miss Ellen Lawless Ternan, late of Houghton Place, Ampthill Square, in the county of Middlesex.'

Other criticism was levelled at the outset, which Forster attempted to forestall in the third volume of the *Life*: 'Of the charge of obtruding myself to which their publication [the letters] has exposed me, I can only say that I studied nothing so hard as to suppress my own personality.' His first volume had not gone without comment among Dickens's friends, none of whom had been asked for contributions. At a *Punch* dinner on 7 December, 1871, the biography had been much discussed. The magazine's editor, Shirley Brooks, recorded that '[Wilkie] Collins & [G.H. Lewes] Lewes stayed till 11. Forster & Dickens talked of – they call it "Life of J. F. with notices of C. D."'

According to James A. Davies, in *John Forster: A Literary Life* (1983), 'There is, as G. H. Ford has shown, a long tradition of regarding the biography as an expression of Forster's egotism.' Worse, 'As is well known, he manipulated and falsified documents to emphasise Dickens's reliance upon him and to counter the fact that the two had been less close in later years.' Apparently Dickens had turned eventually to the company of the younger Wilkie Collins, whose bohemianism contrasted with Forster's 'increasing staidness and intense respectability', according to Michael Slater. One wonders, though, even if all this is true, whether it makes a great difference to this compelling portrait of the novelist, or whether it greatly changes our view of the biographer, whose standing in his day remained high.

Other omissions include Forster's unwillingness to speculate on Dickens's obsession with Mary Hogarth in death. He simply reports, 'His wife's next younger sister, Mary, who lived with them, and by sweetness of nature even more than by graces of person had made herself the ideal of his life, died with a terrible suddenness that for the time completely bore him down. His grief and suffering were intense, and affected him, as will be seen, through many after-years.' He gives us Dickens's frequent references to her – his longings for their kinship in death and his brooding on not being buried beside her – without speculation or relating this to Dickens's character.

Also, Forster in his discretion does not name Dickens's first and thwarted love, 'the real' Dora, whom he immortalized as the frothy, girlish Flora Finching. On the fated love for Maria Beadnell, he simply quotes the author: 'No one can imagine in the most distant degree what pain the recollection gave me in

Copperfield.' Had he known of its existence, Forster would have censored a letter of February 1855, in which the author wrote to her, 'My entire devotion to you, and the wasted tenderness of those hard years which I have ever since half loved, half dreaded to recall, made so deep an impression on me that I refer to it a habit of suppression which now belongs to me, which I know is no part of my original nature, but which makes me chary of showing my affections, even to my children, except when they are very young.'

Although the biography is admired today, according to James A. Davies at the time 'there was much agreement that Forster had harmed his friend's reputation by stressing his lowly background and lusts for lucre. *The Times* was typical: Dickens had been "uneasy in society, and… lacking, in a word, the manners of a gentleman."' Yet his friends admired it. In February 1874 Carlyle wrote, 'I have read your third volume of *Dickens* with continued interest and pleasure – and with a glad surprise, moreover, which heightens all these feelings. Surprise I say, for the narrative flows with limpid clearness, soft harmony, perfection of phrase and idea; not a trace it in it anywhere of the horrid state of pain in which I too well know you to have been all the while.' And, as his recent biographer Claire Tomalin wrote, *The Life of Charles Dickens* is a 'great book': 'On page after page he brought Dickens alive with "the passionate fullness of his nature", his energy, charm and brilliance and also his anger and obsessiveness. He presented a genius but not a saint, and he suggested that the same forces that had driven him to achieve so much also drove him to break up his life.'

Dickens may be considered today 'a darker, more turbulent, and altogether more complex figure' than he was once, as Michael Slater observed. But there is still truth in John Forster's most revealing and poetic insight into where the man and the fiction meet. It is in Dickens's best self. For the Dickensian soul is Christmas: 'He had identified himself with Christmas fancies. Its life and spirits, its humour in riotous abundance, of right belonged to him. Its imaginations as well as its kindly thoughts, were his; and its privilege to light up with some sort of comfort the squalidest places, he had made his own.' Dickens's writerly soul continues to sparkle in John Forster's *Life*.

LESLIE STEPHEN: LIFE, LETTERS & LIT.

For a publicly taciturn and privately thin-skinned Victorian, Leslie Stephen (1832–1904) remains remarkably good company. The voice in his literary essays stays with us, amiably authoritative, honest and ironic, its resonance unsullied by what we learn of the man's literary insecurity – and of his petty domestic tyranny. Had it not been that he is now remembered mostly as the intimidating father of Virginia Woolf and her sister, Vanessa Bell, we might say of him – as he wrote of Sir Walter Scott – 'he has, at least, this merit, that he is one of those rare natures for whom you feel not merely admiration but affection'. Affection? We are a less tolerant age and would probably not subscribe to Stephen's subsequent exemption: 'We may cherish the fame of some writers in spite of, not on account of, many personal defects.'

If not a great, daring critic like Arnold, Stephen – editor, biographer, essayist, literary critic, historian, mountaineer – proves, at least, to have been one of the most interesting of Victorian intellectuals in the sheer range of his accomplishments, in the spirit of his prose and in the contradictions of his character.

David D. Zink expressed succinctly his contribution to literature in *Leslie Stephen* (1972): 'He merits serious consideration as a pioneer critic of the English novel, as a leader in the Victorian rehabilitation of the Augustan age, and as one who early recognized the consequences of the social matrix for literature.' In these he helped shape the taste of the largely middle class audience he addressed, and for that has not been ignored by discriminating critics. There are two outstanding biographies, by Frederick W. Maitland (1906) and Noel Annan (1984), a well edited two volume collection of selected letters by John W. Bicknell (1996) and – recently begun – a multi-volume series of Stephen's shorter essays, edited by S. T. Joshi.

According to Annan, Stephen was born 'into the professional

middle class and into a talented family, into a clan which was establishing itself as an aristocracy of the intellect by dominating so many of the eminent positions within the cultural establishment'. His 'clan' was the Clapham Sect, a loose group of evangelical Christian social reformers. Later Stephen was to distance himself from Evangelicalism, turning towards its antagonist, Rationalism, in a spirit of scientific humanism.

He was educated (and bullied) at Eton from 1842, then Kings College, London (1848) and, after illness, at Trinity Hall, Cambridge from 1850. His childhood weakness turned to wiry strength. The vigour he would show in his writing life, he proved as an athlete at Cambridge. A popular radical there, he remembered, 'I was held to be... rather a sociable person than otherwise. I dined out a good deal and talked and smoke and drank to general satisfaction.' Two years later he achieved first class honours in the Mathematics Tripos (twentieth wrangler) and was appointed to a fellowship (1854).

Stephen became a junior tutor in 1856 and was ordained in 1859. He took up rowing, ultimately turning to coaching, in which role he proved an inspiration to student crews. To them he seemed the personification of a 'muscular Christian'. Manliness became an obsession and a favourite expression of his. Later he would become celebrated as a pioneer mountaineer and serious walker, leader of a like-minded group for the twenty-plus miles of the 'Sunday Tramps', a walking club he co-founded in 1879.

His father, a significant influence on his moral and religious views, died in 1859, a time when doubts disturbed the recently ordained Stephen, partly those occasioned by the publication of *On the Origin of the Species*, a book whose author he came to revere. Soon he found he could no longer accept the Thirty-nine Articles of the Church of England, which summarised its beliefs and centred worship on *The Bible*. As Annan expressed it, 'Stephen was thought to be a rather modern clergyman concerned more with ethics than theology, and the sudden collapse of his faith came, therefore, as a shock even to his intimate friends.' He himself underplayed the agonising he endured, focussing instead on his recognition of the impossibility of belief: 'I had to take part in services where the story of the flood or of Joshua's staying the sun to massacre the Amorites were solemnly read as if they were authentic and edifying narratives – as true as the stories of the Lisbon earthquake or the battle of Waterloo.'

He would make the most explicit statement of his theological opinions in a letter of 1873: 'I do not believe the New Testament narrative to be true. To my mind, the whole history of Christ, in so far as it is supernatural, is legendary... As to natural religion, I think its two great doctrines – God and a future state – more probable than not; and they appear to me to make all the difference to morality. Take them away and epicureanism seems to me the true and proper doctrine.' He expressed the view, also, that religion provided evidence of mankind's need for love and belief in a higher self.

When Stephen resigned his Cambridge tutorship in 1862, he was allowed to keep his fellowship, though soon there remained little that he valued to do there ('It is a lazy sort of place for men who, like me, had no share in the teaching.') Consequently he resigned that, too, two years later, moving to London to live with his mother and sister in Porchester Terrace.

Once in London his barrister brother came to his assistance. Fitzjames Stephen also enjoyed success as a journalist for the *Saturday Review* (the *Saturday Reviler*, according to John Bright), being a master of a scathing and spirited style – 'a Bill Sykes converted by Jeremy Bentham' (John Morley) – and a force to be reckoned with, as Matthew Arnold discovered to his irritation.

The older brother found Stephen some initially congenial employment with the *Review*: 'I find that I can pick up a pretty good living by writing for the papers, and like the work so far,' he reported. 'Meanwhile it is rather an effort to turn out of a warm, easy place like Cambridge, where I have been vegetating for near fifteen years in comfort. I had a luxurious set of rooms. I walked about in a gorgeous cap and gown, and every one that I met took off their hats to me. Now in London I find that people don't instinctively recognise me.'

According to Maitland, at Cambridge marriage generally signalled the end of a career. Not for Stephen. Through family connections he met and, in 1867, married the daughter of the late novelist W. M. Thackeray. He set up home with Harriet ('Minny') and her sister, Anne, a writer. These were good years for Stephen. In 1869 he reported, 'I feel like a frozen animal that has been taken in & thawed by benevolent people & am sensible of being expanded & improved in every faculty I possess.' His nearest relations had become near neighbours in South Kensington.

Stephen soon learned his craft as a journalist, privately adopting the easy, light-hearted cynicism that went with it. In a November letter of 1866 he characterised his situation as follows: 'I read some of the greatest rubbish that appears in the English language in order to criticise it in the papers and to do facetiousness, which I think to be very poor, because editors are always begging for "light articles" – damn them!' In another letter he talked of being 'driven to supplying the "padding" & other secondrate parts of newspapers'. He went on to complain that 'respectability & conservatism wraps a man around like a cloak', though – his fantasy of a bohemian life aside – he considered London *the* place to live.

By late 1867 he had found a balance in grinding 'steadily away, sneering at virtue & enthusiasm in the Saturday Review & airing some of my pet crotchets elsewhere'. He much preferred work of an intellectual nature: 'If I don't get much money, I can at least thank God that I have no accounts to keep & no wearisome papers to tie up in red tape.' And in December 1869 he even condescended to admit that 'a journalist is doing a very necessary bit of work in the world & if he is an honest man… & speaks the truth with some vigour, he may help things on a bit'.

The journalist could also increase his work rate (of a review and an article a week) with the arrival of the *Pall Mall Gazette*, his political articles for the New York *Nation*, and then the *Cornhill* in 1866 – 'the cherished "Cornhill"'(Henry James). Stephen would then manage three or four articles in a week, writing at speed. These *Cornhill* essays – published later in three volumes as *Hours in a Library* – comprise thirty-two essays written between 1868–1882. They generally deal with the moral and intellectual life and work of an author. Despite his disclaimer of March 1884, that 'Hours in a Library and all that kind of stuff is not my real taste and therefore I can produce only third-rate work', it is chiefly for these literary essays that Stephen is still read today.

In the essay on Charlotte Brontë, he clarifies his critical methodology: 'though criticism cannot boast of being a science, it ought to aim at something like a scientific basis, or at least to proceed in a scientific spirit. The critic, therefore, before abandoning himself to the oratorical impulse, should endeavour to classify the phenomena with which he is dealing as calmly as if he were ticketing a fossil in a museum… Our literary, like our religious creed, should rest upon a purely rational ground, and be exposed to logical tests.' The 'scientific' perspective from which Stephen wished to write should not surprise us, given his training in mathematics, though it translates really as a logical approach.

He also shared the very Victorian belief in the moral benefits of art. On one occasion he stated it explicitly: 'Art provides the most powerful, though the least obtrusive, means by which the standard of morality is affected.' Art, in other words, must teach morality, and the author is the exemplar: 'The whole art of criticism consists in learning to know the human being who is partially revealed to us in his spoken or his written words.' We should look, he advised in a lecture given in St. Andrews in March 1887, 'to make a personal friend of the author'. This is how Stephen approached his subjects. For instance, in his essay on Samuel Johnson, he wrote from the heart, 'The love which we feel for Johnson is due to the fact that the pivots upon which his life turned are invariably noble motives, and not mere obedience to custom.'

How does the Victorian reader learn this love? Firstly, by

showing 'instinctive sympathy' for the author. Even great enthusiasm is acceptable, but ultimately a reader must apply 'with rigid impartiality such methods as are best calculated to free us from the influence of personal bias'. And these methods include learning to 'know the very trick of his speech, the turn of his thoughts, the characteristic peculiarities of his sentiments, of his imagery, of his mode of contemplating the world of human life'.

If we apply this to Stephen's comments on Laurence Sterne, we have a better understanding of what he means: 'To read a book in the true sense – to read it, that is, not as the critic but in the spirit of enjoyment – is to lay aside for the moment one's own personality, and... to breathe [the author's] air, and therefore to receive pleasure and pain according as the atmosphere is or is not congenial.' An alternative view might be that in reading we may domesticate our authors and bring them into our world.

What, then, of the moral dimension, since Stephen is decidedly against Sterne's morals? Fortunately for his argument, 'The qualification must, of course, be understood that a great book really expresses the most refined essence of the writer's character. It gives the author transfigured, and does not represent all the stains and distortions which he may have received in his progress through the world.' It seems we are approaching a secularized version of the soul here.

Articulated in this way, the sense of identification between reader and writer is very intimate. 'I confess that I at any rate love a book pretty much in proportion as it makes me love the author', he wrote. Unsurprisingly, therefore, Stephen showed great interest in biography. He expanded several of the *Cornhill* essays into full biographies for Morley's *English Men of Letters* series (Johnson, Pope, Swift, Eliot, Hobbes) and contributed 378 articles – about a thousand pages in total – to the *Dictionary of National Biography*, appearing in all but three volumes (according to Zink). He relaxed a little with the pieces collected in *Studies of a Biographer*, though he had even less pride in them than in the *Cornhill* essays. But as Maitland observed, near death 'He told his nurse that his enjoyment of books had begun and would end with Boswell's *Life of Johnson*.' Like his master Sainte-Beuve he believed fruit and tree, books and author, were as one.

With his easy conversational tone and his evident enjoyment of his writers, it seems (characteristically) paradoxical that Stephen never came to feel comfortable in his role as literary critic, nor ultimately to especially value the genre (At the end of his life he would write 'of the sentiment which grows upon me, of the small value of literature in general'). 'I always feel', he wrote once, 'that a critic is a kind of parasitical growth, and that the best critic should come below a second-rate original writer', and he described his breed to Thomas Hardy, in May 1876, as 'generally a poor lot, horribly afraid of not being in the fashion, and disposed to give ourselves airs on very small grounds'.

Of course, it was always personal. Stephen had explained to Norton earlier, in January 1870, that 'I have an instinct, derived I suppose from anonymous scribbling wh. always makes me ashamed of everything of mine that appears in print.' And to the mathematician and philosopher W. K. Clifford he confessed, 'What always vexes me when I write is that my views look so hideously commonplace and obvious when I have got them in black and white that I fancy everybody wondering at my taking the trouble to express them. Let us hope that this peculiar effect is due to their undeniable truth.' Either way, he dreaded 'the criticism of intelligent people'.

Although Stephen had a memory for poetry uncommon in that age, he claimed to be 'very fallible' on its merits. And so the essays largely concern prose, offering shrewd judgments, common sense and wit. From 'Autobiography', for instance: 'A man who expects that future generations will be profoundly interested in the state of his interior seems to be drawing a heavy bill upon posterity.' And writing of Rousseau's personal contradictions: 'Your proper biographer glides over these difficulties, or tries to find some reconciliation. The man who tells his own story reveals them because he is unconscious of their mixture.'

Of Gibbon, he ventured, 'it requires a certain moderation of character to be satisfied with a history instead of a wife'; and of Defoe, pithily: 'He is simply a reporter *minus* the veracity.' He wrote of Balzac, on whom he is very good and imaginative ('He did not so much invent characters and situations as watch his imaginary world, and compile the memories of its celebrities.') Here he is even a little liberal: 'Balzac, indeed as compared with our respectable romancers, has the merit of admitting passions whose existence we scrupulously ignore; and the further merit that he takes a far wider range of sentiment, and does not hold by the theory that the life of a man or a woman closes at the conventional end of a third volume, but he is above all things a dreamer, and his dreams resemble nightmares.'

Stephen had a great admiration for George Eliot, for her intelligence and for her early novels. Referring ironically to common criticisms of her, he wrote: 'She is convicted upon conclusive evidence of having indulged in ideas; she ventured to speculate upon human life and its meaning, and still worse, she endeavoured to embody her convictions in imaginative shapes, and probably wished to infect her readers with them. This was, according to some people, highly unbecoming in a woman and very inartistic in a novelist. I confess, that for my part, I am rather glad to find ideas anywhere. They are not very common.'

Where necessary, Stephen felt free to be plain-spoken, as he was of Walter Savage Landor: 'His principles are not the growth of thought, but the translation into dogmas of intense likes and dislikes, which have grown up in his mind he scarcely knows how, and gathered strength by sheer force of repetition instead of deliberate examination.'

He reckoned his favourite essay in the first series of *Hours in a Library* was the one on Jonathan Edwards, which concluded: 'Clearing away the crust of ancient superstition, we may still find in Edwards's writings a system of morality as ennobling, and a theory of the universe as elevated, as can be discovered in any theology. That the crust was thick and hard, and often revolting in its composition, is, indeed, undeniable; but the genuine metal is there, no less unmistakeably than the refuse.'

Stephen acknowledged that others liked best his Wordsworth essay. Here he did not shrink from pointing out the poet's faults: his 'too facile optimism'; the fact that 'There are times… when [his] moralising tendency leads him to the regions of the namby-pamby or sheer prosaic platitude.' There are other 'moral defects': 'the want of quick sympathy which shows itself in his dramatic feebleness, and the austerity of character which caused him to lose his special gifts too early and become a rather commonplace defender of conservatism; and that curious "diffidence" (he assures us that it was "diffidence") which induced him to write many thousand lines of blank verse entirely about himself.'

And yet, as Stephen acknowledges near the beginning of 'Wordsworth's Ethics', 'We love him the more as we grow older and become more deeply impressed with the sadness and seriousness of life; we are apt to grow weary of his rivals when we have finally quitted the regions of youthful enchantment. And I take the explanation to be that he is not merely a melodious writer, or a powerful utterer of deep emotion, but a true philosopher. His poetry wears well because it has solid substance. He is a prophet and a moralist, as well as a mere singer.'

Wordworth proved something more to Stephen, beyond being an illustration of the essential moral faculty at work ('the vigour with which a man grasps and assimilates a deep moral doctrine is a test of the degree in which he possesses one essential condition of the higher poetical excellence'). He is also a personal guide to 'the refining influence of sorrow'. On at least on two occasions in his life – at the loss of his wives – Stephen needed desperately to transmute sorrow into such strength.

Despite the weight of his literary criticism, Stephen could still speak disparagingly of it. He told Norton in December 1877, 'I am cramming with a view to more *Hours in a Library*. If I go on for a few more years more I shall have written something like a big book – big, but not very first rate, after all, I am no Sainte-

Beuve; but the work amuses me, and gives me some ideas.' Partly he felt – as did Arnold – remote from public esteem. When John Morley wrote soliciting work for a proposed magazine he cautioned, 'I don't draw. The public is indifferent to me, and, though my name would be a respectable item in your list of contributors, I don't think that I could write the kind of article that tells upon circulation.'

George Murray Smith had rescued him from journalism in 1871with the offer of the editorship of the *Cornhill*, a monthly family magazine famously once edited by his late father-in-law, Thackeray. While the pay was not 'magnificent', Stephen reckoned that with this £500 a year and a like amount from other work, he and his wife could live comfortably enough. The post had the advantage of allowing him time to make progress on what would be his major book, *The History of English Thought in the Eighteenth Century*.

The *Cornhill* did not suit him intellectually, as it excluded 'the only subjects in which reasonable men take any interest: politics and religion'. The following year he told author and art professor Charles Eliot Norton, 'I have nothing to do but to provide healthy reading for the British public & to be sure that our Mag. may lie on the table of the most refined female without calling a blush to her cheek.' For his own more controversial pieces on religion, politics, and university reform, however, he had *Fraser's* and the *Fortnightly*.

While his criticisms may have been just to an extent, as an editor Stephen published some important contemporaries: Matthew Arnold (notably parts of *Literature and Dogma*), Robert Browning, Thackeray (posthumously) and his daughter, Anne, Alfred Austin (fortunate to be appointed Poet Laureate in 1896), George Meredith, Thomas Hardy, Henry James and R. L. Stevenson, plus others who would 'condescend to be popular', though he found it difficult to find 'some good writer in the popular scientific line'. In all he also contributed seventy-five articles of his own to the *Cornhill* over thirty-five years, on literary and social subjects.

Stephen the editor proved firm but fair. To give examples of his manner: to one contributor he wrote, 'I do not think that I need to make any suggestions; for, though I differ from you on some points, I could not ask you to alter your opinions.' To another, Robert Louis Stevenson, he was most encouraging: 'I think very highly of the promise shown in your writing and therefore think it worth while to write more fully than I often do to contributors. Nor do I set myself up as a judge. I am very sensible of my own failing in the critical department & merely submit what has occurred to me for your consideration.'

His literary career thriving, Stephen's first great sorrow came suddenly, with his wife's death from eclampsia in 1875. 'His love for Minny had been protective, jocular, cossetting', according to Annan. Now he felt bereft of purpose. He continued to share a house with his mercurial sister-in-law, who 'manages to be always in two places at once & was constantly driving about in a carriage, invariably just missing everybody & meeting everybody else'. Depressed, he retreated into the work he rarely left, his 'sedative' as he described it, while all the time editing the *Cornhill* and dealing with his grief and their little girl. He also turned for comfort to a widowed neighbour and mother, the 'good and beautiful' Julia Duckworth, whom he was to marry in 1878. She would be the mother of his famous daughters.

Stephen's editorship in the *Cornhill* years had coincided, ironically, with a sharp decline in the fortunes of the magazine – from a circulation of 20,000 readers in 1871 to 12,000 by 1882 – though in no small part owing to competition from new titles on the market. His publisher, Smith, kept the news from him until he offered Stephen another project, which would become perhaps his greatest achievement: the *Dictionary of National Biography* ("THE MAGNUM OPUS OF OUR GENERATION', according to *Truth* magazine). For this he would need a team of contributors, all of whom must be kept in line with respect to word count (and hyperbole). Stephen edited the quarterly

Dictionary from 1885 to 1891. It closed in 1900 after 63 volumes, though he had left the project in poor health.

In the previous twenty years, he had maintained a remarkable publishing pace. In 1871 *The Playground of Europe* (his 'little collection of Alpine stories') had appeared and in 1873 his *Essays on Freethinking and Plainspeaking*. The following year came the first of three *Hours in a Library*, and in 1876 the *History of English Thought*. Two years later, the year of his second marriage, appeared the first of his biographies for the *English Men of Letters* series.

In 1893 came *Agnostic's Apology and other Essays* and, two years on, Stephen's second wife died. To Noel Annan, 'In Julia he recognised a deeper and more sensitive character than his own and one who had borne sorrow, as he would have wished to bear it, but could not. He worshipped her with an unalterable devotion.' He had been, despite himself, a trial to both his wives and his children, being both needy and demanding. In middle age Stephen had styled himself 'a sort of harmless misanthrope'. According to Sheldon M. Novick (biographer of eminent jurist Oliver Wendell Holmes), in his last years he deteriorated: 'Leslie was cut off by deepening bitterness and by growing deafness; visitors were obliged to shout at him, and he groaned loudly to himself.' Yet he wrote on. In 1898 he published *Studies of a Biographer* and in 1900 *English Utilitarians*. In the year of his death, 1904, came his Ford lectures.

Despite the rigours of a long and enormously productive writing life and a lived life that ended sourly and in sorrow, Stephen seems to have made a number of intimate friends. Although he professed himself hardly sure that they understood him fully, he acknowledged that he could rarely express himself completely or candidly, in letters or in conversation. His closest friends had included George Meredith and the blind economist Henry Fawcett, an early influence, on whom the news of Stephen's first engagement produced the amusing anecdote he reported to 'Minny', as follows:

Miss T. is the youngest, isn't she Stephen? Yes.
Does she write as well as her sister – No.
Doesn't she write occasionally – No.
Doesn't she help her sister to write?
Wouldn't she write well if she did write?
&c &c &c

Later valued friends included John Morley, the legal historian Frederick W. Maitland, and three Americans: Norton, Holmes and the poet and diplomat, James Russell Lowell. Being abolitionist by family background and personal conviction, Stephen had first visited Boston in 1863, during the Civil War, searching for clarity on the issues. While many in the British government favoured the South, hoping for the failure of the American experiment in democracy, Stephen championed the North. He was shrewd enough to realise that slavery was to many northerners a political rather than a moral issue, given that it anchored the South's economy and status. He made important New England friendships on that visit.

Stephen's letters across the Atlantic over the years provide something of a diary of his emotions. They are generally affectionate and frequently amusing at the expense of his correspondents. He compared America's 'lumbering continent' to his 'small but unparalleled island' and affected sympathy for his friends' distance from his beloved Alps, where he climbed whenever possible. Fostered by occasional visits, his closest American friend was Charles Eliot Norton.

After Norton had been in London for some months in 1873, following the death of his wife and prior to Stephen's own first loss, he received an affecting letter, which reveals the emotion Stephen generally withheld: 'You dont know what your friendship has been & will be to me. I have not, & never have had, many intimate friends; & for some reason or other, it is so happened that even my best friends have generally been in sympathy with me only on one side & that not the most sensitive side... It is really odd that, of all the men I know, you & perhaps Morley (I can't think of a third) are the only ones with whom I can be sure of finding thorough sympathy in such conversations as we used to have. My brother always wants to argue & so do I – but an argument always ends by worrying me.'

In his American letters Stephen would readily confess his failings: 'I have an infernal turn for inappropriate modesty'; 'I am of the thin-skinned breed; and a chance remark about me sometimes makes me swear like Beelzebub for hours together.' An affectionate letter to Norton from 1894 ends, 'My letter, I see, will not take a cheerful turn, but I feel better generally after swearing, and you must imagine that as I cease to write, I fill my pipe and take my book and feel that my mind is lightened by discharging my ill-humour on my friend. It is wrong, but it is rather my way.'

The revelation that stays with us is also to be found in a letter to Norton. In March 1876 he had written that 'unhappiness tries my temper. I am more fretful and irritable by disposition than you perhaps know'. In his *Mausoleum Book*, written for the children, he confessed his 'tempers and irritabilities' as an unchangeable aspect of his character. All this chimes with accusations of his domestic cruelty, of his bullying his daughter, Vanessa, over the household accounts. It no doubt led to Woolf's depiction of him as Mr Ramsay in *To The Lighthouse*, as a man who seems to take a delight in disillusioning his children, who 'was incapable of untruth; never tampered with a fact; never altered a disagreeable word to suit the pleasure of or convenience of any mortal being, least of all his own children'. In 'A Sketch of the Past' (1940) she wrote of him as friend, author and father. Unfortunately, she did not know him as the first of these.

One insider who would have known some of this but wrote with perfect tact was his biographer, Maitland, who joined Stephen's 'Sunday Tramps' in April 1880 and later married the niece of Stephen's second wife. Lord Acton described Maitland as England's ablest historian and Holmes described his work on legal history to Stephen as being 'of the truly scientific kind – accurate investigation of details in the interest of questions of philosophical importance'.

Maitland's scrupulousness is apparent in his *The Life and Letters of Leslie Stephen* (1906), which came out two and a half years after his friend's death. He explained in his introduction that he has been licensed to 'write a short article or "appreciation" or a notice in a biographical dictionary'. Stephen had recommended him: 'He, as I always feel, understands me.' Maitland chose to write his full biography because, he argued, he lacked the skill to write a short one. His substantial use of Stephen's letters proved very rewarding, as the biography remains highly readable today. Noel Annan referred to it as a 'masterly commemorative biography'.

One tactic Maitland adopted was to allow Stephen to confess his failings himself through his letters, though he does say in summary, 'We should not claim for him all the Christian virtues. He was hot-tempered, and he could be impatient, which no clergymen ought to be; and though he was very modest, we could not call him meek; but he was incapable of bearing malice.' To more than balance criticism, since he believed Stephen made too much of his own failings, he quoted many encomiums from former students and friends throughout his book.

At the end, quoting Stephen's 'Can you not praise the dead man sufficiently unless you tell lies about him?' he declared again, 'I have told no lies. I have said the worst that I know. Stephen's temper was "honestly coltish"; he had a low flash-point; there is a trace of the ancestral "wild duck" in him, and more than a trace of the sensitive plant.' He then focussed on Stephen the writer, countering criticism with a remark of Sir George Trevelyan's: 'He seemed never to think an ignoble, a feeble or a timid thought.' One is left in no doubt of Maitland's affection for his friend: 'For my own part I should say of him what he said of Thackeray. "His writings" – at all events his later writings – "seemed to be everywhere full of the tenderest sensibility, and to show that he valued tenderness, sympathy, and purity of nature, as none but a man of exceptional kindness of heart knows how to value them."'

Modestly in this case, Maitland shared Stephen's Victorian belief that biography offered only a superficial reading of character. Forty-five years later, Noel Annan published *Leslie Stephen: His Thought and Character in Relation to His Time*, which he revised and extended in 1984 as the widely admired *Leslie Stephen: The Godless Victorian*. Annan certainly penetrated beneath both the surface of the life and the times. He made it clear in the revised edition where *his* interest lay: 'I still believe that his writings are of greater interest than his life and that to understand Stephen is to understand Evangelical morality and Victorian rationalism, the strongest influences of the age.' Consequently, the life events were explored in the first one hundred and twenty-five pages of his book. There then followed a further two hundred and twenty-five pages that connected the life to Stephen's character, to Evangelicalism, Rationalism, Comte and Darwin, to his Augustan Age, Agnosticism, and Morality (in Society, Biography and Literature).

Annan attributed Stephen's limitation as a critic to his scepticism about his role, as well as to the conventionality of his views (which, as we have seen, included the muddying of aesthetics with ethics). He saw the scepticism as, 'typical of Stephen's determination to be honest but it makes his literary criticism undeniably less impressive… we recognize his voice at once: but it does not woo or command us'. The critic would have been in sympathy with these observations, since he acknowledged in his *Mausoleum Book* that what limited his achievement had been 'my want of proper self-confidence or, in the early days, of ambition'.

But Stephen also knew his worth, despite a lifetime's self-deprecation: 'I know, of course, that I am a man of not inconsiderable literary ability. I think again that I am a man of greater ability than a good many much more popular authors. I have been approved by many men whose approval is worth having.' And he also knew that he might have achieved more: 'The sense in which I do take myself to be a failure is this: I had scattered myself too much. I think that I had it in me to make something like a real contribution to philosophical or ethical thought. Unluckily, what with journalism and dictionary making, I have been a Jack of all trades.'

Virginia Woolf remembered her father telling her, as they walked around the croquet lawn at Fritham, that he possessed, 'Only a good second class mind'. Time seems to have borne out, to a degree, evidence of his judgement. An otherwise admiring obituary in *The Spectator* (27th February, 1904) concluded (like Annan later): 'we doubt if he will ever greatly affect our judgment or enjoyment of the books he has written of". John Gross, in his masterly *The Rise and Fall of the Man of Letters* (1969) concurred, in calling him a writer of 'the second rank (though wearing better than others)'. Second again. And again, when Annan began *Leslie Stephen: Selected Writings in British Intellectual History* (1979) he declared him 'the second most important man of letters in the late Victorian age' (after Matthew Arnold). Would it have mattered to the man himself?

It is unlikely. In January 1884, with so much work behind him, Stephen could still write to Charles Eliot Norton, 'I don't know why it never struck me before, but it has suddenly become evident to me that literary criticism is not my proper line. I stumbled into it somehow, and have never become acclimatised. I feel that I am out of my element in this kind of work, and, when I have made my bow and earned my wages, I shall shake the dust off my shoes and find more congenial occupation in writing a book which is dimly shaping itself in my mind [*The English Utilitarians*]. It will probably come to little enough; but at least it will let me talk my own dialect and not be a-mouthing of effete criticism.'

ROBERT BROWNING: HOW IT STRUCK A CONTEMPORARY

A Handbook to the Works of Robert Browning (1885) & *Life and Letters of Robert Browning* (1891) by Mrs Sutherland Orr

I only knew one poet in my life:
And this, or something like it, was his way.
– 'How it Strikes a Contemporary'

Frederic William Maitland held that 'a biographer rarely penetrates far below the surface, and that he yet performs a useful office if he is fairly diligent, moderately intelligent, and scrupulously sincere'. His own superb biography of Sir Leslie Stephen (1906) exposed the modesty in such a claim. So too does John Forster's *Dickens* and Alexandra Sutherland Orr's biography of Robert Browning, which set the temper and the terms of our understanding of the poet. These writers approached their subjects from the position of intimate friends of the recently deceased and opted to tell the life with the assistance of the letters (and the family). This afforded glimpses of their subject's perspective on events to support the portraiture. In this, Mrs. Orr (1828–1903) had the hardest task, given that the Browning letters to which she had access generally lack charm (not being 'vigorous or characteristic or light', according to his old friend, William Wetmore Story).

Mrs. Orr proved a discriminating Browning scholar and had the mature, detailed reminiscences of his unmarried sister, Sarianna, to assist her in her work. She would not have subscribed to G. K. Chesterton's observation, in his characteristically lively *Robert Browning* (written for the 'English Men of Letters' series in 1920), 'On the subject of Browning's work innumerable things have been said and remain to be said; of his life, considered as a narrative of facts, there is little or nothing to say.' A later

Browning scholar, Maisie Ward, judged that Mrs. Orr had succeeded in painting a vivid picture 'of a mind so many-sided that no one has succeeded in fully penetrating it'. In her pioneering study, Mrs. Orr had no intention of simply telling the life as a series of unsurprising events. She had an insight into an essentially coherent personality upon which they impacted, a Browning who was to bring her the disapproval of the poet's intimates.

Alexandra Leighton (Mrs. Sutherland Orr) was born in St Petersburg in 1828, where her physician grandfather, Sir James Leighton, attended the Russian royal family. She had been named after the Empress, her godmother. Being of independent means her father, also a doctor, ensured that the family travelled widely in Europe. At sixteen Alexandra Leighton developed rheumatic fever, which resulted in a partial loss of sight and eventually necessitated the assistance of an amanuensis.

Her younger brother, Frederic Leighton, became a highly successful artist in the academic style and a friend of Browning's from the time they met in Rome. The poet first turned to him to design the funeral monument for his wife, Elizabeth Barrett Browning, in 1861 and three years later wrote an impassioned short poem to accompany Leighton's provocative painting of the 'Eurydice and Orpheus' myth. In his collection, *Balaustion's Adventure* (1871), Browning would refer to Leighton as 'a great Kaunian painter'.

Miss Leighton had met Browning in Paris in 1855, two years before she married Colonel Sutherland Orr. She followed her husband to India when he joined his regiment, the 3rd cavalry. Shortly after, the 'Indian Mutiny' necessitated her escape from the city of Aurangabad. Her problems were then compounded by the death from dysentery of her husband in 1858. Returning to her family in England, she took up residence in Bath and in London in 1869, where she was to resume her friendship with Browning and his sister. Her intimacy with the poet would create rumours – the norm for the widower Browning and his female admirers –

though their relationship seems to have been platonic. She devoted herself to his work and he confided in her. While Sarianna proved useful discussing the events of her brother's life, Mrs. Orr listened to his opinions and sought his assistance in untangling some of his poems' obscurities.

In the portraits for which Miss Leighton/Mrs. Orr sat for her brother, she is depicted as delicate, pretty and refined. To some she appeared less conventionally so in person. Author Julian Hawthorne – the son of Nathaniel Hawthorne – wrote of her as a disconcerting presence: 'a little creature in black: her fingers and shoulders jerked nervously, her face twitched, her forehead was bulbous, her eyes very far apart; she was an intellectual woman, a Positivist, but told me she had been forbidden by her doctor to use her brain; when one looked her in the face, her eyes seemed to rush away to right and left: she adjured me not to write at night – else I would perish in my youth'.

Mrs. Orr's scholarly interests and admiration for the poet's work led her to publish papers on it (as well as on other subjects), to financially support the Browning Society (a source of some internal conflict on at least one occasion) and to publish *A Handbook to the Works of Robert Browning* (1885) with his tacit approval. After his death in 1889 she wrote her *Life and Letters of Robert Browning*, published two years later.

Writing of the Browning Societies in her biography, Mrs. Orr described the poet's 'passive assent' to their establishment but remained ambivalent about them herself. She recognised the poet had thereby 'made himself public property' and suggested that, as far as his work was concerned, the contagion of enthusiasm (even of emotion during the poet's lifetime) 'detracted from its intellectual worth'. On the other hand, she understood that the societies improved Browning's sales 'and with it their distinct influence for intellectual and moral good'. She was connected with that celebrated group which met monthly at University College London from 1881, founded by Frederick James Furnivall and Emily Hickey.

Later she accepted that, on balance, they provided a healthier outlet to admiration: 'The hysterical sensibilities which, for some years past, he had unconsciously but not unfrequently aroused in the minds of women, and even of men, were a morbid development of that influence, which its open and systematic extension tended rather to diminish than to increase.' Illustrating the strength of admiration for Browning, she quoted a letter from an American wife who addressed the poet about her husband in the following words: 'You are the great enthusiasm of his life.'

Recognising this kind of need, Mrs. Orr produced *A Handbook to the Works of Robert Browning*. She explained in a Preface that at the urging of members of the Browning Society she had set out to compose a 'primer' on the poems, but that her work had 'naturally shaped itself into a kind of descriptive Index, based partly on the historical order and partly on the natural classification of the various poems'. Its organisation had weighed heavily upon her during and since its completion and, with becoming modesty, she voiced her regrets 'that the arrangement is clumsy and confusing', and that there were 'some blunders of a more mechanical kind, which I might have been expected to avoid'.

Despite Mrs. Orr's reservations, the *Handbook* offered an informative guide to the interested reader – expensive, as Frederick Furnivall complained in a fit of pique during a society disagreement, and even 'dull' he suggested. Perhaps, but even at this distance in time it is a useful source to dip into for the events of a poem. The indivisibility of Browning's oeuvre is first acknowledged ('Mr. Browning's work is himself') and then artificially divided (into dramas, argumentative poems, didactic poems, critical poems, etc.). While no boundary is airtight here, Mrs. Orr sees a natural divide in the poems: '" The Ring and the Book" was written at what may be considered the turning-point… in the author's artistic career: for most of his emotional poems were published before, and most of the argumentative after it.'

With the poetry itself Mrs. Orr shows greater confidence. In her opening remarks ('General Characteristics') she argues that 'His genius always shows itself as dramatic and metaphysical at the same time.' As a dramatic poet, unlike Shakespeare, he does not disappear into his characters ('His personality may be constructed from his works.') In fact he 'defends them from their own point of view'. And he is metaphysical, not in thinking but in examining his characters' thoughts ('He is a constant analyst of secondary motives and judgments.') She writes of 'the drama of motive' in his work: 'He had been inspired as dramatic poet by the one avowed conviction that little else is worth study but the history of a soul; any outward act or circumstance had only entered into his creations as condition or incident of the given psychological state.'

Carlyle once said of Browning, 'It's a very strange and curious spectacle to behold a man in these days so confidently cheerful' and G.K. Chesterton would describe him as 'the only optimistic philosopher except Whitman'. Mrs. Orr acknowledges this optimism as being at the heart of his appeal, while implicitly cautioning his readers, 'So much of Mr Browning's moral influence lies in the hopeful religious spirit which his works reveal, that it is important to understand how elastic it is, and what seeming contradictions it is competent to unite.' The alternative, she explains, would set one poem against another.

She also addresses here the perennial question of Browning's difficulty: 'He has never intended to be obscure, but he has become so from the condensation of style which was the excess of significance and of strength.' This she acknowledges as an issue, given that 'With all his love for music, Mr. Browning is more susceptible to sense than to sound. He values thought more than expression; matter, more than form; and, judging from a strictly poetic point of view, he has lost his balance in this direction, as so many have lost it in the opposite one.' In point of fact Browning is formally very adventurous. Mrs. Orr further argues that the poet remains unchanging in his commitment: 'Mr Browning's position is that of a fixed centre of thought and feeling. Fifty years ago he was in advance of his age. He stood firm and has allowed the current to overtake him, or even leave him behind.' Such critical observations balance the author's admiration.

In the course of her *Handbook* Mrs. Orr leads the reader through the events of the poems (with some commentary), the longer ones requiring a great deal. *The Ring and the Book*, for instance, requires forty-six pages. Her descriptions are generally illuminating. So, of her brother's painting of Orpheus and an urgent Eurydice, she offers: 'But the face of Leighton's Eurydice wears an intensity of longing which seems to challenge the forbidden look, and makes her responsible for it.' And Browning's masterly 'Andrea Del Sarto', which Mrs. Orr links with 'Sordello' ('the soul of a true artist must exceed his technical powers') is 'the lament of an artist who has fallen short of his ideal – of a man who feels himself the slave of circumstance – of a lover who is sacrificing his moral, and in some degree his artistic, conscience to a woman who does not return his love. It is the harmonious utterance of a many-sided sadness, which has become identified with even the pleasures of the man's life; and is hopeless, because he is resigned to it.'

For the general reader Mrs. Orr's assistance clearly proved valuable, since the book went through several editions. While not directly involved, Browning assisted her on occasions. She refers in her biography to the incidence of a fever which interrupted the writing of 'Artemis Prologuizes', when he 'gave me these supplementary details for the *Handbook*'. The book turned out to be of some use to Browning, who avoided all discussion of his poetry with outsiders whenever possible, even to the point of allowing misreadings. It also increased his earnings, which improved from £100 in 1881 to £1,252 in 1888. According to Maisie Ward, 'at times Browning seemed to endorse [the *Handbook*] totally – even telling people to read it to find out what he had meant in a given poem; yet at others his own account simply contradicted the book's interpretations'.

In the *New Letters of Robert Browning*, collected by DeVane and Knickerbocker (1951), there are two occasions where Browning promotes – blindly, as it were – the work of Mrs. Orr, showing his faith in her judgement (They also illustrate the fact that his ambition remained a living thing.) He began a letter to George Smith in May 1873 with, 'Here is a note I return to you as rather for your consideration than mine: but it gives me the opportunity of saying that Mrs. Orr has pleased to write another article on the new Poem [*Red Cotton Night-Cap Country*] – which the *Fortnightly*, – to which it was highly commended by Mr. [George] Lewes, – don't want: I have not read a word of it, of course, – but on every account I should be glad if there were any way to its appearance: it seems only my duty to such disinterested zeal (and considerable intelligence too) that I should bring the fact that there *is* a paper of the kind going a-begging – under your notice; so the duty is done.' Browning added the following day a note accompanying the text, which included the words, 'if you can do nothing for it, please return it as soon as convenient, as she may try her luck (and mine) in other quarters'. The piece would finally appear, not in Smith's *Cornhill Magazine*, but in the *Contemporary Review* that summer.

In November of the same year the poet replied to an offer from its editor, James Thomas Knowles. of an article: 'I may say, while I have the opportunity, that Mrs. Orr will be glad to write the article you suggested, as I shall be abundantly satisfied with whatever she pronounces. If you would like to see her – she will always be cheerfully visible at 11, Kensington Park Gardens, W.' The long article in question, 'Mr. Browning's Place in Literature', appeared in May 1874.

Given such essays, the *Handbook*, and their personal history (Browning acknowledge her, along with his sister, as his best, frankest critics in the discussion of his poems, and read to her twice-weekly). Mrs. Orr became the obvious family choice to write *Life and Letters of Robert Browning*.

Their friendship is occasionally invoked in the biography ('He has said more than once, when its reminiscences have been invoked'; 'I well remember Mr. Browning's telling me how…'). When writing, for instance, of his formative debt to Keats and especially to Shelley, she writes approvingly, 'no one who has ever heard him read the *Ode to a Nightingale*, and repeat in the same subdued tones, as if continuing his thoughts, some line from [Shelley's] *Epipsychidion*, can doubt that they retained a lasting and almost equal place in his poet's heart'.

Because she is driven by her admiration for the man ('No one who loved Mr. Browning in himself, or in his work, can…'), Mrs. Orr felt the injustice of the under-appreciation of his poetry: 'Few men so much "reviewed" have experienced so little', for 'the independent judgment which could embrace at once the quality of his mind and its defects, is almost absent… from the volumes which have been written about him.' Yet she remained clear-eyed, as the reference to 'defects' suggests, both in her observations of life and work.

This makes for an acute portrait, one which hardly pleased family and friends. The American sculptor William Wetmore Story, a long-standing friend of Browning's who lived in Rome, contributed his reminiscences to Mrs. Orr's biography. On reading the published result in 1891, he commented that it seemed rather colourless, but then that social vivacity was hard to capture.

More bluntly, Pen Browning described the biography to William Lyon Phelps as 'a very bad book' and reckoned that he had not been shown it until the proof stage, when it was too late to make changes. According to Ward, 'The supreme point of irritation lay perhaps in the small proportion given in the book to that central fact which concerned both son and sister: Browning's family life. To some extent this omission was, like Mrs. Orr's own anonymity, a tribute paid to Victorian convention. But her statement that "the paternal instinct was the weakest in his nature" was not likely to please Pen.'

Interesting as this judgment is, William Irvine and Park

Honan were perhaps closer to the mark in their comprehensive 1974 biography, *The Book, The Ring, & The Poet*, when they wrote of the book's having dismayed Pen for its portrait of the poet as a lifelong valetudinarian. They reported the Michael Fields (poets Katherine Harris Bradley and Edith Emma Cooper) as noting in 1895 that Pen 'hates Mrs. Orr's life as we do, – the puling invalidism attributed to a man who never stayed in bed'.

The idea appears early in the biography. Having established Browning as 'healthy, even strong, in many essential respects', he nevertheless seems to his biographer to have inherited something of his mother's delicacy: 'he was conscious of what he called a nervousness of nature… He imputed to this, or, in other words, to an undue physical sensitiveness to mental causes of irritation, his proneness to deranged liver, and the asthmatic conditions which he believed, rightly or wrongly, to be produced by it.'

A consequence was that 'He had the pleasures as well as the pains of this nervous temperament; its quick response to every congenial stimulus of physical atmosphere, and human contact.' This may have led him to 'overdraw' on his strength, she continues, and although 'Many persons have believed that he could not live without society' his socialising exacted a toll: 'the excited gayety which to the last he carried into every social gathering was often primarily the result of a moral and physical effort which his temperament prompted, but his strength could not always justify. Nature avenged herself in recurrent periods of exhaustion, long before the closing stages set in.'

Mrs. Orr determines to impose this interpretation on the narrative, as she tells the reader: 'I shall subsequently have occasion to trace this nervous impressibility through various aspects and relations of his life.' His mother's precarious health, allied with his father's 'placid intellectual powers' – as her argument goes – allowed for a 'transmutation into poetic genius' with its attendant pain.

Her thesis, allied with the fact that Browning lived quietly during his marriage to Elizaeth Barret Browning, has the attendant benefit of addressing his tendency to dominate conversations and exhibit excessive social zeal (dubbed by some 'vulgarity'). These would prompt Henry James, in his 1892 story *The Private Life*, to posit the simultaneous existence of two Brownings: the hidden writer and the loud social being. It also accords with less charitable memories of the old poet. Mary Gladstone complained in her diary of being constantly sent into dinner with 'old Browning', who 'always places his person in such disagreeable proximity with yours and puffs and blows and spits in your face. I tried to think of 'Abt Vogler' but it was no use – he *could* not have written it.'

This, Mrs. Orr ascribes to Browning's disappearance from society: 'It is on record that during the fifteen years of his married life, Mr. Browning never dined away from home, except on one occasion… and we cannot therefore be surprised that he should subsequently have carried into the experience of an unshackled and very interesting social intercourse, a kind of freshness which a man of fifty has not generally preserved.' Of course to argue that the Brownings lived a life of social isolation is clearly untrue. Even in a small way, they were never socially unattended.

On the subject of the poet's loquaciousness, she admits that 'Mr. Browning was a brilliant talker; he was admittedly more a talker than a conversationalist.' She defends him, however, from the charge of conceit: 'He never willingly monopolized the conversation.' She then adds generously, 'but would at time be carried away by his "great mental fertility"'. Also, he might show a lack of restraint when, 'Feeling, imagination, and the vividness of personal points of view, constantly thwarted the attempt at a dispassionate exchange of ideas.'

Browning's social 'performance' is, in Mrs. Orr's view, attributable to the nerves mentioned above: 'We cannot doubt that the excited stream of talk which sometimes flowed from him was, in the given conditions of mind and imagination, due to a nervous impulse which he could not always restrain; and that the effusiveness of manner with which he greeted alike old friends and new, arose also from a momentary wanted self-possession.'

As to the charge of Browning's loudness, she is slightly more guarded in his defence: 'The loud voice, which so many persons must have learned to think habitual with him, bore also traces of this half-unconscious nervous stimulation. It was natural to him in anger or excitement, but did not express his gentler more equable states of states of feeling.' Mrs. Orr interjects a note from the poet's sister explaining that he spoke loudly from the habit of talking to deaf friends, though she adds warily: 'This fact necessarily modifies my impression of the case, but does not quite destroy it.'

There is another quality in Mrs. Orr's portrait which will not have endeared it to the family: a charge of fatalism. She contrasts his intellectual vigour with an 'aversion to every thought of change', a passivity which 'disposed him too much to make a virtue of happiness' and to ignore 'many standing problems of human suffering'. She acknowledges that 'It seems still harder to associate defective human sympathy with his kind heart and large dramatic imagination.' Yet to her he became a prisoner of his own point of view, a creative artist inevitably 'self-centred'.

The thematic core of her portrait aside, his biographer structures her materials with some care. She intervenes in her narrative to pace it and to direct her reader's response. So, when Browning's sister comes to live with him, the author instructs us to remember that 'Her presence with him must therefore be understood wherever I have had no special reason for mentioning it.' When raising the subject of Browning and medical science she tells us, 'As I shall have occasion to show, no knowledge of either disease or its treatment ever seems to have penetrated into his life.' And later, 'A long interval in the correspondence, at all events so far as we are concerned, carries us to the December of 1864.' She writes elsewhere of a fact 'which falls practically into the present period of our history'.

With respect to Browning's spiritual and intellectual allegiances, Mrs. Orr presents her readers with an evangelical

Christian Browning, a believer in subjective idealist philosophy, who avowed that 'he knew neither the German philosophers nor their reflection in Coleridge, who would have seemed a likely medium between them and him'. He is also described as a patriotic Liberal of the old school.

She shows a knowledge of his talents (his potential as an actor, for example), his tastes (how music seemed 'to pass out of his life altogether'; how 'the fashionable routine of country-house visitings' became tiresome) and his idiosyncrasies. She presents him, for example, as a man with the 'marked peculiarity' of 'an habitual aversion for the paraphernalia of death'. Here Mrs. Orr adds honestly, 'He shrank, as his wife had done, from the "earth-side" of the portentous change; but truth compels me to own that her infinite pity had little or no part in his attitude towards it. For him, a body from which the soul had passed, held nothing of the person whose earthly vesture it had been.'

Equally she is quite open on the relationship between the Brownings, beginning with his confession that early on 'There was so much pity in what I felt for her!' She captures the intimacy of their marriage in a letter of Elizabeth's from the winter of 1859: 'Nobody exactly understands him except me, who am in the inside of him and hear him breathe. For the peculiarity of our relation is, that he thinks aloud with me and can't stop himself.'

She tells us that both Brownings suffered distress at the lack of interest in Browning's poetry, quoting Elizabeth: 'At the same time, his treatment in England affects him, naturally, and for my part I set it down as an infamy of that public – no other word… But nobody there, except a small knot of pre-Raphaellite [sic] men, pretend to do him justice.'

Mrs. Orr is also candid in her judgement on the relative merits of the two poets 'He regarded Mrs. Browning's genius as greater, because more spontaneous, than his own: owing less to life and its opportunities; but he judged his own work as the more important, because of the larger knowledge of life which had entered into its production.' To Mrs. Orr this is simply, 'wrong in the first terms of his comparison: for he underrated the creative, hence spontaneous element in his own nature, while claiming primarily the position of an observant thinker; and he overrated the amount of creativeness implied by the poetry of his wife. He failed to see that, given her intellectual endowments, and the lyric gift, the characteristics of her genius were due to circumstances as much as those of his own.'

On the subject of Browning's relations with men and women generally, Mrs. Orr writes of 'the reserve which, I believe, habitually characterised Mr. Browning's attitude towards men. His natural, and certainly most complete, confidants were women.' Pamela Neville-Sington, in *Robert Browning: A Life After Death* (2004), lists them: 'Isa Blagden, Annie Smith, Alexandra Orr, Eliza Fitzgerald – but he was to them as a loving brother, no more.' She further speculates that, 'For Louisa Ashburton, Robert had felt physical attraction without tenderness; for Julia Wedgwood tenderness without physical attraction. The poet's letters to Katharine Branson exude both warm affection and sensuality.'

As to his admiration of women, Mrs. Orr offers a critical rider: 'He never quite understood but the strongest women are weak, or at all events vulnerable, in the very fact of their sex, through the minor traditions and conventions with which society justly, indeed necessarily, surrounds them. Still less did he understand those real, if impalpable, differences between men and women which correspond to the difference of position.... He would say on occasion: "You ought to *be* better; you are a woman; I ought to *know* better; I am a man.' He approved of women being given the vote, though against their agitation for it under the umbrella of Women's Rights.

The biographer's authority is evident throughout. She challenges the poet's understanding on further occasions, as she does with remarks in his Shelley essay: 'I venture, however, to think, that in his various and necessary concessions, he lets slip the main point; and for the simple reason that it is untenable.'

Later, on the pressing subject of unintelligibility, she first quotes Browning's understandable irritation at being incorrectly printed. She then adds her own qualification to redress the balance: 'He also failed to realize those conditions of thought, and still more of expression, which made him often on first reading difficult to understand.'

Such observations illustrate the fact that while Mrs. Orr makes every attempt to be supportive of Browning, she also enlightens the reader with respect to his flaws of character and views. There are many instances of her discretion, as well as the odd reference to the restrictions she either embraces ('One or two characteristic utterances of Mr. Browning are, however, the only ones which it seems advisable to repeat here') or endures (his vitality 'also reveals itself in his letters in so far as I have been allowed to publish them'). Elizabeth Barrett Browning's letters are more memorably excerpted in the course of the biography.

Mrs. Orr takes it upon herself to correct the record on Browning's behalf, as she does in the case of his play, *A Blot in the 'Scutcheon*, with respect to the falling out with Macready over his desertion of the principal role. Similarly, she 'cannot refrain' from dispelling some wrong assertion that young Robert Browning derived his nickname Pen from a statue, or dismissing the myth that the poet met Stendhal.

Her vigilance includes correcting William Sharp's *Life of Robert Browning*, a rival, lesser biography which appeared the year before her own. She points out, for instance, how he wrongly interprets Browning's intention in 'Two in the Campagna'. And again, excusing one intemperate poem ('Lines to Edward Fitzgerald') listed in the bibliography of Sharp's book, she writes: 'I owe it to him to say – what I believe is only known to his sister and myself – that there was a moment in which he regretted those lines, and would willingly have withdrawn them.' Finally she is able, having severely qualified Sharp's comment on Browning's 'message' with the words, 'This statement is relatively true', to end her book by waxing eloquently on Sharp's erroneous idea that 'a new star appeared in Orion' on the night Browning died.

On the other hand, Mrs. Orr is also scrupulously fair to her sources. One footnote reads: 'The term Gothic has been applied to Mr. Browning's work, I believe, by Mr. James Thompson, in writing of *The Ring and the Book*, and I do not like to use it without saying so. But it is one of those which must have spontaneously suggested themselves too many other of Mr. Browning's readers.' She is also authoritative without affecting omniscience. While comprehensive on the poet, Mrs. Orr makes no claim to be entirely exhaustive on others. When referring to the work of a Browning uncle, *History of the Huguenots*, she is content to quote another's opinion ('a work we are told…').

Mrs. Orr biography is not without its failings, however, though some are more of period than perception. She has that stylistic delicacy of expression we associate with Victorian propriety: 'Husband and wife had both determined to forgo any pecuniary benefit which might accrue to them from this event [the death of their friend, Kenyon]; but they would not be called upon to exercise their powers of renunciation.'

Although she is capable of a certain toughness of expression ('he blew out his brains'), her descriptions can founder in the sentimental: 'She rallied surprisingly and almost suddenly in the sunshine of her new life, and remained for several years at the higher physical level… But her ailments were too radical for permanent cure, as the weak voice and shrunken form never ceased to attest.' Elsewhere she writes of their friend Isa Blagden's perspective on Browning's response to Elizabeth's death: 'so deeply poetic were the ravings which alternated with the simple human cry of the desolate heart: "I want her, I want her!" But the ear which received these utterances has long been closed in death.'

Less excusable to our tastes is Mrs. Orr's snobbishness, albeit characteristic of a highly class-conscious period. She tells an otherwise amusing anecdote about Pen playing as a boy with a friend 'not of his own class' and how had the boy been objectionable 'neither Penini nor his parents would have endured the association'. In a later part of the biography she refers to Browning having learned to accept London as his home again 'in spite of the refuse of humanity which would sometimes yell at the street corner, or fling stones at his plate-glass' – a reminder of the deeply divided society.

If one measure of a good biography is the degree to which it offers a compelling portrait of its subject, another is the extent to which it holds its own in the canon over the passage of time. Mrs. Orr's has done both. Her version of Browning is plausible, and it is clear from all subsequent biographies that she has a great deal to offer, mostly on the narrative of Browning's life, admittedly, but also for her interpretations. All acknowledge use of *Life and Letters of Robert Browning*.

Typical, perhaps, is Maisie Ward's two-volume *Robert Browning and His World* (1967 and 1969). She uses Mrs. Orr to propel her narrative ('She tells us'; 'She declares'; 'Mrs. Orr is convinced) and only occasionally challenges her predecessor's reliability. The poet's most recent biographer is Iain Finlayson, in *Browning: A Private Life* (2004). Finlayson is more cautious in taking Mrs. Orr at her word: 'She can sometimes, in her emphases and suppressions, be inspired to what we now recognize as spin.' Surely this is a congenital pitfall of the genre.

While the informed reader today might choose to read the sparklingly clever Chesterton biography, the Irvine and Honan for its abundant colour and detail, or one of the later biographies mentioned above, Mrs. Orr's is still a lively source. She would certainly have taken issue with Chesterton's breezy summary that Browning 'combines the greatest brain with the most simple temperament known in our annals'. With unremitting attention and sincere admiration she sought to resolve the congestions in the poetry and the contradictions in the man.

LOOKING FOR LEWES: GEORGE HENRY LEWES'S *LIFE OF GOETHE* (1855)

George Henry Lewes is underknown. A Victorian intellectual of varied interests vigorously pursued, he is difficult to pin down. To add to that, he remains overshadowed in our minds by our admiration for his partner, George Eliot. Nevertheless, Lewes (1817–1878) distinguished himself as a stimulating critic (lecturer, author and editor) in literary and dramatic criticism, the theatre, philosophy, physiology, and botany. To narrow the focus alarmingly, my intention here is to consider the Lewes behind his most celebrated work, the *Life of Goethe*. I begin with two potted biographies.

Lewes, the grandson of a well-known comic actor, periodically yearned for the theatre. He appeared on stage from time to time (including membership in Dickens's troupe), and translated plays when he needed money to support himself and his dependants. An illegitimate son – radical and bohemian in his younger years – he had been raised in England and France, entering the literary world of London via a friendship with the critic Leigh Hunt. In 1841 he married Agnes Jervis, the daughter of an MP and minor poet. They would eventually separate after his wife gave birth to children by his friend and fellow *Leader* editor, Hunt's son, Thornton Leigh Hunt. Thomas Carlyle wrote to his sister of their socialist paper, describing this Hunt as 'a really clever, little brown-skinned man, and true as steel in his way' and Lewes as 'an *airy* loose-tongued merry-hearted being with more sail than ballast'.

In the early 1850s Lewes began a relationship with George Eliot (Mary Ann Evans). Being in legal terms 'complicit in adultery', he could not gain a divorce. Together they visited Weimar and Berlin in 1854, Lewes to research the Goethe biography on which he had worked for some time. In Germany he and Eliot were welcomed, despite their unorthodox relationship. His literary status confirmed by the best-selling biography, Lewes continued to devote himself to his writing (including a stint as editor of *The Fortnightly Review*). Through the years he also encouraged, guided and championed Eliot's fiction, which eventually made them wealthy. With time, their *de facto* marriage became increasingly accepted within London's literary community.

Elizabeth Hardwick, an admirer, once referred to him as being like someone from Dostoevsky, while in his day he had been described as 'the ugliest man' in London. Henry James, writing to his mother, once recounted a dinner where 'I sat next to Lewes, who is personally repulsive; (as Mrs. Kemble says "He looks as if he had been gnawed by the rats – & left;") but most clever & entertaining. He is rather too much the professional *raconteur* – he told lots of stories; but he recounts very well – chiefly in French.'

At the same time Lewes was valued for his intellect and goodness, as the Scottish academic David Masson reported: 'he is, indeed, a most kindly, genial, guileless person, & with versatility & accomplishment that make him a miracle. All who really know him, like him, & appreciate him highly.'

It is important to balance Lewes's youthful radicalism with his professionalism. As a writer he knew and addressed his audience with care. At one time he worked for George Smith, for *The Cornhill Magazine* and *The Pall Mall Gazette*. William Baker, editor of *The Letters of George Henry Lewes* (1995), cites one (ironic) instance of Lewes's circumspection in his role there: 'By April 1861, Lewes has become Smith's reader, commenting probably on a part of Anthony Trollope's *Framley Parsonage* as unsuitable, on moral grounds, for serialization in the *Cornhill*: "among the immense public of the C. M. there will infallibly be many family men and women who will seriously object to any love making whatever with a married woman."'

Lewes's obsession with Johann Wolfgang von Goethe (1749–1832) was perhaps inevitable given the correspondence of their interests. Germany's greatest writer had been born in Frankfurt and studied at Leipzig University. He briefly took up the law, while also writing essays and lyrical verse and plays. His drama *Goetz von Berlichingen* (1773), about a poet and adventurer, brought him national prominence. About this time he began early work on his great tragedy *Faust* (1806/1831) and his Shakespearean play *Egmont* (1788). In 1774 came *The Sorrows of Young Werther* (1774), an epistolary novel of love and suicide which caused a sensation. He journeyed to Weimar in 1775 at the invitation of Karl August. The duke became his intimate friend and Goethe held a number of positions in the government there over the years. Of a restless intellect, he also explored botany, anatomy and optics in the course of an increasingly honoured life.

Lewes's 1855 *Life of Goethe* was published to some acclaim (and a little German envy). It sold a thousand copies within three months, later reappearing in several editions in England and Europe. The book succeeds in combining biography and criticism with aspects of cultural history, its attention focused on the major works and as much detail as Lewes could manage on the incidents in the life set against the times. With such an impressive scope it admittedly requires some patience from the reader.

He is, however, clear about his task: 'It is not the biographer's province to write a history of an epoch while telling the story of a life; but some historical indication is necessary, in order that the time and place should be vividly before the reader's mind.' And so we have the overview: 'It was the middle of the eighteenth century: a period when the movement which had culminated in Luther was passing from religion to politics, and freedom of thought was translating itself into liberty of action. From theology the movement had communicated itself to philosophy, morals, and politics. The agitation was still mainly in the higher classes, but it was gradually descending to the lower. A period of deep unrest: big with events which would expand the conceptions of all men, and bewilder some of the wisest.' Periodically Lewes returns to contextualise his subject's progress ('The French

Revolution is as yet only gathering its forces together').

Writing of the 1770s in Germany, the author explains 'the spirit of the Revolution issued from the study and the lecture hall; it was a literary and philosophical insurrection, with Lessing, Klopstock, Kant, Herder, and Goethe for leaders. Authority was everywhere attacked, because everywhere it had shown itself feeble or tyrannous.' We may hear a personal disenchantment in the following: 'It was a sceptical epoch, in which everything established came into question. Marriage, of course, came badly off among a set of men who made the first commandment of genius to consist in loving your neighbour *and* your neighbour's wife.' Lewes goes on to summarize: 'The cause of the disease was want of faith. In religion, in philosophy, in politics, in morals, this eighteenth century was ostentatious of its disquiet and disbelief.'

The autobiographical air is another interesting dimension to the book, from the point of view of this essay. The analogies to Lewes's life and attitudes are sometimes implicit (as above) but nonetheless there, given the correspondence between both men's life experience, attitudes, mutual interests in dramaturgy and science (and in the writings of Spinoza, the Jewish Dutch philosopher of the Enlightenment). This is not to suggest that Lewes had chosen Goethe as a subject in order to voice his own views. Rather it is his sincere admiration for the poet as artist that explains his interest.

Perhaps the most immediately anticipated resemblance for his contemporaries was that between Lewes – with his open marriage and subsequent cohabiting with Eliot – and Goethe's notorious, if slightly less unconventional, romantic life and late marriage. In an essay of March 1843 Lewes argued that in Goethe's case 'ethics became subordinate in fact to aesthetics'. 'Here', according to Rosemary Ashton in *The German Idea* (1980), 'is the germ of the thesis which was to inform the *Life of Goethe*.'

And yet Lewes's approach is more tactful, in the interests of his audience. On the subject of the poet's marriage to the much younger Christiane Vulpius (after they already had children together) he offers: 'Better far had there been no connexion at all; but if it was to be, the nearer it approached a real marriage, and the farther it was removed from fugitive indulgence, the more moral and healthy it became. The fact of the *mésalliance* was not to be got over. Had he married her at first, this would always have existed. But many other and darker influences would have been averted. There would have been no such "skeleton in the closet of his life" as, unfortunately, we know to have existed.'

The temperature in the biography *is* allowed to rise in at least one instance, as Lewes deals with the liaison with the seemingly provocative Charlotte von Stein. Here the narrative switches tenses (Note the italics and yet the firm 'pedestal'): 'Hitherto he has been captivated only by very young girls, whose youth, beauty, and girlishness, were the charms to his wandering fancy; but now he is fascinated by a *woman*, a woman of rank and elegance, a woman of culture and experience, a woman who, instead of abandoning herself to the charm of his affection, knew how, without descending from her pedestal, to keep the flame alive.'

We are intended to know that Lewes has weighed such judgements, a number in defence of Goethe's treatment of women: 'Such, after mature deliberation, I believe to have been the real story', one concludes. Another is equally temperate: 'After this exposition of what I conceive to be the real case, it will be easy to answer the outcry of the sentimentalists against Goethe's "faithlessness" and his "cruel treatment of Fredrika"', for 'he was perfectly right to draw back from an engagement which he felt his love was not strong enough properly to fulfil'. Lewes is ever ready to speculate on such affairs: 'As far as I can divine the states of things in the absence of [Frau von Stein's] letters, I fancy she coquetted with him'; ''I am persuaded that if Lotte had been free, he would have fled from her as he had fled from Fredericka.'

One is tempted to read a reflection on Lewes's own marital situation into: 'The thoughtlessness of youth, and the headlong impetus of passion, frequently throw people into rash engagements; and in these cases the *formal* morality of the world, more careful of externals than of truth, declares it to be nobler for such rash engagements to be kept, even when the rashness is felt by the engaged, than that a man's honour should be stained by a withdrawal.'

He takes the opportunity to impart such wisdoms to the reader as he leads us through the poet's life. In doing this, the thirty-eight year old biographer assumes a maturity his subject lacked: 'He knew little, and that not until late in life, of the subtle interweaving of habit with affection, which makes life saturated with love, and love itself become dignified through the serious aims of life.' And with parenting, Lewes also stands on the side of common sense: 'whatever sympathy we may feel with the poet, yet, as we are all parents, or hope to be, let us not permit our sympathy to become injustice; let us admit that the old Rath had considerable cause for parental uneasiness'.

The two men come closer in their world views. Although Goethe is most associated with early German Romanticism and, more properly, with classicism, Lewes celebrates that aspect of his character and work most closely allied with his own belief in realism. 'What is Art but Representation?' he writes. His fervent commitment to realism in literature – as befits the partner of George Eliot, the primary exponent of the genre in his day – is announced when discussing *Werther*: 'While emphatically declaring that the artist must take his materials from reality, must employ his own experience, and draw the characters he has really known, we must as emphatically declare that he is bound to represent his experience in forms sufficiently different from the reality to prevent the public reading actual histories beneath his invention.'

This 'is commanded by morality', and *Werther* has disappointed, then, when revealed as a *roman à clef*. There is another proviso. Despite Lewes commitment to truth he is also, conventionally, opposed to licence: 'The artist is not justified in painting every truth; and if we in this nineteenth century often carry our exclusion of subjects to the point of prudery, that error is a virtue compared with the demoralizing licence exhibited in French literature.'

He defends Goethe in discussion of his *Elective Affinities*, a novel about sexual chemistry, by rejecting charges of immorality. Lewes naturally sides with those 'who look at life as it *is*, not as it might be; who accept its wondrous complexity of impulses, and demand that Art should represent reality'. He sees tragedy in this tale but not immorality, 'for the tragedy lies in the collision of Passion with Duty'. To him 'Goethe was an Artist, not an Advocate', who painted a 'true picture' of sexual relations.

Another cause for empathy between subject and biographer is their role as outsiders. Lewes had faced social disapproval after his German sojourn with Evans, as Goethe had on his return from Italy: 'Every one will understand this, who has lived for many months away from the circle of old habits and old acquaintances, feeling in the new world a larger existence more consonant with his nature and his aims; and has then returned once more to the old circle, to find it unchanged, – pursuing its own paths, moved by the old impulses, guided by the old lights, – so that he feels himself a *stranger*.'

And yet travel is the most certain of teachers. Lewes is experienced in its benefits: 'Foreign travel, even to unintelligent, uninquiring minds, is always of great influence, not merely by the presentation of new objects, but also, and mainly, by the withdrawal of the mind from all the intricate connexions of habit and familiarity which mask the real relations of life. This withdrawal is important, because it gives a new standing-point from which we can judge ourselves and others, and it shows how much that we have been wont to regard as essential is, in reality, little more than routine.'

That the two writers were passionate about the theatre is another attraction of the German poet for Lewes, though he is not without criticism of Goethe's view of 'literary' theatre and of Shakespeare, on whom the poet had worked. As a theatre critic and theorist, Lewes brings in his own views of what is required and what Goethe achieved. In discussing greatness in the drama, he singles out Shakespeare, above all, and Moliere as the two who can combine art with entertainment. Goethe and Schiller, he points out, fell into 'the error of supposing that a Drama could be more successful as Literature than as the reflection of national life'. Being pragmatic he writes, 'It is all very well for a poet or a philosopher to scorn the fleeting fashions of the day, and to rely on the verdict of posterity; but the Drama appeals to the public of the day, and while the manager keeps his eye on posterity, the theatre is empty.' He also faults Goethe's understanding of Shakespeare.

Biographer and poet shared an active enthusiasm for science. As well as being an amateur scientist (the noun was then a recent coinage), Lewes was always something of an ambassador for scientific inquiry: 'it is necessary for the development of science that science should cease to be the speculation of a few, and become the minister of the many; from the constant pressure of unsatisfied *wants*, science receives its energetic stimulus; and its highest reward is a satisfaction of those wants'. In the biography he deals sympathetically with Goethe's 'passionate study of science', excusing the poet's stubborn misconstruing of Newton's work with prisms and colour.

Errors aside, Lewes applauds Goethe merit as 'a *thinker in science*', though not possessing 'the merit of an industrious discoverer and collector of details'. 'Let it be distinctly understood,' he writes, 'and that not on the testimony of the admiring biographer, but on some of the highest scientific testimonies in Europe, that in the organic sciences Goethe holds an eminent place – eminent not because of his rank as a poet, but in spite of it.'

With Goethe, as with Lewes, the scientific community largely closed ranks against his experimentation: 'The veriest blockhead who had received a diploma considered himself entitled to sneer.' Lewes seems dispassionate, if cynical, in considering the matter:

'The mass of men, simply because they are a mass of men, receive with difficulty every new idea, unless it lies in the track of their own knowledge; and this opposition, which every new idea must vanquish, becomes tenfold greater when the idea is promulgated from a source not in itself authoritative.'

As a fellow artist and occasional author, Lewes also assumes an affinity with Goethe's thinking when treating the poet's reluctance to print his poems: 'If I may interpret according to my own experience, the explanation is, that his delight in composition was rather the pure delight of intellectual activity, than a delight in the result: delight, not in the *work*, but in the *working*.' He reveals an understanding of the effects of criticism on its recipients: 'Judging from a tolerably extensive acquaintance with authors in relation to criticism, I should think it highly probable that the longer Goethe pondered on Herder's letter the fainter became his pleasure in the praise, and the stronger his irritation at the blame.'

Above all though, Lewes's *Goethe* is intended to establish for British readers the greatness of 'a Poet, whose religion was Beauty, whose worship was of Nature, whose aim was Culture' and whose 'mission was to paint Life'. He argues that Goethe is *the* German phenomenon, a man who was in fact 'by nature... more Greek than German'. This is underlined by the fact he stands alone in German literary genius, since Germany is 'not rich in works written with the perfection which France and England demand'.

There are references to Goethe's charisma, estimates by friends, extracts from the work translated and analysed, all delivered in the confident hope that though 'Every public man is in some respects mythical... evidence so strong as these pages furnish may be held more worthy of credence than anything which gossip or ignorance, misconception or partisanship has put forth without proof'. 'Partisanship' has so muddied Goethe's reputation that Lewes's feels the need to be defensive. Partly this is the result of Goethe's prodigious output; perhaps more is the result of his behaviour. Lewes concedes that the very abundance of the poetry led to unevenness. To him, 'the weak pages are prose' and 'his immense activity was forced to expend itself on minor works, because he dimly felt himself unripe for greater works.'

The biographer's loyalty turns to rhetoric in his defence of the man: 'Pitiful and pathetic is the thought that such a man can, for so many years, both in his own country and in ours, have been reproached, nay even vituperated as cold and heartless! A certain reserve and stiffness of manner, a certain soberness of old age, a want of political enthusiasm, and some sentences wrenched from their true meaning, are the evidences whereon men build the strange hypothesis that he was an Olympian Jove sitting *above* Humanity, *seeing* life but not *feeling* it, his heart dead to all noble impulses, his career a calculated egotism.'

Lewes is not beyond special pleading. At one point, introducing an anecdote which illustrates the poet's generosity, he writes bathetically, 'But the tribute of affectionate applause is claimed now we have arrived at a passage in his life so *characteristic* of the delicacy, generosity, and nobility of his nature, that it is scarcely possible for any one not to love him, after reading it.' He petitions the reader for their favour when discussing Schiller's revision of his early opinion of Goethe: 'Let the reader who has been led to think harshly of Goethe, from one cause or another, take this into consideration, and ask himself whether he too, on better knowledge, might not alter his opinion.' He would also rescue Goethe's wife from the sharp tongue of posterity: 'as I have taken great pains to represent the young Goethe, so also have I tried to rescue the young Christiane from the falsifications of gossip, and the misrepresentations derived from judging her youth by her old age'.

Although grandly impressed with the best of the work (*Werther*, *Faust, Part One*, *Wilhelm Meister*, and so on) Lewes sees weakness elsewhere. He finds the master insensitive to the nature of political freedom, for example, though he defends Goethe when accused of living only in his art. He takes issue with *Dichtung und Wahreit* (*Poetry and Truth*, 1833) concluding, 'This is to write autobiography when one has outlived almost the memories of youth, and lost sympathy with many of its agitations.' Also, missing the charm of letters, *Italian Journey* 'is on the whole, a very disappointing book'; 'criticism makes sad work with' *Egmont* as a tragedy; Goethe's *Wanderjahre* has 'almost every fault a work can have.'

The second part of *Faust* is deemed wrong even in its conception: 'In the presence of this poem, I feel more embarrassment than with any other of Goethe's works.' Goethe has committed the cardinal sin in giving way to his growing impulse 'towards mysticism and over-reflectiveness'. Lewes offers a shrewd assessment of the old Goethe when he concludes, 'finding himself a prophet when he meant only to be a poet, he gradually fell into the snare, and tried to be a prophet now he could no longer be so great a poet as before'. To Lewes, 'The primary requisite of poetry is that it shall move us; not that it shall instruct us.'

As a critic Lewes is briskly confident of his opinions: 'Our own contemporary Literature seems so poor to us, not because there are no good books, but because there are so many bad.' He judges the Romantic School guilty of a 'brilliant error' since 'The desire to go deeper than Life itself led to a disdain of reality and the present. Hence the selection of the Middle Ages and the East as regions for the ideal; they were not present, and they were not classical.'

His *bête noire* is the 'philosophical critic'. In writing of *Wilhem Meister* he pours scorn upon the German tendency to pursue boundless possibilities in reading into a literary work ('Of all horrors to the German of this school there is no horror like that of the surface'): 'The critic is never easy until he has shifted his ground. He is not content with the work as it presents itself. He endeavours to get *behind* it, beneath it, into the depths of the soul which produced it. He is not satisfied with what the artist has *given*, he wants know what he *meant*. He guesses at the meaning; the more remote the meaning lies on the wandering tracks of thought, the better pleased is he with the discovery; and he sturdily rejects every simple explanation in favour of this exegetical Idea. Thus the phantom of Philosophy hovers mistily before Art, concealing Art from our eyes.'

As a biographer he offers personal involvement, which adds a little warmth to proceedings: 'Two letters, quite recently discovered, have fallen into my hands'; 'In the room which they show to strangers in his house in Frankfurt, there is also a specimen of his engraving – very amateurish; but Madam von Goethe showed me one in her possession which really has merit.' There are moments of personal loss as well: 'Of all his unrealized schemes [for a poem], this causes me the greatest regret.'

Lewes is for clarity and order. With one eye to his reader's stamina, he makes frequent references to his own shifts of focus in this comprehensive work. They also serves to underline his careful preparation: 'We now return to the narrative, some points of which have been anticipated in the preceding chapter'; 'The current of narrative in the preceding chapter has flowed onwards into years and events from which we must now return' ; 'if this chapter were not already too long, I should be glad to linger over many details, but must now content myself with the briefest indication of the general aspects of the poem'.

He translates the letters and poetry with modesty, telling us on the second page, 'it is unfair to the poet, and to the writer quoting the poet, to be forced to give translations which are after all felt *not* to represent the force and spirit of the original. I will do my best to give *approximative* translations, which the reader will be good enough to accept as such, rather than be left in the dark.' He does not translate the French passages on the assumption his countrymen will not have difficulty here.

Lewes's writing style is enviably clear. He favours taut lines ('He made it his study to subdue into harmonious unity the rebellious impulses which incessantly threatened the supremacy of reason' ; 'He was fond of dissipation, into which he carried an air of supreme gravity'). We also note the didactic tone of a man of the world: 'The fathers of poets are seldom gratified with the progress in education visible to them; and the reason is that they do not know their sons to be poets, nor understand that the poet's orbit is not the same as their own.'

While there is, then, something of the coolly authoritative about Lewes, his style can rise to the richly metaphorical, particularly early in the biography where facts are limited: 'experience even of the worst sides of human nature will be sublimated into noble uses, as carrion by the wise farmer is turned into excellent manure'; neglected authors are only visited 'by spiders of an inquiring mind'. Or more allusively, on the fragment that exists of *Prometheus*: 'It lies there among his works, like the torso of the Theseus, enough to prove the greatness of the artist, if not enough to satisfy the spectator.' The imaginative works well with a thumbnail sketch, such as that of the translator Major von Knebel: 'As one looks upon his rough, genial, Socratic head, one seems to hear the accents of an independent thoroughly honest nature give weight to what he says.'

Equally Lewes can be highly fanciful, addressing no doubt the tastes of his readers. At his subject's difficult birth we have the high drama, the *sturm und drang*, of 'an infant, black, and almost lifeless', revived by heavenly concession: 'But if the town was heedless, not so were the stars, as astrologer's will certify; the stars knew who was gasping for life beside his trembling mother, and in solemn convocation they prefigured his future greatness.' Then there is, 'In the groves of Sesenheim she was a wood-nymph; but in Strasburg salons the wood-nymph seemed a peasant.'

Emotion is inescapable in romantic terrain: 'He suffered greatly at this destruction of his romance: nightly was his pillow wet with tears; food became repugnant to him; life had no more an object.' We learn also that 'Long before celebrity had fixed all eyes upon him he was likened to an Apollo', not least because 'The brow was lofty and massive, and from beneath it shone large lustrous brown eyes of marvellous beauty, their pupils being of almost unexampled size.' And here he is *en route* to genius:

'Through hail, frost, and mud, lonely, yet companioned by great thoughts, he rode along the mountainous solitudes.'

There are moments of wit to relieve such twaddle. Lewes writes of 'a certain Herr Buff, on whom the reader is requested to fix his eye, not for any attractiveness of Herr Buff, intrinsically considered, but for the sake of his eldest daughter, Charlotte'. At another moment he writes of the company drinking toasts to someone's mistress, then smashing their glasses 'to prevent their being desecrated by other lips after so solemn a consecration (a process which looked less heroic when *item'd* in the bill next day)'. Or perhaps, 'But just as he was never known to lose his head with wine, so also did he never lose himself entirely to a woman: this stimulus never grew into intoxication.'

I share Rosemary Ashton's view of the *Life of Goethe*, that it is 'undogmatic yet scholarly, admiring of Goethe but stopping short of idolatry, honest but not unnecessarily shocking, [and] deserves the fame it achieved'. It is uneven, admittedly, though overall still recognizably a real achievement. At the time it pleased the demanding Thomas Carlyle, who had helped with the proofs and who called it 'well-formed, clear, free-flowing'. This was the highest praise for Lewes, whose interest in German literature had been kindled by the eminent Scot.

The book inevitably had its critics, too, beyond the carping German scholars irritated by the presumption of an Englishman's writing of their great man. There were those at home, like the *Edinburgh Review*, who contested Lewes's calmness in the face of Goethe's notorious womanizing. Fifty years ago Edgar W. Hirshberg, while admitting the book's continuing usefulness, argued that 'judged by modern standards it is in many respects ponderous and wordy, with much superfluous detail and sometimes too exhaustive criticisms of the works'. And David Williams, in *Mr George Eliot* (1983), while admiring the biography notes that 'The Victorians liked pomp and amplitude in their biographies of eminent persons and Lewes supplied these trimmings.' While conceding something to these views, I have to say that I could not find serious fault with the book.

Besides, the *Life of Goethe* is a well-tempered biography quite revealing of George Henry Lewes. And it brought to mind George Eliot's remark in *The Mill on The Floss* that 'It is only by a wide comparison of facts that the wisest full-grown man can distinguish well-rolled barrels from more supernal thunder.'

JAMES ANTHONY FROUDE: THE BIOGRAPHER AS ARDENT APOLOGIST

[This essay is based on a reading of the abridged and edited *Froude's Life of Carlyle* by John Clubbe, published in 1979.]

> 'Froude is easy to deplore. His imperialism, his chauvinism, his apparent racism, his unabashed religious bigotry, and his worship of strong men are all attributes so deeply distasteful to modern sensibilities'. Ciaran Brady *James Anthony Froude: An Intellectual Biography of a Victorian Prophet* (2014)

> 'Carlyle was an unbridled racist and imperialist who venerated the strong, recommended the planned emigration of 'surplus' workers, revealed a savage contempt for the common people and supported authoritarian rule.' Terry Eagleton *Critical Revolutionaries* (2022)

For reasons baldly stated in these epigraphs, the 'constitutionally atrabilious' historian and philosopher Thomas Carlyle saw his influence begin to wane even in his lifetime, while James Anthony Froude's rarely waxed uninterruptedly. Many Victorians, in thrall to the former, vilified the latter for the biographical portrait of his hero as a deeply flawed human being. The biography, though, is outstanding, and it reveals much about its author.

In a real sense Froude's is the biography of Carlyle's marriage to Jane Welsh, during which he proved so monumentally irascible as to effectively destroy their relationship. Rarely has someone so enamoured of his subject written such a painfully honest, psychologically acute portrait. For all its celebration of Carlyle's genius, it is an indictment of the man. The Carlyle that emerges is also hypochondriacal and arrogant, a driven man yet verbally intoxicating and capable of great generosity and humour. The book's small supporting cast includes Carlyle's mother – the closest in his affections and the furthest from his written accomplishments – and in the later stages the appearance of Froude himself.

Thomas Carlyle (1795–1881) was born in Ecclefechan, Dumfries, close to the English border. The precocious son of a stonemason, he attended Edinburgh University, avoiding first the vocation of Presbyterian minister his parents expected of him, then the law and teaching, both of which he sampled. An interest in German literature (Goethe, Schiller) led him to translation. In that same decade, the 1820s, Carlyle married Jane Welsh, an eminent doctor's daughter. The two lived for six years on a remote farm of the Welshes, Craigenputtock (Dumfriesshire) where the isolation enabled Carlyle to write *Signs of the Times* (1829) and *Sartor Resartus* (1833–4), the latter making his reputation.

Withdrawing to London where he felt uneasy at first, they purchased a house in Cheyne Walk, Chelsea, which was later much modified to block street noise. In 1837 Carlyle published his vigorous *The French Revolution: A History*, a great success. Slowly earning the status of a sage, he wrote on a variety of subjects, including works on *Chartism* and *On Heroes* and, in 1858–65, his biography of Frederick the Great. The sudden death of his wife effectively ended his writing career in 1866, a career that had become to seem reactionary. Matthew Arnold, for one, disliked Carlyle (a 'moral desperado') and also remained ambivalent toward Froude, whom he knew quite well. Nevertheless, Carlyle was dubbed the voice of the age at his eightieth birthday tribute.

James Anthony Froude (1818–1894) made his name as a historian and editor. Born in Devon, the son of the Archdeacon of Totness, he was raised in a difficult family environment. He first attended Westminster School and then Oriel college, Oxford, before being elected as a fellow of Exeter College in 1842. Froude had been a student at the time of the Oxford Movement (1830s), a proto-Catholic group which sought to resurrect ancient high church traditions, fearing the liberalisation of Anglican rituals, and which drove many Christians into religious doubt. Initially Froude had been much influenced by John Henry Newman, assisting in the latter's *Lives of the English Saints*, though the experience began to crystallise his doubts about the authenticity of biblical claims: 'The more I saw and the more I read, the more the individual figure of the great saints of Ireland dissolved into the mist… It was impossible to separate the truth from the wilderness of nonsense.'

Froude turned against Newman at the latter's move to embrace Catholicism. When his 1849 novel, *The Nemesis of Fate*, brought notoriety (which included his tutor's burning a copy in the college, incensed by its questioning of faith) it effectively led to his apostasy. He resigned his fellowship, which had involved ordination, married and turned to journalism in London. Between 1856 and 1870 he produced a twelve volume history of England, which helped to assure his reputation, as did his editing of *Fraser's Magazine* (1860–1874).

Froude then returned to Carlyle, another early influence, adopting some of his polemical force and views, including those on the superior individual's impact on his age and the virtue of power. These informed his various dramatic histories, (on Henry V111 and *The English in Ireland in the 18th Century*). He knew a great deal about Ireland from his time there, though his Protestantism gave him a negative perspective. Visits to South Africa, Australia and New Zealand resulted in books which mixed travel with his imperialist views. In 1892 he returned to Oxford to teach modern history.

Froude remained ever controversial as a man and a brilliant but erratic historian (There were accusations of bias and inaccuracies in his admittedly exhaustive use of sources). In Ciaran Brady's words: Froude 'was also a wilful, unpredictable, and offensive mind. Possessed of a troubled and trouble-making voice from the beginning of his career to its close, he seemed to have made a practice of deliberately provoking enemies and deliberately disappointing friends. At one time or another almost everyone in British public life had good reason to feel mortally offended by Froude.' To Brady, Froude the moralist has been obscured by the imperialist, which is why he has all but disappeared from view.

In his *Life of Carlyle* we learn that for twenty years, when the two were in London, they met two or three times a week. Froude's involvement in the biography began in June 1871 when Carlyle brought him his late wife's papers (eventually the damning *Reminiscences of Jane Welsh Carlyle*): 'He explained, when he saw me surprised, that it was an account of his wife's history, that it was incomplete, that he could himself form no opinion whether it ought to be published or not, that he could do no more to it, and must pass it over to me.' To Froude, 'this action of Carlyle's struck me as something so beautiful, so unexampled in the whole history of literature, that I could but admire it with all my heart… In his most heroic life there was nothing more heroic, more characteristic of him, more indicative at once of his humility and his intense truthfulness.'

At the time there was to be no biography, but the interest of others prompted Carlyle to seek out Froude's help again to write 'an authentic portrait' after his death; and therefore at the close of 1873 he delivered more papers, 'a collection overwhelming from its abundance'. His instruction was to tell the truth 'and if shadows there were, that least of all should I conceal them'. Froude, on his part, felt the need to write the biography of this 'prophet', for his own time and for posterity. In his preface he offers the idea tentatively: 'Carlyle, like [Isaiah and Jeremiah], believed that he had a special message to deliver to the present age… He has told us that our most cherished ideas of political liberty, with their kindred corollaries, are mere illusions, and that the progress which has seemed to go along with them is a progress towards anarchy and social dissolution. If he was wrong, he has misused his powers. The principles of his teaching are false.' Later in the volumes, however, he links Carlyle with the noun 'prophet' on at least four occasions.

Rosemary Ashton offers a modern perspective: 'During the

1840s and 1850s Carlyle continued his self-appointed task of warning his contemporaries of the dangers of political and economic *laissez-faire* on the one hand and social revolution on the other.' He believed in strong government, a feudal society in which men possessed the only important 'liberty' which was to work, and found, in Ashton's words, such duty extended even to the rebelling West Indian sugar workers who had "inherited" their duty as slaves. However uncompromising Carlyle's ideas, they were expressed in essays and histories that engaged a Victorian readership, for much of his early career at least.

In 1873 the great Russian novelist Ivan Turgenev astutely observed: 'It is a very easy thing to love despotism – at a distance. Some years ago I had the pleasure of visiting Carlyle. He also was loud in his denunciation of democracy, and was very unreserved in his expressions of sympathy with Russia and her Emperor.' Such views coupled with his admiration of 'heroes' (like Cromwell and Frederick the Great of Prussia) would later recommend him to C20th fascists.

Froude establishes in his preface that he shuns the allure of hagiography ('It would have been easy, without suppressing a single material point, to draw a picture of a faultless character.') This would have run counter to his own instincts and Carlyle's injunctions. There are grounds, he argues, for adopting the strictest approach: 'When a man has exercised a large influence on the minds of his contemporaries, the world requires to know whether his own actions have corresponded with his teaching, and whether his moral and personal character entitles him to confidence. This is not idle curiosity; it is a legitimate demand.' But Froude – given his narrowly partisan perspective – could not countenance his failure to convince his readers of Carlyle's entitlement.

Besides, he is imbued with the spirit of his teacher's instruction. He draws the reader's attention to Carlyle's defence of biographical integrity in a review of John Gibson Lockhart's *Life of Scott* (1837), where he dismissed the common herd of biographers: 'How delicate, decent is English biography, bless its mealy mouth! A Damocles' sword of *Respectability* hangs forever over the poor English Life-writer (as it does over poor English Life in general), and reduces him to the verge of paralysis.' He could not abide, he wrote, the 'vague ghost of a biography, white, stainless; without feature or substance; *vacuum*, as we say, and wind and shadow'. Part way into his biography, Froude quotes another of Carlyle's pithier judgments on the genre: '"The biographies of English men of letters," he says somewhere, "are the wretchedest chapters in our history, except the Newgate Calendar."'

This devotion of the biographer to his subject is consistent with Froude's view that he had been intellectually rescued by Carlyle as a young man: 'I, for one (if I may so far speak of myself) was saved by Carlyle's writings from Positivism, or Romanism, or Atheism, or any other of the creeds or no creeds which in those years were whirling us about in Oxford like leaves in an autumn storm.' From student days, he says, he has pledged his faith to his guide: 'Carlyle taught me a creed which I could then accept as really true; which I have held ever since, with increasing confidence, as the interpretation of my existence and the guide of my conduct, so far as I have been able to act up to it. Then and always I looked, and have looked, to him as my master. In a long personal intimacy of over thirty years, I learned to reverence the man as profoundly as I honoured the teacher.'

This notion of Carlyle as his 'master' is also repeated later in the biography. Not only does Froude see his own debt to Carlyle, he thinks of his readers' debt too, once freed from the 'Ark of the Church': 'Truth must stand henceforth by its own strength, and what is really incredible will cease to be believed. Very much of the change in this happy direction is due to Carlyle's influence; in this direction, and perhaps also in the other, for every serious man, of every shade of opinion, had to thank him for the loud trumpet notes which had awakened the age out of its sleep.'

It is a fact that Froude's biography assumes our agreement as to Carlyle's genius. Assertion repeatedly substitutes for evidence from the writings. The following comment on the man's humility and integrity gives some idea of Froude's approach: 'He was simply a man of high original genius and boundless acquirements, speaking out with truth. If we asked who he was, we heard that his character was like his teaching; that he was a peasant's son, brought up in poverty, and was now leading a pure, simple life in a small house in London, seeking no promotion for himself, and content with the wages of an artisan.'

If Froude had remained on this theme throughout the four volumes, Carlyle's many friends would have had nothing to cavil about. And yet the portrait is incomplete without its dark side. For all his virtues, the harsh reality we learn is that, 'Nature had made him weak, passionate, complaining, dyspeptic in body and sensitive in spirit, lonely, irritable, and morbid.' He could also be 'fierce and uncompromising. To those who saw but the outside of him he appeared scornful, imperious, and arrogant.' To intimates he could be an 'autocrat in his own circle' and 'made from nature sufficiently despotic'. In sum he is a case of arrested development: 'With all his splendid gifts, moral, intellectual, Carlyle was like a wayward child – a child in wilfulness, a child in the intensity of remorse.'

Froude is then both defence and prosecution in the case. One could be forgiven for wondering what is the text and what the subtext of his biography. The great man's faults are a wound that Froude never ceases to return to and which cumulatively undermine his optimistic belief that 'His faults do not blemish the essential greatness of his character, and when he is fully known he will not be loved or admired the less because he had infirmity like the rest of us.'

What makes that certain is the mental cruelty inflicted on the stoical, duty-bound Jane Welsh Carlyle. She is the fated heroine of Froude's book and the biographer appears half in love with her. She is introduced as having a 'slight, airy, and perfectly graceful' figure' and 'large black eyes shining with soft mockery' (the 'mockery' is repeated). 'She was called beautiful, and beautiful she was even to the end of her life, if a face be beautiful which to look at is to admire. But beauty was only the second thought which her appearance suggested; the first was intellectual vivacity.' Furthermore, 'She was a cultivated, proud, beautiful woman, who had ruled as queen in the society of a Scotch provincial town.'

After first turning down this stonemason's son, the socially superior Jane shared in a fateful decision. Froude is clear though whose fault it was: 'Men may sacrifice themselves, if they please, to imagined high duties and ambitions, but they have no right to marry wives and sacrifice them.' He is opaque regarding the implication that Carlyle had been impotent: 'His infirmities, mental and bodily, might make him an unfit companion for her or indeed for any woman.' To Jane, Carlyle would provide a 'brilliantly distinguished' husband, according to Froude, 'a compensation for the disappointment of her earlier hopes', which lay in a marriage to her most appealing suitor. The Scottish clergyman Edward Irving, who had befriended Carlyle, could not free himself from his engagement to another woman. (This may have been a disguised mercy in a way, since Irving, founder of the Catholic Apostolic Church and a mesmerizing preacher, won fame, then exhaustion and an early grave.)

Marriage dispelled Jane's lofty ambitions, bringing loneliness and weakening her health. Although both were of 'exceptional originality and genius' and 'two extraordinary persons', they began and remained incompatible. Of 'the six years' imprisonment on the Dumfriesshire moors', Froude writes, 'Miss Welsh had looked forward to being Carlyle's intellectual companion, to sharing his thoughts and helping him with his writings. She was not overrating her natural powers when she felt being equal to such a position and deserving it. The reality was not like the dream. Poor as they were, she had to work as a menial servant.' We may also note, as Froude does, that love her as Carlyle did, 'The strongest personal passion which he experienced through all his life was his affection for his mother.'

Carlyle's principal fault lay in the fact that he believed his wife, 'should do the work of a domestic servant as his own mother and sisters did; and he was never able to understand that a lady differently educated might herself... find a difficulty in accepting such a situation. He was in love, so far as he understood what love meant.' Certainly the future for which Jane Welsh sacrificed her happiness would be grim: 'his wife would see but little of him, and that little too often under trying conditions of temper'. Even early in their marriage, Froude writes, 'He observed nothing, as through his life he never did observe anything, about her which called away his attention from his work.'

The couple left Craigenputtock for London and then returned: 'She was without society, except on an occasional visit from a sister-in-law or a rare week or so with her mother at Templand. Carlyle... was unable to bear the presence of a second person when busy at his desk. He sat alone, walked alone, generally rode alone. It was necessary for him some time or other in the day to discharge in talk the volume of thought which oppressed him. But it was in vehement soliloquy, to which his wife listened with admiration perhaps, but admiration dulled by the constant repetition.' They had sacrificed their evenings with their 'brilliant little circle'. This Froude follows rather limply with, 'Carlyle observed these symptoms less than he ought to have done.'

A return to London helped but did not resolve the conflict. Jane was, in her own words, 'married past redemption!' To her friend, the novelist Geraldine Jewsbury, the problem was lovelessness: 'Bear in mind that her inmost life with solitary – no tenderness, no caresses, no loving words; nothing out of which one's heart can make the wine of life.... He suffered too; but he put it all into his work. She had only the desolation and barrenness of having all her love and her life laid waste. She did not falter from her purpose of helping and shielding him, but she became warped.'

Froude admits that Carlyle 'consulted her judgement about his writings, for he knew the value of it', but it was too little acknowledgement for her: 'From the first she saw little of him, and as time went on less and less; and she, too, was human and irritable.' Here he at last humanizes his abused heroine: 'Mrs. Carlyle was fiery and generous, but with a keen sarcastic understanding... [she], as well as her husband, was not an easy person to live with. She had a terrible habit of speaking out the exact truth, cut as clear as with a graving tool, on occasions, too, when without harm it might have been left unspoken.'

Jane's diary of her misery was begun in 1855. An entry for November 6 reads, 'Mended Mr C.'s dressing-gown. Much movement under the free sky is needful for me to keep my heart from throbbing up into my head and maddening it. They must be comfortable people who have the leisure to think about going to Heaven! My most constant and pressing anxiety is to keep out of Bedlam! That's all.'

When they were apart Carlyle could be tender and affectionate with Jane, not always with the desired result: 'His letters had failed to assure her of his affection, for she thought at times that they must be written for his biographer.' This was especially true when he fell under the spell of the aristocratic Lady Ashburton. According to Jewsbury 'to her there was a complicated aggravation which made it very hard to endure. Lady A. was admired for sayings and doings for which she was snubbed. She saw through Lady A.'s little ways and *grand-dame* manners, and knew what they were worth. She contrasted them with the daily, hourly endeavours she was making that *his* life should be as free from hindrances as possible.' The editors of Jane Welsh Carlyle's letters, Alan and Mary McQueen Simpson, concluded, 'He was having a love affair of a kind. It was a literary intimacy like his own courtship of Jane.' And it led her to wonder if Carlyle even loved her.

To Froude, Jane was more aware of such implications than her husband: 'Carlyle regarded the Ashburtons as "great people," to whom he was under obligations: who had been very good to him:

and of whose train he in a sense formed a part. Mrs Carlyle, with her proud, independent, Scotch republican spirit, imperfectly recognised these social distinctions.' Travelling with them, she told Carlyle she would 'be going merely as part of your luggage – without self responsibility'. There is no question that Froude sides with Jane – it is woven into all his remarks on their dysfunctional relationship – but he will not finally censure his subject. For both men, genius must have its way. After all, what of 'Carlyle's insistence on *Entsagen* (renunciation of personal happiness) as essential to noble action'.

During Jane's lifetime, Froude admits only to having been so blinded by Carlyle's presence and his 'stream of splendid monologue', that he misinterpreted Jane's mental state: 'Though I knew things were not altogether well, and her drawn, suffering face haunted me afterwards like a sort of ghost, I felt for myself that in him there could be nothing really wrong, and that he was as good as he was great.' Once, he recalls having provoked a 'bright assenting laugh' from Jane when he said, 'the true way to look at marriage was as a discipline of character'. At the time, the ironist missed the sarcasm. At all events Jane died in 1866 at the age of sixty-five, fifteen years before her husband, giving both men time to reflect on missed opportunities.

We are told repeatedly of Carlyle's remorse following Jane's death. It remains insufficient to redeem his character in the reader's eyes, though Froude offers it: 'For many years after she had left him, when we passed the spot in our walks where she was last seen alive, he would bare his grey head in the wind and rain – his features wrung with unavailing sorrow. Let all this be acknowledged.' He then implicates us in the wrongdoing: 'let those who know themselves to be without either these sins, or others as bad as these, freely cast stones at Carlyle'. As a defence, this is a heavy leaning on John 8:7. He returns to the charge later: 'there are many, perhaps the majority of us, who sin deeper every day in their lives in these very points in which Carlyle sinned'. Such guilt is hardly palliated by this.

Another defence of his hero's indefensible behaviour is the *sui generis* plea: 'Selfish he was, if it be selfishness to be ready to sacrifice every person dependent on him, as completely as he sacrificed himself to the aims to which he had resolved to devote his life and talents. But these objects were of so rare a nature, that the person capable of pursuing and attaining them must be judged by a standard of his own.'

Froude offers us Carlyle as victim of his own character, while most chilling of all is his following claim: 'Though the lives of the Carlyles were not happy, yet if we look at them from the beginning to the end they were grandly beautiful. Neither of them probably under other conditions would have risen to as high an excellence as in fact they each achieved; and the main question is not how happy men and women have been in this world, but what they have made of themselves.'

Such nonsense aside, Froude's style is admirably simple and effective, his narrative pace assured and involving. He is lightly ironic as a defence against earnestness ('Reticence about his personal suffering was at no time one of his virtues') and he enjoys deploying mythological and heroic allusions ('The days of the loaf – her first baking adventure, which she watched as Benvenuto Cellini watched his Perseus – were not yet'.) Jane Welsh Carlyle is the sacrificed Iphigenia and Carlyle (to editor John Clubbe) an unnamed Oedipus.

Periodically Froude states his views on biography. For instance he sees the need for generosity with lesser talents: 'With great men of the ordinary kind whose names and influence will not survive their own generation, to leave out the shadow, and record solely what is bright and attractive, is not only permissible, but is a right and honourable instinct.' With an enduring great like Carlyle he conceives of his role in dramatic terms, which is partly the reason his biographical portrait is ambiguous: 'The functions of a biographer are, like the functions of a Greek chorus, occasionally at the important moments to throw in some moral remarks which seem to fit the situation.'

Froude likes to dispense little wisdoms and ironies along the way, often generalising about humanity, though with a pointed application to Carlyle's circumstances: 'Men who are out of humour with themselves often see their own condition reflected in the world outside them, and everything seems amiss because it is not well with themselves'; 'Proud men never wholly forgive those to whom they feel themselves obliged.' And, with equal astuteness, 'The English are always restive when other nations are fighting, and fancy that they ought to have a voice in the settlement of every quarrel.'

He also writes with hard-won Christian certainty: 'The secret of a man's nature lies in his religion, in what he really believes about this world, and his own place in it.' Agnostics could never come 'to any greatness in this world', because 'God's law was everywhere: man's welfare depended on the faithful reading of it.'

It seems probable that Froude was aware that he had been set up to fail in offering this frank account of Carlyle's life, and if so there is something noble in his dangerous gesture. He may not have conceived the extent of the negative reception to his biography at first, but he certainly did by the time of the publication of the last two volumes. Prior to the biography, his publication of the *Reminiscences* (1881) brought controversy: accusations that he had blackened Carlyle's name and recriminations within the Carlyle family for misappropriating material. He persevered with the biography out of his sense of justice and at the urging of the brother and sister. That it did not satisfy all his critics is understandable, and is partly the result of Carlyle's and of Froude's own past arrogance.

In his life of Carlyle, *Moral Desperado* (1995), Simon Heffer argued that reviewing the biography *The Spectator* 'attacked what it called Carlyle's "prophetic misanthropy"' and 'The tone of criticism is very much one of a class – the educated, orthodoxly Christian middle class – that had had enough of having its morals and intellectual shortcomings pointed out by Carlyle and now reinforced by his disciples, and was determined (in the light of the new evidence of the sage's own failings) to get its own back.'

Alternatively *The Quarterly Review*, in a lengthy and laudatory review of 1885, began with its admiration for Froude (and his subject), declaring the work one of the finest of biographies. It chose to dwell on Froude's skill and on Carlyle the writer, rather than on the 'Scandalous Chronicle' of the marriage, while nevertheless noting that 'The effect of this rigid insistence on the "Veracities" is tremendous' and that damage had been done as far as 'the general mind' was concerned, perceptively predicting (or encouraging) the scandal: 'nor is it at all certain that his memory will ever wholly shake itself free from these sordid trappings'. Where they were wrong was in supposing Mr. Froude unhurt by the 'hard words that have been flying at the great mausoleum he had now completed to the memory of Carlyle'.

In truth Froude remained haunted by the reception of his Carlyle work. On a West Indies trip, he noted in his journal, 'Bad Carlyle fit on me. What my connection with Carlyle has cost me: my own prospects as a young man; later gave up *Fraser* [the periodical] because Carlyle wanted it for [William}Allingham, and my work on Charles V so as to be free to write Carlyle's biography; then the ten years of worry before the book was finished, and the worry for the rest of my life. Bye and bye the world will thank me, but not in my own lifetime. I ought to shake the whole subject off me, but it is not easy to do… I am surprised that the Carlyle business hangs heavy on me and spoils all.'

One thing Froude never forgot was his debt to the 'prophet'. In July 1874 he had written the following to Carlyle: 'To me, you & you only appeared to see your way in the labyrinth of modern confusion – You have made it possible for me still to believe in truth & righteousness and the spiritual significance of life while creeds & systems have been falling to pieces. – As more & more our inherited formulas are seen to be incredible, so more & more the English speaking world will turn to you for light… My own Self, whatever it be worth, was falling to wreck when I first came to know you. Since that time in whatever I have done or written

I have endeavoured to keep you before my eyes – and at each step I have asked myself whether it was such as you would approve.'

Despite Carlyle's unworthiness as a spiritual guide and his biographer's bigotry, Froude's great nineteenth century biography remains a startling and intense character portrait of two eminent men.

'SUCH A LIFE': ELIZABETH GASKELL & HER CHARLOTTE BRONTË

'Don't you like reading letters? I do, so much', wrote Elizabeth Gaskell to John Forster, later Dickens's biographer, in May 1854. Indeed the general Victorian enthusiasm for the *Life & Letters* format is proverbial and perfectly understandable. Letters offer an unprecedented intimacy, immediacy and atmosphere. The narrator propels the narrative forward by judicious editing, while readers witness the life's momentary dramas secure in the hands of someone who knows exactly how they will play out. In the case of biographies of literary figures, there is generally an extra bonus in that the letters are likely to be well written. All the while, the narrative arc is generally simple: anonymity, success, and then death.

Elizabeth Gaskell's biography of her late friend, Charlotte Brontë (1816–1855), a tale of a fated, courageous spirit, is a case in point. It is an excellent page-turner, laudatory but not quite hagiographic, novelistic but not fanciful. Its strength (almost at times a weakness) lies in the substantial use it makes of these letters. The biography is in fact so dependent upon Brontë's correspondence – given her unusually quiet and short life – that it is tantamount to being co-authored. Perhaps this is partly a consequence of the biographer's urgency in writing it. On June 16, 1855 Gaskell was asked by Patrick Brontë to write the *Life of Charlotte Brontë*; it duly appeared in March 1857.

Gaskell (1810–1865) and Brontë had admired each other's work before they met in Windermere through the kindness of the Kay-Shuttleworths. Charlotte Brontë had already published: *Jane Eyre* (1847) and *Shirley* (1849). *Villette* was to follow in 1853. Elizabeth Gaskell had published only *Mary Barton* (1848). Later they exchanged visits and corresponded. By the time Gaskell completed her biography, she had published *Cranford* (1853) *Ruth* (1853) and *North and South* (1855). She also had short stories, novellas (and poems) to her name and the comfort of wide social and literary circles that included Dickens, who promoted her prose in *Household Words*.

In a letter of August 1850 Gaskell described Brontë at the time of their first meeting as having 'gone through suffering enough to have taken out every spark of merriment, and shy & silent from the habit of extreme, intense solitude. Such a life as Miss B's I never heard of before. Lady K S described her home to me as in a village of a few grey stone houses perched up on the north side of a bleak moor – looking over sweeps of bleak moors.' Here is the moment when the biography was effectively written, a daguerreotype for Gaskell's unchanging portrait of her friend, an almost completely formed, suitably tragic and perfectly believable simplification. Brontë became a novelist's protagonist.

When, in April 1845, Gaskell learnt from the Haworth stationer that Brontë had died a week before, she felt she might have done more to save her friend's life. According to Jenny Uglow, in *Elizabeth Gaskell* (1993), 'This regret intensified her later determination: unable to save Charlotte in life, she would save her reputation in death.' She had the idea of a biography which would present Brontë the woman rather than as the successful novelist, an idea appropriate since Brontë's publishing life had a span of only six years of her thirty-nine.

Crucial to her initial enterprise was Gaskell's desire to draw this as a totally lifelike portrait of Brontë, a singular woman of singular talent. As she wrote to Ellen Nussey, Brontë's lifelong friend and a key source for the biography, 'I am sure the more fully she – Charlotte Brontë – the *friend*, the *daughter*, the *sister*, the *wife*, is known, and known where need be in her own words, the more highly will she be appreciated.'

Her entrance into her subject and her continuing reference point had to be Brontë's own words, not her thinly-veiled fiction. Fortunately she was given access to a substantial number of letters, which she recognised as a rich resource. Initially Gaskell had worried about writing a biography: the need to keep facts in view and the need for an appropriate style, which she felt ought to be elevated but for which she had, mercifully, her husband's assistance (one 'who has an admirable knowledge of language, and an almost fastidious taste as to style'). Of another thing she was certain: her biography would thrive on Brontë's letters because 'her language, where it can be used, is so powerful & living, that it would be a shame not to express everything that can be, in her own words'.

They had a further value. Gaskell saw in them confirmation of an unchanging character, when she found its key: 'In after-life, I was painfully impressed with the fact that Miss Brontë never dared to allow herself to look forward with hope; that she had no confidence in the future; and I thought, when I heard of the sorrowful years she had passed through, that it had been this pressure of grief which had crushed all buoyancy of expectation out of her. But it appears from the letters, that it must have been, so to speak constitutional; or, perhaps, the deep pang of losing her two elder sisters combined with a permanent state of bodily weakness in producing her hopelessness.' I am reminded of her sister Emily's 'Often rebuked, yet always back returning' and its last verse:

What have those lonely mountains worth revealing?
    More glory and more grief than I can tell:
The earth that wakes *one* human heart to feeling
    Can centre both the worlds of Heaven and Hell.

In contrast to the melancholic Brontës, Elizabeth Gaskell appears to have been a vivacious character. The editors of her letters, J.A. V. Chapple and Arthur Pollard, write of her vitality, her kindliness, her social success and her moral seriousness. Despite their differences of temperament, however, biographer and subject shared many ideas that might be considered proto-feminist today. At times when we read Brontë we sense Gaskell's approval. Thinking of Branwell's disastrous independence, for instance, Brontë writes, 'Girls are protected as if they were something very frail or silly indeed, while boys are turned loose on the world as if they, of all beings in existence, were the wisest and least liable to be led astray.' And a little later the biographer considers the different roles men and women must fulfil while being authors, recognising that a man can readily switch between roles, 'But no other can take up the quiet, regular duties of the daughter, the wife, or the mother, as well as she whom God has appointed to fill that particular place: a woman's principal work in life is hardly left to her own choice; nor can she drop the domestic charges devolving on her as an individual, for the exercise of the most splendid talents that were ever bestowed.'

We sense the two have the same view when we read, 'She especially disliked the lowering of the standard by which to judge a work of fiction, if it proceeded from a feminine pen; and praise mingled with pseudo-gallant allusions to her sex, mortified her far more than actual blame.' Hence the Brontë sisters use of pseudonyms (The American poet Elizabeth Bishop would still need to bristle at such treatment a century later.)

Gaskell and Brontë are again alike in their piety, though adherents to different denominations (the former Unitarian, the latter Anglican). Gaskell feared that her friend's husband had a low opinion of dissenters like herself. She writes of one of Brontë's letters, 'the wholesome sense of duty in it – the sense of the supremacy of that beauty which God, in placing us in families, has laid out for us, seems to deserve especial regard in these days'. Both writers had known bereavement and Gaskell would empathise with Brontë's comments on the loss of Emily and Anne, 'These things would be too much, if reason, unsupported by religion, were condemned to bear them alone.' And at another time, 'The strength, if strength we have, is certainly never in our own selves; it is given us.'

Gaskell's admiration of Brontë goes beyond their shared values as Christian women authors, of course. She defends her character, also. There is, for instance, the aloofness: 'The deep and exaggerated consciousness of her personal defects – the constitutional absence of hope, which made her slow to trust in human affection, and consequently slow to respond to any manifestation of it – made her manner shy and constrained to men and women, and even to children.' All the while aware of her disadvantages of temperament and circumstance, she venerates Brontë for her response to publishers' rejections: 'She had the heart of Robert Bruce within her, and failure upon failure daunted her no more than him.' Equally, Gaskell seeks to disarm her friend's critics: 'I do not deny for myself the existence of coarseness here and there in her works, otherwise so entirely noble. I only ask those who read them to consider her life, – which has been openly laid bare before them, – and to say how it could be otherwise.'

As the biographer-friend, she feels the need to address the matter of her subject's appearance. Privately she first described her as being 'very little & very plain. Her stunted person she ascribes to the scanty supply of food she had as a growing girl, when at that school of the Daughters of the Clergy.' To another she wrote of her as having 'a reddish face; large mouth & many teeth gone; altogether plain'. Even here Gaskell prefaced the remark with admiration of her new friend's commitment: 'Miss Brontë I like. Her faults are the faults of the very peculiar circumstances in which she has been placed; and she possesses a charming union of simplicity and power; and a strong feeling of responsibility for the Gift, which she [*sic*] has given her.' Gaskell celebrates her 'unusual power of attraction – though so plain in feature'.

The significance of the above becomes clear in the biography, for Gaskell creates a psychological portrait which involves reckoning with the self-image of the author of *Jane Eyre*. It would appear that Brontë's plainness, beyond depressing her spirits in Gaskell's opinion, robbed her of confidence as a woman. The biographer loyally summons the case against this plainness: 'Much of this nervous dread of encountering strangers I ascribed to the idea of her personal ugliness, which had been strongly impressed upon her imagination early in life, and which she exaggerated to herself in a remarkable manner. "I notice," said she, "that after a stranger has once looked at my face, he is careful not to let his eyes wander to that part of the room again!"' A more untrue idea never entered into anyone's head. Two gentlemen who saw her during this visit, without knowing at the time who she was, were singularly attracted by her appearance; and this feeling of attraction towards a pleasant countenance, sweet voice, and gentle timid manners, was so strong in one as to conquer a dislike he had previously entertained to her works.'

There are occasions when her depiction of Charlotte Brontë betrays a novelist's overzealousness (to contemporary taste at least): 'She bent her whole energy towards the fulfilment of the duties in hand; but her occupation was not sufficient food for her great forces of intellect, and they cried out perpetually, "Give, give," while the flat and comparatively stagnant air of Dewsbury Moor told upon her health and spirits more and more.' And again, 'The interests of the persons in her novels supplied the lack of interest in her own life; and Memory and Imagination found their appropriate work, and ceased to prey upon her vitals. But too frequently she could not write, could not see her people, nor hear them speak; a great mist of headache had blotted them out; they were non-existent to her.'

In creating Brontë as the victim of circumstances there is a danger of underplaying her ambition and disguising the more articulate and philosophical side of her nature, which became increasingly apparent to the outside world as the author was taken up by her publisher. Gaskell comes to this view late in the biography when she writes, 'There is one other letter, addressed to Mr [Sydney] Dobell, which developes [*sic*] the intellectual side of her character, before we lose all thought of the authoress in the timid and conscientious woman about to become a wife.' Gaskell also burnishes her social image: 'She never expressed an opinion without assigning a reason for it; she never put a question without a definite purpose; and yet people felt at their ease in talking with her. All conversation with her was genuine and stimulating… instead of rousing resentment, she merely convinced her hearers of her earnest zeal for the truth and right.'

Her frankness appealed to Gaskell; her fatalism moved her. In 1849 Brontë confessed, 'Sometimes when I wake in the morning, and know that Solitude, Remembrance, and Longing are to be almost my sole companions all day through… I have a heavy heart of it. But crushed I am not, yet.' She would not wish her circumstances on anyone. In an exchange of letters two years on, Brontë remarked, 'You charge me to write about myself. What can I say on that precious topic? My health is pretty good. My spirits are not always alike. Nothing happens to me. I hope and expect little in this world, and am thankful that I do not despond and suffer more.'

Another character in the biography is the village of Haworth, which plays its part in the defeat of the Brontës. It is an isolated, bleak and monochrome part of the West Riding, hard on its tough inhabitants. The *Life* begins with a description of Keighley and travels with the 'slight feeling of disappointment at the grey neutral tint of every object, near or far off' along the four miles that separates the town from Haworth, with its Parsonage and Church – and its gravestones'. The spirit of place and the Yorkshire folk with their Puritan traditions and myths are treated with pointed interest. The latter are described as self-willed, independent and not easily trusting: 'There is little display of any of the amenities of life among this wild, rough population. Their accost is curt; their accent and tone of speech blunt and harsh.' They are not entirely alien to Gaskell, for she likens the Yorkshire and the Lancashire people she lived among. They are given to the concealment of feelings beneath a bantering exterior.

Brontë had stimulated Gaskell's imagination on a visit two years before her death, as Gaskell recounted, besotted with imagery, in a letter to John Forster: 'The sinuous hills seemed to girdle the world like the great Norse serpent… On the Moors we met no one. – Here and there in the gloom of the distant hollows she pointed out a dark grey dwelling – with Scotch firs growing near them often, – & told me such wild tales of the ungovernable families, who lived or had lived therein, that Wuthering Heights even seemed tame comparatively. Such dare-devil people, – men especially, – & women so stony & cruel in some of their feelings & so passionately fond in others. They are a queer people up there.' She referred to life in the Parsonage with the wind 'piping & wailing and sobbing around the square unsheltered house in a very strange unearthly way'.

Gaskell conveys some of the atmosphere in her biography: 'if you walk to it from Birstall Station about meal-time, you encounter strings of mill-hands, blue with woollen dye, and cranching [crunching] in hungry haste over the cinder-paths bordering the high road'. And, in another instance, an explanation of why Mr Brontë carries a revolver summons up a vivid account of an earlier riot involving a vicar and a factory owner. There is also a Whiggish ring to some of her observations, which captures the mood of the times: 'We forget, now-a-days, so rapid have been the changes for the better, how cruel was the condition of numbers of labourers at the close of the great Peninsular war'; or 'He had been much abroad and spoke French well, of itself a suspicious circumstance to the bigoted nationality of those days.'

After Brontë and Haworth, the family–Patrick Brontë aside – pale in comparison. The three sisters together are presented two-dimensionally, as virtuous but shy in the extreme, as focused only on themselves or on the local community. Their fears over Branwell are disabling: 'They began to lose all hope in his future career. He was no longer the family pride; an indistinct dread was creeping over their minds that he might turn out their deep disgrace But, I believe, they shrank from any attempt to define their fears, and spoke of him to each other as little as possible.'

Almost equally disheartening was the need to take up employment, specifically as governesses. Gaskell concedes that that the upbringing of the motherless sisters had not prepared them to understand children. Brontë's early experience proved deadening. There is little wonder she could write, 'a private governess has no existence, is not considered as a living rational being, except as connected with the wearisome duties she has to fulfil'. Yet the fact that their 'definite acquirements were few' necessitated that both Charlotte and Emily seek further education in Brussels, which led to the abortive project of opening their own school.

Otherwise, their domestic routine in Haworth remained the height of comfortable monotony, a life of sewing, praying, suffering illnesses, walking the moors and running the old parsonage. To visit others, to holiday, seemed 'a dereliction of duty'. They were freed only at nine p.m. each evening, 'to pace up and down (like restless wild animals) in the parlour, talking over plans and projects, and thoughts of what was to be their future life'. Later they turned to discussing and reading from their works in progress.

All this drove their creativity, their desire to be acknowledged. Gaskell writes, 'It is well that the thoughtless critics, who spoke of the sad and gloomy views of life presented by the Brontës in their tales, should know how such words were wrung out of them by the living recollection of the long agony they suffered.' For all that, Gaskell's portraits of Emily and Anne, neither of whom she met, are superficial. She suggests that they 'were bound up in their lives and interests like twins. The former from reserve, the latter from timidity'. They 'avoided all friendships and intimacies beyond their sisters'. When she writes, 'Anne, like her eldest sister was shy; Emily was reserved' she prefaces the comment with the distinction that to be shy suggests a desire to please, whereas 'reserved' suggests an indifference.

For Brontë, Emily had been 'Stronger than a man, simpler than a child, her nature stood alone.' To Gaskell, the 'tall, long-armed' Emily is an enigma. She is presented as a child of the elements, a 'free, wild, untameable spirit, never happy nor well but on the sweeping moors that gathered round her home'. There is, in contrast, strikingly realistic detail in Brontë's response to meeting George Henry Lewes: 'the aspect of Lewes's face almost moves me to tears; it is so wonderfully like Emily, – her eyes, her features, the very nose, the somewhat prominent mouth, the forehead, – even, at moments, the expression.'

Gaskell admits at one point, 'all that I, a stranger, have been able to learn about her has not tended to give either me, or my readers, a pleasant impression of her. But we must remember how little we are acquainted with her, compared to that sister, who, out of her more intimate knowledge, says that she "was genuinely good, and truly great."'

Anne is rendered even more vaguely in Gaskell's biography, always 'docile, pensive' and 'always patient and tractable', one who 'would submit quietly to occasional oppression, even when she felt it keenly'. To Brontë, Anne possessed through her asthma and the fatal consumption, 'an extraordinary heroism of endurance'. The scene of her death, in Scarborough, is movingly drawn by Gaskell. The ill-fated, incorrigible Branwell is given his due as a talented, magnetic character ('full of noble impulses, as well as of extraordinary gifts'), but spoiled, self-indulgent, then conscience stricken by his affair with a married woman, which is said to have led to drink and drugs and his early death.

Patrick Brontë *was* known to Gaskell and yet remains oddly as enigmatic as Emily in the biography. Meeting him on a visit to Charlotte, she privately confessed, 'He was very polite & agreeable to me; paying rather elaborate old-fashioned compliments, but I was sadly afraid of him in my inmost soul; for I caught a glare of his stern eyes over his spectacles at Miss Brontë once or twice which made me know my man; and he talked *at* her sometimes.'

Gaskell was fascinated and appalled by the fact of Brontë's dining alone, though Charlotte was his last child alive. In the biography she describes him as, 'even in old age... a striking looking man, above the common height, with a nobly-shaped head, and erect carriage'. He is possessed of a 'strong, passionate,

Irish nature', 'in general, compressed down with resolute stoicism'. Yet he is also capable of violent outbursts against domestic possessions. He can be cold and remote and is said to carry that loaded pistol for defence of his boldly stated opinions, which can be 'wild and erroneous, his principles of action eccentric and strange, his views of life partial, and almost misanthropical'.

There follows another admission of the biographer's – that she has not explained the man: 'But I do not pretend to be able to harmonize points of character... I have named these instances of eccentricity in the father because I hold the knowledge of them to be necessary for a right understanding of the life of his daughter.' And yet Patrick Brontë, for all that, provided the spark and materials for the *Life*, had been proud and encouraging of his children, and ultimately judged Gaskell's biography as 'worthy of what one Great Woman, should have written of Another'.

Was his estimate of the biography correct? I think Gaskell felt she could to be perfectly honest within the parameters of the taste of the time, her sense of duty to the dead, and her imagination. To the novelist, her friend's life had been that of the dutiful, oppressed heroine of romantic fiction. Elizabeth Jay's introduction to the Penguin *Life* puts this bluntly: 'For all the evidence, written and oral, that Gaskell had, so impressively and so swiftly, assembled, her Charlotte was an imaginative creation and, as such, took on a life of its own.' As a veteran novelist, Gaskell deployed such devices as character simplification (the suppression of discordant traits); the shifting of the timing of events; and the accentuation of the isolation, relative poverty and oddity of her heroine's background.

For Jenny Uglow Gaskell had a greater agenda: 'The concentration on private life, relationships and character rather than on public achievement would make Gaskell's book both convention-ally yet subversively "feminine", a contrast to the current model lives (by male authors) of successful men.' This view has the support of Hilary Fraser, in *English Prose of the*

Nineteenth Century (1996), who reminds us that, 'the epigraph from Elizabeth Barrett Browning's *Aurora Leigh* signals the emphasis she is to take' ['How dreary 'tis for women to sit still / On winter nights by solitary fires / And hear the nations praising them far off]. 'Gaskell's heartfelt portrait of Charlotte Brontë stresses precisely the disjunction between the public figure of the acclaimed author and the private suffering woman which Barrett Browning represents as the condition of the female writer in the nineteenth century.'

I am not entirely convinced, however, by this feminist angle, which seems a little ambitious. Gaskell, for example, is at times at pains to celebrate her heroine's modesty and timidity as becoming. I do not share Fraser's view that 'Gaskell's careful inclusion of Charlotte's hesitant and apologetic correspondence with various famous literary men is also designed to emphasise the gendering of professional literary work in the period.' In reality, I think, the character portrait emerged partly through its author's inexperience ('Oh! If once I have finished this biography, catch me writing another!'), partly through protectiveness of her subject, and partly though compromise.

The biography lends itself to other, negative interpretations that would have wounded Gaskell. In *Victorian Poetry, Drama, and Miscellaneous Prose 1832–1890* (1989) Paul Turner wrote, 'Setting out to "show what a noble, true, and tender woman Charlotte Brontë really was"... Mrs Gaskell tried to do so, not by idealizing her friend's character, but by using the rest of her family as foils. Thus her father's violence, her brother's depravity, and her sister Emily's ruthlessness (as when she punched her dog's "red fierce eyes" until it was half-blind) serve to make Charlotte relatively appealing. Some of the best stories about these foils turn out to have been apocryphal; but they added to the pleasure of reading the book, and the resultant portrait of Charlotte seemed entirely realistic, especially against the almost surreal savagery of her background.'

And Juliet Barker, in *The Brontës* (1994), focuses on what she sees as the glaring omission in Gaskell's biography of certain of Charlotte's character traits and shortcomings: 'The portrayal of Charlotte as the martyred heroine of a tragic life, driven by duty and stoically enduring her fate, served its purpose at the time. Charlotte's wicked sense of humour, her sarcasm, her childhood *joi de vivre* which enlivens the juvenilia, are completely ignored. So, too, are her prejudices, her unpleasant habit of always seeing the worst in people, her bossiness against which her sisters rebelled, her flirtations with William Weightman and George Smith and her traumatic love for Monsieur Heger. What remains may be a more perfect human being, but it was not Charlotte Brontë.'

With respect to Brontë's 'flirtations': Weightman, her father's curate, had been admired for his good looks and easy kindness. There exist a number of letters to Constantin Héger, principal of the boarding school in Brussels, which Gaskell had read and suppressed, since Brontë had been recently wed. She wrote anxiously to her publisher George Smith in August 1856, 'I can not tell you how I should deprecate anything leading to the publication of those letters [to M. Héger].' They appeared in print in 1913.

As to the reference to George Smith, neither party confirmed 'flirtation'. Charlotte Brontë wrote in an 1850 letter, 'We both know the wide breach time has made between us; we do not embarrass each other, or very rarely, my 6 or 8 years of seniority, to say nothing of lack of all pretension to beauty, etc., are a perfect safeguard.' Smith told Mrs Humphry Ward in 1898, 'I never could have loved any woman who had not some charm or grace of person, and Charlotte Brontë had none. I liked her and was interested by her, and I admired her... I never was coxcomb enough to suppose that she was in love with me.'

In Barker's opinion, then, Gaskell was at fault in her partisan portrait of Charlotte. She also goes on to criticise the portrayal of the other Brontës: the obsessive Emily; Anne of the unconventional views (a 'cypher' here); Branwell, all but invisible;

and their father 'who took such tender care for his young children, campaigned incessantly on behalf of the poor of his parish and espoused unfashionable liberal causes'. He 'is unrecognizable in her malicious caricature of a selfish and eccentric recluse'.

So the biography divides readers. Where there is no disagreement is in the chief handicap Gaskell faced in writing the biography: how to present characters still living. The principals – aside from Patrick Brontë and his daughter's husband, Arthur Bell Nicholls – had died but others, some of whose influence on her subject's life may be said to have been pernicious, still lived. In the first edition of the biography, when she comes to Brontë's time as a governess, Gaskell has to circumvent this as best she can: 'I intend carefully to abstain from introducing the names of any living people, respecting whom I may have to tell unpleasant truths, or to quote severe remarks from Miss Brontë's letters; but it is necessary that the difficulties she had to encounter in her various phases of life, should be fairly and frankly made known, before the force "of what was resisted" can be at all understood.'

Gaskell's aim, however worthy, proved insufficient to protect the book from censure. The Penguin Classics *Life* reproduces the first edition, of March 1857, where the biographer felt she could express her opinions on her heroine's treatment most frankly. Subsequent editions had to excise her accusations of criminal neglect and sadism *in lieu* of the threat of legal action. Shaming had not been an act of recklessness on Gaskell's part, in fact, since as Jay's scrupulously prepared edition of the *Life* notes, 'she had asked her publisher [George] Smith in October 1856, "Do you mind the law of libel?" for she had three people she wished to "gibbet", Lady Scott, Mr Newby and Lady Eastlake'. Lady Scott she intended to libel, since she was 'that bad woman who corrupted Branwell Brontë, encouraging his infatuation and then deserting him to protect her inheritance'.

She had written in the biography of this 'wretched woman, who not only survives, but passes about in the gay circles of

London society, as a vivacious, well-dressed, flourishing widow'. She hoped that with the book 'there may be awakened in her some feelings of repentance'. Several pages later she returns to the fact that 'she goes flaunting about to this day in respectable society; a showy woman for her age; kept afloat by her reputed wealth'.

It was not only the case that individuals were targeted in themselves or portrayed in ways they might have felt unjustified, but also that guilt could be surmised, with a little help from the biography in tandem with Brontë's fiction. There was the association of fictional places and characters with their real-life originals. So, for example, the school at Lowood in *Jane Eyre* could be identified as the Cowan's Bridge School, run by William Carus Wilson, which had been responsible for the health hazard that had killed the older Brontë sisters.

Future editions of the biography would temper the criticisms. Gaskell negotiated these problems at some artistic and emotional cost. She had intended to be away from England when the reviews arrived, since she dreaded, as always, 'supercilious, or personal ones, or impertinently flattering ones'. According to J.A.V. Chapple (1980) in *Elizabeth Gaskell: A Portrait in Letters*, 'The life was published in March 1857 whilst she was away with Marianne and Meta on holiday in Italy. It raised a storm of protest. Her husband, himself enmeshed in complicated problems of his own as Chairman of Trustees for Manchester New College at a critical time in its history, was forced by threats of legal action to issue a public retraction and apology on her behalf through William Shaen, their friend and solicitor. She came back on 28 May into this "Hornet's nest". She had felt it her "duty" to tell "painful truths"; now she was being asked to take out passages and prepare a revised edition.'

Gaskell confided the extent of her injury to Ellen Nussey on 16 June, 1857: 'I am writing as if I were in famous spirits, and I think I *am* so *angry* that I am almost merry in my bitterness, if you know that state of feeling; but I have cried more since I came home than I ever did in the same space of time before; and never needed kind words so much, – & no one gives me them. *I did so try to tell the truth*, & I believe *now* I hit as near the truth as any one *could* do. And I weighed every line with all my whole power & heart, so that every line should go to its great purpose of making *her* known & valued, as one who had gone through such a terrible life with a brave & faithful heart.'

There were compensations for Elizabeth Gaskell's honest endeavours and time brought them: satisfied readers, admiring critics and financial rewards. George Smith paid her £800 for the *Life* and in March 1858 she wrote to him again to thank him for an extra £200. She goes on to say, 'This last, 3rd edition, – if it has been read at all by those who cared to correct mistakes, – has only elicited expressions of approval; even Mr Carus Wilson has written to approve. I have had curious proofs of the great interest felt in her, – a letter from a young Russian lady…; odd Australiasian [*sic*] islands, – Americans by the dozen, all full of her.'

Other, more professional, biographies have followed since Gaskell's *Life*, biographies of each of the Brontës and of Gaskell herself. Some redress imbalances – Jay's and Barker's reservations are telling – but none is more pleasurable to read and none more evocative of a time and place – and a character.

III: The Age of Terror

EDMUND WILSON'S *PATRIOTIC GORE*

Writing of an impromptu buffet supper with the Kazins in May 1962, Edmund Wilson noted in his diary: 'I took Alfred back to a couch and talked to him about his review of *Patriotic Gore*. He showed a certain indignation over my Introduction: 'I and my people "had it made" and didn't sympathize with the Negroes [*sic*] and people like him, the son of immigrants, who had found in the United States freedom and opportunity. He is still full of a romantic faith in American ideals and promises, and it is hard for him to see what we are really doing.' Though Kazin loved the rest of the book, calling it 'the most profound considerations on literature in this country that I have ever seen', Wilson remained unrepentant about his introductory essay. A patriot, he was nevertheless at war with the America of its day and of a century before.

Patriotic Gore: Studies in the Literature of the American Civil War (1962) was Wilson's great, partially sighted contribution to American literary history and biographical criticism. 'The period of the American Civil War was not one in which belles lettres flourished,' he wrote, 'but it did produce a remarkable literature which mostly consists of speeches and pamphlets, private letters and diaries, personal memoirs and journalistic reports.' His book explores a sample of these, with a cast of some thirty men and women. He opens with the novelist Harriet Beecher Stowe and ends with his hero, Supreme Court Justice Oliver Wendell Holmes Jr, contributing something to the American myths he examines and explodes along the way. Lost in the atmosphere of individual cases, the reader is likely to forget Wilson's passionate rejection of American power in his introduction.

Yet that introduction – not the omission of black American voices – was the sticking point for some on the book's appearance, since it was thought to undermine the heroism, defiance and patriotism he goes on to celebrate. Propelled by moral indignation despite its loftier assertion to the contrary, it offers an anti-war tract against the predatory role of nations, taking curious symbolism from a Disney film of greater sea slugs ingurgitating smaller ones. Wilson writes of explaining 'the general point of view which gives shape to my picture of the past'.

This involves discarding the 'pretension to moral superiority', to the deceitful rhetoric of such euphemisms as 'democracy', 'liberty' and 'destiny' when used to cloak American imperialism – what Ellen Glasgow called in *The Sheltered Life* (1932) 'empty' words. In the book Wilson is also sketching a history of America's aggression against its own peoples in that other 'country' of the South.

Although he makes supportive comments on the rights of Native Americans and African Americans in *Patriotic Gore*, he fails to capitalize on the written records of the latter's experience (David. W. Blight – an authority on African-American studies – – was among those to articulate this in his qualified admiration for *Patriotic Gore* in a 2012 *Slate* article.) The reason, I suspect, is that Wilson's first intention is to highlight the aggression of the bigger sea slug: the Federal government ('There is in most of us an unreconstructed Southerner who will not accept domination.') The moral blight of the Southern institution of slavery nevertheless comes into focus immediately the book begins.

The letters Wilson wrote on the issue in *Letters on Literature and Politics 1912–1972*, edited by his wife, Elena, offer interesting glimpses of the long evolution of the book and its changing purpose. At one time it was to be an exploration of nineteenth century American literature, a more critical version of the work he admired by Van Wyck Brooks: 'We have set our values straight about the Hawthorne-Emerson-Melville generation but are still quite in the dark as to what is first-rate and what is second-rate after that' (April 1947). Shortly after he wrote of showing interest in 'the effect of the war on the writers who had fought in it and survived it'. He was sure that most fiction about the war paled in comparison to the letters, diaries and memoirs.

In April 1961 he wrote of wanting 'to show the whole career of all my major subjects, how they lived, what they thought about, and what their personalities were'.

And so *Patriotic Gore*, after its inflammatory introduction, turns into a different book; and then turns again because its author, when addressing the effect of war on his subjects, fell to admiring them. As Robert Penn Warren astutely noted at the time, 'What touches Wilson's heart most deeply is some courageous manifestation of the old virtues.' Warren cites the portraits of Holmes, Robert E. Lee, U.S. Grant, Alexander Stephens and General Sherman. He might have extended this to almost every character we meet for all have, if not eminence or virtue, some dogged saving grace that Wilson is moved to admire, if it only the courage to be wrong-headed. We find ourselves immediately immersed in their stories.

Another chief pleasure of *Patriotic Gore* is Wilson's willingness to let characters speak at length in their own words. He quotes substantially from novels and letters – in fact at times he approximates the anthologist. Occasionally the curtain lifts a little to suggest the research that has gone into the book: 'If one examines the files for the eighties and nineties of the Century Magazine, one sees very clearly the falling-off... in the quality.' When he rescues scenes from novels which are 'hard to get hold of nowadays and unlikely to be read in the future by anyone except literary historians', you see he has been there.

There is no pedantry here. Wilson's genuine enthusiasm licenses moments of humour and mythmaking. He dryly remarks of Francis Grierson's work in California: 'it shows signs of that exalted lightheadedness which is likely to seize prophets in that part of the world'. Of Harriet Beecher Stowe he writes, 'If there is something to be said for the author's claim that *Uncle Tom's Cabin* was written by God, it is evident that the nine novels which followed it were produced without divine intervention.' And with a wild simile: 'The experience of reading them seems to become more and more like grasping an unwieldy bath sponge; you squeeze out a gallon of words and then find that you have in your hands the diminished but resistant residuum of a dry and fibrous substance, which the author will re-dip for another novel.'

Carl Sandburg's biography of Lincoln is a popular butt. When he quotes that biographer's fanciful imaginings about the young Lincoln in his mother's arms ('A trembling took his body and dark waves ran through him sometimes when she spoke so simple a thing as, "The corn is getting high, isn't it?"') Wilson punctures the image with, 'The corn is getting high, indeed!' As far as embellishing myths is concerned, he completes his realistic portrait of Lincoln with noting a dramatically apposite martyrdom, the equal of popular tradition. Similarly, in his brief portrait of Sherman's family, he wonders if the general's wife's zealous Catholicism and her Jesuit son's calling were not expiation for his ruthless march through Georgia during the war.

The first part of *Patriotic Gore* deals with the decline of much New England theology as a consequence of its rigour and exclusiveness. Wilson writes of 'the tyranny of the Calvinist tradition' and its denial of empathy, hence the mediocrity of much early nineteenth century fiction. He observes its ambivalence in the face of slavery and a distracting tendency to mysticism, confronted in the work and thought of Stowe, her husband Calvin Stowe, Francis Grierson and Julia Ward Howe. He discusses the religious fervour that galvanised much public opinion and the 'apocalyptic aspect' it took on for many patriots. He gives consideration to Howe's 'The Battle Hymn of the Republic', a work like Stowe's which the writer felt to be something of a conduit for supernatural forces.

Wilson's Stowe was aware that slavery could not be squared either with the founding principles of freedom or equally with Christian teaching. Wilson judges *Uncle Tom's Cabin* positively as prose narrative: We become 'aware that a critical mind is at work, which has the complex situation in a very firm grip'. David M. Potter offered the contrary, more conventional view in *The Impending Crisis, 1848–1861* (1976): 'It may plausibly be argued that Mrs. Stowe's characters were impossible and her Negroes [sic] were blackface stereotypes, that her plot was sentimental, her dialect absurd, her literary technique crude, and her overall picture of the conditions of slavery distorted. But without any of the vituperation in which the abolitionists were so fluent, and with a sincere though unappreciated effort to avoid blaming the South, she made vivid the plight of the slave as a human being held in bondage.'

Her narrative, Wilson reminds us, had such a life – –immense sales and influence, immortalized characters, epigones and a famously crude melodramatic version – that its post-war eclipse might have been occasioned by its own distorted success. He concedes, however, that her later fiction is given to Dickensian deathbed scenes, stock characters and melodramatic attention to social problems. Finally, despite her intelligence and observational skill, her tone was too much that of the minister's wife to hold posterity's attention.

Wilson finds the long-suffering Calvin Stowe 'an odd Yankee character who, in spite of his hypochondria, inspires respect and sympathy'. A scholar friendly to Judaism, pragmatic and yet idealistic, he is yet a man tortured by lifelong visions that stemmed from the terrors of dwelling on Original Sin. He is representative even in that, according to Wilson: 'There were many such household devils and supernatural visitants – a heritage, as in Stowe's case, from the old theology – still alive in the practical North on the eve of the Civil War' (And *after* the war he might have added– – see Drew Gilpin Faust's unnerving *This Republic of Suffering*, 2008). Hallucinations lead to spiritualism. Enter the enigmatic composer and spiritualist Francis Grierson, whose real interest to Wilson is in his recollections, *The Valley of Shadows*, which perfectly captured Middle West life on the eve of the Civil War. It is here that Wilson seems to believe the real 'medium' in Grierson is to be found, as the reader comes to feel 'that a great moment of history has lived itself through him'.

Lincoln, the most mythologized American, is Wilson's next

subject. He produces a subtle, conflicted portrait, which cuts away levels of hagiography. In the introduction Lincoln is compared to Lenin and Bismarck, a 'dictator' and 'repressive' in his measures. Here he is admirable in many ways. The often maligned biography of Lincoln by his law partner, William Herndon, is an approved source for Wilson. Using Herndon, he establishes that the sceptical Lincoln's only gods were evolution and the law, yet that he had a strong sense of a calling. He traces through speeches and writings Lincoln's increasing adoption of Christian terminology ('terms that would not be repugnant to the descendants of the New England Puritans and to the evangelism characteristic of his time') and ultimately – amid the enduring tragedy of war – his conception of his mission in Christian terms.

Having established this, Wilson examines the great President's character through his writings: 'This is a Lincoln intent, self-controlled, strong in intellect, tenacious of purpose.' He fleshes out a portrait with, 'from those who knew Lincoln best, we learn that he was naturally considerate, but essentially cold and aloof' outside the immediate family, seriously unconventional socially and bearing a superiority in manner. These qualities are supported by sources. He does not overlook Lincoln's ambition, but omits that wonderful comment in Herndon's politically incorrect but wonderfully frank biography, 'His ambition was a little engine that knew no rest.'

Finally and with real insight, he points out that Lincoln shaped his own legend in publicly expressing his conception of the direction and meaning of the Civil War and his role in it ('We have, in general, accepted the epic that Lincoln directed and lived and wrote.') Elsewhere – in an essay on James Branch Cabell – he describes Lincoln as 'a superior man who has been vulgarized rather than exalted by the popular myth about him' (In a 1958 essay, 'The Old Stone House', he even struck an emotional note – thinking perhaps of his own father, a lawyer greatly influenced by Lincoln's example – when he wrote, his 'miseries burden his grandeur' and agonizingly, 'I can hardly bear the thought of

Lincoln.') I have to say I am not as admiring of Wilson's conclusion, regarding the dramatic inevitability of his sacrifice, though it neatly returns us to the subject of mysticism.

In a two-part essay, 'General Grant', Matthew Arnold wrote appreciatively of *Personal Memoirs* for its author's 'high merit of saying clearly in the fewest possible words what had to be said, and saying it, frequently, with shrewd and unexpected turns of expression'. Wilson seconds this, acknowledging Grant's habitual understatement. His portrait is as concerned to bring out the fine qualities of the man as it is to study the undeniable literary quality of his writing. He begins with Twayne's assistance in the publishing of the memoirs, so that the dying and bankrupt Grant could make an excellent financial return from his agonizing labours to help his family.

He traces Grant's humble beginnings, through a period of 'moral collapse' after the Mexican War (of which Grant disapproved), his period of drunkenness and then intense involvement when the Civil War came. Wilson is fascinated by Grant's widely reported 'poise and detachment' when in the field, coupled with a tendency to revert to alcohol at times. His performance as President is inevitably contrasted with his brilliance as a commander and here Wilson offers comments by Charles Francis Adams, who served with Grant, and his brother, the historian Henry, who reacted negatively to the hapless if honest politician, a complete failure as a two-time President, a favourite gull of business interests. Wilson paints a moving picture of the courage shown by the 'humiliated, bankrupt and voiceless' former President working through his last days. Grant died a week after completing his *Personal Memoirs*.

Whereas Grant is tact itself in his prose – his problems kept invisible – General Sherman is frank, equally if differently stylish, and better educated. William Tecumseh Sherman assumed that his *Memoirs* would prove interesting to veterans devoted to '"the cause" which moved a nation to vindicate its own authority'. 'Authority' and 'progress' were his watchwords (the latter included 'substituting for the useless Indians the intelligent owners of productive farms and cattle ranches'). Wilson's Sherman, though a ruthless Northerner, is redeemable, even heroic and likeable (albeit with a faint whiff of possible insanity). An amateur painter given to quoting Shakespeare and reading Dickens, he had lived a colourful life in ante-bellum America, being raised in a senator's household.

We accompany Wilson and Sherman on his infamous campaign in spring 1864. Once a demoralized man, he is seen here exalted by leadership. 'We cannot help sharing his excitement, we cannot help being swept along' writes Wilson. In fulfilling his desire 'to make Georgia howl' Sherman is living his belief in the cruelty and the beauty of war, his actions bearing unmistakeable comparison to the total war ethos of the Nazis. This contradictory figure, we learn, is fighting neither for the end of slavery nor the protection of democracy (being in his own words 'almost a monarchist') but simply for maintaining the status quo: 'Unionism'. He can even be gallant and yet in a long fascinating exchange of justifications quoted here with his opponent General Hood, we learn that Sherman indulged in intimidation, 'anticipating the *Schrecklichkeit* [terror] exploited by the Germans' in two wars.

Post-war, Wilson finds Sherman avoiding the political messes of Washington, being 'much shrewder than Grant in a worldly way and self-willed to the point of truculence'. Yet the nationally famous and socially desirable Sherman was not to catch up on the life he had missed with his family. Though they had a number of children, the Shermans often remained apart, and he found his wife's Catholicism at times obstructive (Wilson reports him defending his decision not to be nominated as Republican presidential candidate by citing a fear his wife might fill the White House with priests). The loss of their eldest son and the desertion of another to the Jesuit order apparently hit him hard and the last part of this chapter deals with the fascinating story of that son, Tom, who led something of a scandalous life, before dying insane.

There follow two chapters concerning Northerners in the South: Frederick L. Olmsted, John T. Trowbridge, Charlotte Forten (the only African-American studied in the book) and Colonel Thomas Wentworth Higginson. The first two offer interesting views of the South, 'ante' and 'post' bellum (A most spirited guide to those states during Secession is William Howard Russell's *My Diary North and South*). Olmsted, landscape architect and much more, influenced many with his negative appraisal of Southern society in *The Cotton Kingdom* (1861). He described its antagonistic, resentful classes, its unruly slaves and hardly viable plantations, its lack of incentive and culture: a general seediness. The travels of Trowbridge in 1864 and 1865 confirm Olmsted's judgements, tinted with religious conviction. Wilson is very good in widening out that zealotry with numerous examples in recognition of a 'deeply theocratic' age.

The highly intelligent Charlotte Forten, 'who modestly wrote a little and sometimes appeared in print' was the daughter and granddaughter of civil rights activists. She chafed at the discrimination she suffered, then found some measure of satisfaction in educating freed slaves in the South Carolina Sea islands. Wilson peeks into her diary and her loneliness: 'The need for more intimate companionship has taken the odd form, in her diary, of impelling her to create an imaginary confidante to whom she can recount her sensations.'

Colonel Higginson, a Unitarian parson whom she met there, had been an active supporter of the fanatic John Brown and later the 'dear preceptor' of Emily Dickinson. A prominent war veteran, Higginson was an active abolitionist and writer ('His limpid and elegant style has a flavor of artistic personality'). Immersed as always in his characters, Wilson reads into Higginson's tone and exploits a smugness: 'We can imagine his attitude toward Charlotte Forten: sympathetic, approving, instructive, very sure of his own benevolence.' This is not perhaps altogether different from his interest in Dickinson, whom Wilson thinks a little overrated as a poet.

A chapter on the diaries of three Confederate Ladies: Kate Stone, Sarah Morgan and Mary Chesnut follows. Civil War diaries from the home front have a disturbing immediacy, as well as providing information of inestimable value about social class, domestic and economic life, information that outsiders like Olmsted and Trowbridge could not access. Always immersed in tragedy, these accounts are explored by Wilson through the literary merit and the relative complexity of their generally conventional attitudes.

Kate Strong is 'the typical Dixie heroine', a Yankee hater who celebrates the murderers of Lincoln and the attempted murderer of Secretary of State Seward. They have 'won the love and applause of all Southerners'. Wilson mines her 'wooden' prose and that of the 'considerably more interesting Sarah Morgan' for attitudes, such as the 'reckless hot headedness' which he identifies as characteristically Southern and which he sees as a major component of the indiscipline that bedevilled the Confederacy and its feudal society. Morgan's diary illustrates the moral difficulties facing the privileged in wartime, such as her consternation about taking the oath of allegiance, or having the enemy protecting the family home: 'It was a singular situation: our brothers off fighting them, while these Federal soldiers leaned over our fence, and an officer standing on our steps offered to protect us.'

Wilson acknowledges the heroism of these proud, spirited women ('Pshaw! There are *no* women here!' writes Sarah Morgan. 'We are *all* men!'). Strong, of the professional class, disdains conventional hatreds and as Wilson writes, 'What is interesting here is an aristocratic sense that has detached itself from planter solidarity.' He reads into her passion and high spirits the Natasha of *War and Peace*, while her grounding had been in Walter Scott's historical romanticism. He notes that it seems inevitable to think in terms of Russian society when writing of the South. To its ladies the comparison to victims of the French Revolution seemed more appropriate.

The greatest of the Dixie diarists is generally held to be Mary Chesnut of South Carolina (though her work was actually written up twenty years later, based on war journals). The great Southern historian C. Vann Woodward wrote of her, 'Mary Chesnut was a shrewd and original observer of the human comedy… Flirtations, philanderings, fornications, courtships, and marriages passed under review, and marriage came off little better than the patriarchy and slavery as an institution.' Wilson is also enamoured of her 'masterpiece', since she has both an understanding of the national crisis and Confederate politics, as well as 'a decided sense of the literary possibilities of her subject'. Also, as the wife of a lawyer (a one-time senator and now a member of President Davies's staff), she lived close to the heart of the Confederacy (in Montgomery, then Richmond).

With his chapter on 'Southern Soldiers', Wilson turns to Richard Taylor, John S. Mosby and Robert E. Lee. General Taylor was the son of the Tennessee President Zachary Taylor, the third shortest serving U.S. President. Taylor – author of one of the duller memoirs of the period in my view – fought with 'Stonewall' Jackson, which prompts Wilson to discuss that eccentric, lightning commander, a 'single-track embodiment of will'. Atypically, Jackson was driven by ambition, and here Wilson takes us into yet another interesting characteristic of the Southern gentleman: his preference for playing the knightly role rather than aspiring for position.

'The Gray Ghost', that daring cavalry commander Colonel John Singleton Mosby, turns out to have been an articulate and well-read lawyer, his *Reminiscences* invoking Homer, Virgil, Gibbon, Sterne, Byron, Moore, Macaulay and Longfellow. A pragmatist, he claimed to have fought simply 'for success and not for display'. Like the most efficient soldiers of the war, he could be particularly ruthless when it suited his purposes, charming otherwise. Mosby seems to have been amused by his myth: 'I can now very well understand how the legendary heroes of Greece were created', he wrote. In fact in his legendary wiliness he seems to have been something of an Odysseus figure. So caught up in Mosby's derring-do is Wilson that he has to put the brake on himself: 'All this is the TV Mosby', he writes.

There is more to be said about such Southern cavaliers than about their sober leader, Robert E. Lee: 'There is nothing about Lee that is at all picturesque, but his dignity and distinction are impressive.' Once superintendent at West Point, opposed to Secession and for the ending of slavery, he turned down the offer of the rank of major general with a role defending Washington to fight for Virginia, his own state, knowing the South could not win the war but preferring defeat to the loss of Virginia's autonomy. Lee gives Wilson less to work with as a character, since he never wrote his memoirs and his letters are 'monotonous', though he remains symbolic of the virtue attached to what were then considered the highest ideals of service. His humility in defeat can be seen in his acceptance after prison of a lowly role as president of a ruined Virginia college.

The chapter on 'Diversity of Opinion in the South: William J. Grayson, George Fitzhugh, Hilton R. Helper' ends justly with: 'To such mental and moral confusion were the thinkers of the South reduced by their efforts to deal rationally with the presence among them of four million kidnapped and enslaved Africans.' The three 'thinkers' are a sorry bunch: malcontents and white supremacists, lacking the integrity of the memoirists. There is the slave apologist, Grayson, writing in heroic couplets; and the Virginia lawyer, Fitzhugh, whose writings were extreme, fantastical, 'pernicious' and 'rambling' (An instance here of the unconventional Wilsonian empathy: 'One cannot, in spite of this, refuse a certain respect to a man who argues with consistency so bold and unconventional a case.') Helper, 'seething with class resentment', wrote an attack on slavery as the source of economic ruin, though Wilson finds something of *Mein Kampf* in its ideology.

Alexander H. Stephens, Vice-President of the Confederacy, provides an altogether more complex proposition and a fascinating chapter: a long-serving congressman, opponent of secession, a man 'revered as a statesman and sage'. Allan Nevins wrote of 'How brilliantly capable [he] was and how truly national in outlook!' before noting his debilitating quick temper and stubbornness over detail. Wilson is an admirer, especially of his fortitude, 'his moral force, his ratiocinative passion… stimulated by physical weakness to extraordinary feats of assertion, of endurance, of inspired longevity'. Incarcerated in execrable condition after the war, he wrote a prison diary and subsequently a justification of the right to Secession (in 1,455 pages) based on his interpretation of a crucial constitutional issue: the sovereignty of each state as enshrined in the Constitution.

For all his impressive understanding, Stephens proved blind on the institution of slavery, which he believed to have been morally right but practically abused. It undid the case he carefully built: 'From the moment this man of principles has established a principle that makes slavery obligatory, every step of the course of the South follows logically from his previous postulates.' Wilson takes us through Stephens's jail time, his key ideas, his thoughts on Lincoln (an admirable former friend, turned despot) and their meeting at the peace commission at Hampton Roads in February 1865 (an incident portrayed in Spielberg's movie 'Lincoln'). He traces Stephens's life in Georgia after the war and leaves us with the image of the man returned to Congress 'shrunk to pure principle, abstract, incandescent, indestructible'.

'The Myth of the Old South' deals with its poetry – not Edmund Wilson's strongest suit. Here he discusses the fervently Confederate verse of Sidney Lanier. Wilson points out that the idealized South of poets and apologists like Lanier was actually some mythical rereading of the eighteenth century splendour of eastern Virginia tobacco plantation life, not the immediately ante-bellum cotton period one might expect. Authors William Gilmore Simms and John Esten Cooke ('master of that agreeable glibness, that bland and somewhat flimsy charm that is still characteristic of one type of Southerner') dwell in it also. Mark

Twain, like Wilson, was also given to regional stereotyping and is quoted blaming Sir Walter Scott for Southern chivalric notions and, by extension, for the war itself. He quotes at length from Lanier, whose florid exhalations apparently run through his correspondence as well as his work, 'And yet there was in Sidney Lanier something that commands our respect, even our admiration.' In essence it is Wilson's own professional virtue: the absolute commitment to talent.

Despite acknowledging that war-related poetry (really 'patriotic journalism') makes for 'barren reading', Wilson presses on, excerpting Henry Howard Brownwell and John W. De Forest (He includes a mention of my childhood favourite: Whittier's stirring 'Barbara Frietchie'). While admitting that John Greenleaf Whittier and James Russell Lowell were in fact poets, he thinks 'It is a gauge of the mediocre level of the poetry of the Civil War that Lowell's 'Ode' should have been thought to be one of its summits.' Melville, too, wrote 'versified journalism'. That leaves the field clear for Walt Whitman, Emily Dickinson and Frederick Goddard Tuckerman, for whom he makes a decent case (though perhaps in claiming his 'style that never lapses like Wordsworth's, though it cannot sustain the level of Yeats' might be one analogy too far).

Wilson rightly admires Poe for the critical, if severe, attention he gives to contemporary poets. He touches on Stephen Crane's singular poetry and offers illustrations from the tragic, capable verse of Adelaide Crapsey, before returning to Lanier whose later work had been 'stimulated' by Whitman's example; we are given six pages of the readable 'The Revenge of Hamish'. Whereas Wilson acknowledges Lowell's excellent dialect verse in *The Biglow Papers*, he finds the prose dialect humour of George Washington Harris, in his Southern 'cracker' Sut Lovingood tales, to be popular, offensive and malevolent. His description of the character of Lovingood as 'a peasant squatting in his own filth' is supported by the examples we read.

Wilson has a fascinating chapter on the post-war novelists of the South: Albion W. Tourgée, George W. Cable, Kate Chopin and Thomas Nelson Page. According to Daniel Aaron in *The Unwritten War* (1973), 'Tourgée, converted to Unionism and antislavery shortly before the War, stubbornly kept the faith as soldier, Carpetbagger, novelist, and publicist.' The author of six novels infused with narrative verve and social history, he is the most interesting to the critic, being an obdurate and unconventional character. Tourgée proved a remarkably resilient soldier and later, when living at his peril in the South after the war, a scourge of racism. *A Fool's Errand* was a sensational seller, dealing with experiences of Reconstruction based on his family's plight. Tourgée again fits Wilson's image of a Southerner, 'in his insolence, his independence, his readiness to accept a challenge, his recklessness and ineptitude in practical matters, his romantic and chivalrous view of the world'.

Cable, son of a failed steamboat owner in New Orleans, saw war service too and then, as an accountant and journalist with a strong puritanical streak, took an interest in political and social reforms. He turned to civil rights activism before publishing his magazine stories as *Old Creole Days* in 1879. According to Wilson he proved to be more than a writer of local colour but one who had 'a remarkable literary gift' and 'a kind of all-round intellectual competence'. His best novel, *The Grandissimes*, is 'partly tedious, partly brilliant' and infused with his characteristic tragic ironies. His work became increasingly hampered by his social conscience and by the demands of his publishers, forcing him to turn to writing romances like *The Cavalier*, in which 'most of the characters in the story, male or female, high or low, seem preoccupied, at the expense of the war, with the problem of whether Ned and his hampered sweetheart will win through to the final embrace'.

Wilson makes it clear that in advocating equal civil rights for African-Americans, authors like Tourgée or Cable (or the abolitionists themselves) were not advocating social equality, racial intermarriage or suggesting the 'God given' equality of white and black. They were concerned with 'justice', and were dismissed at best as quixotic by the South they lectured to. In contrast Thomas Nelson Page of Virginia offered readers the romanticising that would lead eventually to *Gone with the Wind*. He invented plantation types that would charm and soften the realities of the old regime 'and Page also struck in his stories a note of reconciliation that everybody wanted to hear'. Not so the unconventional Kate Chopin, who lived after her marriage in Louisiana with her French Creole husband. A widow with six children after twelve years of marriage, she nevertheless pursued her vocation as a writer. Her novel best remembered today and scandalous at the time was *The Awakening* (1899): 'quite uninhibited and beautifully written [it] anticipates D.H. Lawrence in its treatment of infidelity'.

Ambrose Bierce – that most bitter of witnesses – is the subject of the next chapter and Wilson is no admirer: 'Even the best of his fiction is monotonous and almost monomaniacal in its compulsive concentration on death, and the general run of his journalism would seem to have been equally sterile and even more disagreeable in its monotony of personal abuse.' Of this death-obsessed figure, a veteran of war who railed against it and yet found army life congenial, Wilson continues, 'His idea of whimsicality is almost invariably homicidal' and his obsession with political corruption seems motivated by the desire 'to imagine macabre scenes in which the miscreants are received in Hell or left to survive alone in a universe divested of life'. To Wilson he lacks tragic status, given his contempt for mankind. Bierce's disappearance and reputed death in Mexico with Villa, on the other hand, certainly has kept his legend alive. His more recent biographer, Roy Morris Jr, is probably right to conclude – speaking from the family's perspective – that 'An unsolved disappearance might, after all, be preferable to a known suicide.'

The penultimate chapter of *Patriotic Gore* deals with 'The Chastening of American Prose Style' and John W. De Forest. We are given a number of illustrations of the florid, circumlocutory prose of the period, stuffed with classical allusions and dedicated to the passing of hours. This contrasts with Lincoln's masterly brevity, Grant's plain-spoken prose, Mark Twain's style ('The Lincoln of our literature', according to William Dean Howells) and a post-war turning toward the demotic, which Wilson sees also in British parliamentary debates. Overlooked, he argues, are the sermon and the diary, both of which brought a 'moral character' to American prose pre-war, which was to be less in evidence after.

Hawthorne, Melville and Poe offered at times 'a peculiar clogged and viscous prose characteristic of the early nineteenth century'. Their sluggishness Wilson considers as illustrative of their isolated lives. Interestingly he finds a quickening of pace and drama mid-century, perhaps inspired by newspaper deadlines or industrialism's 'mechanical techniques', or simply the quickened pace of life. Southern writers still steeped in Scott only later accelerated. They wrote, as Mark Twain observed, for the past. Wilson then offers a subtle twist on this. Veterans, he argues, learned to write in this manner but for non-combatants like the Henrys (James and Adams) the opposite was true. There is no urgency in their work, but rather 'a diffidence and a mechanism of self-defence'. It has been noted (by Bernard DeVoto) that American Literature was dominated for the rest of the century by men who might have but had not fought in the war: by James and Adams and Howells and Twain as well. Wilson sees James's 'obscure hurt' (as he called it) as a possible reason for his taking British citizenship in 1915 ('trying to make up in old age for the non-participation of his youth').

Are Wilson's last two pieces in *Patriotic Gore* two of the longest because he was reluctant to complete the book? He is said to have regretted not putting the De Forest portrait in an appendix, though a shorter version might have been preferable. De Forest's work itself does not hold our attention for Wilson's seventy-two pages. What he has to offer are the earliest realistic scenes of warfare in fiction, plus a life of unflagging effort. A financially independent and much travelled writer from Connecticut, De Forest was a veteran of the war (with forty-six days under fire) and a proto-realist admired by Howells (as well as prime contender for coining the term 'The Great American Novel'). *Miss Ravenel's Conversion from Secession to Loyalty* (1867) is his famous novel. Wilson wants to celebrate his accomplishments, but they are limited: 'De Forest has moral indignation, but no fury and no real compassion.' His style while 'an excellent style in its way… is of a kind that almost completely excludes, not only the nuances of atmosphere and the vibrations of unspoken feeling, but also the real pulse of emotion'.

Like Cable's, De Forest's career was blighted by the censorship of editors, publishers and the reading public (heavily female), a market 'which insisted upon prudery and demanded sentimentality'. Worse was to come for realists like himself, Howells and Howells's protégé, Stephen Crane: 'The spreading sordidness, the inundating vulgarity of post-war American life was coming, as the century went on, to dismay all three of these realists.' It was Howells, whom Wilson quotes, who neatly terminates the attention to De Forest: 'Mr. De Forest's books are a part of our literary history; Mr. James's are a part of our literature.'

To an extent Wilson righted his introduction's thematic course with his last subject, a man who both spoke the truth *to* power and spoke the truth *as* power. The fascinating Justice Oliver Wendell Holmes – he of famous dissents – 'stands alone as one who was never corrupted, never discouraged or broken'. Holmes remained a fiercely independent thinker his whole life, capable of both conservative and liberal opinions and judgements. To Wilson, Holmes was a 'truly great man' who trained himself to be a distinguished writer, though as Louis Menand wrote in *The Metaphysical Club* (2001), 'The key to Holmes's civil liberties opinions is the key to all his jurisprudence: it is that he thought only in terms of aggregate social forces; he had no concern for the individual.' One of his secretaries, describing him in old age, wrote of that aloofness, 'His thought was a little cruel, it was so exact and so lacking in human prejudices.' His critics called him 'selfish, vain, thoughtless of others'. Wilson disagrees.

Holmes had viewed the Civil War as a crusade, dropping out of Harvard to enlist (though he did graduate) while always expecting to be killed in it. The collection of his war letters and diary, *Touched with Fire*, reveal the coolness beneath the rough affection which was typical of Holmes. He wrote for instance to his parents in September 1862, immediately before the battle of Antietam, 'I don't talk seriously for you know all my last words if I come to grief – You know my devoted love for you – those I care for know it – Why should I say any more – It's rank folly pulling a long mug every time one may fight or may be killed.'

Though the war was an inescapable subject in his later life – he had been wounded on three occasions, twice seriously – Holmes remained ambivalent about it, doing his best to avoid any discussion even of the issues. To his close friend, Sir Frederick Pollock, he wrote in October 1918, 'I have read half of Lord Charnwood's *Life of Lincoln* under the compulsion of its being sent to me by a cousin. It seems to me artistically done but I hate to read of those times.' Wilson suggests the war accentuated certain traits in his character: 'The young Holmes had brought out of the war a tough character, purposive, disciplined and not a little hard, a clearly defined personality, of which his humor and affable manners, his air of being a man of the world and the ready susceptibility to feminine attraction which he sometimes a little paraded, could never quite embellish the bleakness.'

After reputedly visiting Emerson to discuss a career in philosophy or law, he chose the latter. He married. He adopted the habit of not reading newspapers, presumably to retain his intellectual balance. Of a philosophical, even poetic, temperament, he yet retained a pragmatism harder than that of his friend William James. To Holmes the law was not a sacred institution but the product of needs established over time. He supported the draft for World War 1 and the death penalty. He could support labour and free speech but was inconsistent, famously in denying an extension of time in the Sacco and Vanzetti case (the anarchists executed for 'supposed murder') on the grounds that he had not the jurisdiction.

Wilson concludes, 'He was indeed a very special case. It is plain that his unshakeable self-confidence, his carapace of impenetrable indifference to current pressures and public opinion was due partly to the impregnable security of belonging to the Boston "Brahmin" caste.' Finally, then, Wilson's portrait of Holmes is of the new man built on the rock of the old integrity. A brilliant humanist, effortlessly superior and determinedly ambitious: 'Justice Holmes was perhaps the last Roman.'

Robert Penn Warren was right in seeing the power of *Patriotic Gore* in the affecting accounts of the experience of 'individuals caught in a collision of blind forces – or rather, of forces they understand imperfectly or not at all – and trying desperately and devotedly to make "moral" sense of their experience'. I acknowledge that some of its diction and assumptions are no longer shared (those of Wilson's introduction aside). Most importantly, we readily regret that Edmund Wilson did not widen his perspective to bring African-American writers and their texts into his narrative. Today their absence is glaring. We can only read what is there, however, and what is there is cumulatively astounding.

WELTSCHMERZ: THE REMARKABLE REMARQUE

Writing in *Die Welt* in June 1971, Hans Habe asked of the belated German interest in reviewing Erich Maria Remarque's work, 'How dead does a German author have to be in order to be able to live?' Remarque (1898–1970), an international best-selling author, had generally published in his homeland first, though it was hardly his *heimat* (in the German sense of a secure home and identity). He had been banned under the Nazis and often later disapproved of, being a popular success and an 'American' (naturalized in 1947). Yet in answer to Habe's question: there are greater signs of 'life' in the reissues of Remarque's work this past twenty years.

Readers who reach for Allan Furst or Philip Kerr, or back to Graham Greene, Eric Ambler or Patrick Hamilton, can find similarly convincing European *Weltschmerz* (world-weariness) in Remarque. His fiction, which covers the first half of the last century in Europe, rivals any in its noirish atmosphere, its gaudy world of alcohol and prostitutes, and its fated romance. On the butchery of the First World War and its chaotic aftermath in Weimar Germany to the murky moral universe of the 'low dishonest decade' that followed and on into war again, Remarque is–well–remarkable. Cumulatively he builds a large, convincing cast of cynical veterans and doomed, reflective refugees, always on the run from the authorities and from their pasts, for whom European residency or escape to America is, tantalizingly, barely within reach.

Today Remarque is largely obscured by the film of his great novel, *All Quiet on the Western Front* (1929), though that is truly unfortunate, because his fiction illuminates much more of the grim life experience of a generation. *All Quiet on the Western Front*, *The Road Back* and *Three Comrades* are concerned with outliving the First World War and Weimar Germany. *Flotsam,*

Arch of Triumph, *The Night in Lisbon* and *The Promised Land* depict the struggle for survival of German refugees from the 1930s to the next war's end. Two other novels, *Spark of Life* and *A Time to Love and a Time to Die*, deal with other Nazi horrors: the concentration camp and the Eastern front.

Erich Remark was born in Osnabrück in north-west Germany into a working-class Catholic family with French ancestry (hence the adopted 'Remarque'; the 'Maria' may have been a nod to Rilke). Conscripted into the German army in June 1917, he served a matter of weeks at the front, where he was wounded by grenade fragments. This experience was to provide the basis for his war novel, though first it resulted in some self-fictionalising, some post-war posturing – the adoption of rank and medals he had not earned – for which he was censured. His adoption of a title some years later, met with a similar result. This from a man both shy *and* flamboyant, privately self-doubting and yet publicity hungry, inwardly angst-ridden and outwardly suave.

While Weimar Germany suffered under enormous inflation and ideological chaos, Remarque returned from the war to finish his education. He trained as a teacher and spent unhappy time in the provinces, clashing with school administrations. Giving up the profession, he held a succession of jobs, including playing piano and organ, working as a book keeper and a salesman. Eventually he found direction for his creativity in journalism and writing advertising copy. A little success brought him connections and a lifestyle more suited to a playboy. He married a model, Jutta Zambona, in Berlin in 1925 and was to have her in his life as a dependent long after their open marriage ended. Remarque had been an apprentice author for many years, even publishing two novels, one serialized in a magazine he edited. In 1929 his war novel was tentatively offered for publication. Against expectation – in a war-weary decade – its simple, shocking honesty led to massive sales, making Remarque a wealthy man.

It might have been more appropriate to treat the novels thematically rather than chronologically, especially since one perceived weakness in Remarque's writing – in literary terms – is its failure to show stylistic development (read 'improvement') over the years. That, however, may be something of an advantage for a career as a bestselling author. Yet out of biographical habit I offer a few words on the eight novels I read in sequence over three months.

All Quiet on the Western Front / Im Westen nichts Neues was among the first prose insights into the horrors of the trenches, which poets like Owen, Graves and Sassoon had brought sharply home to English readers. And yet some veterans begrudged its popular acceptance. Sassoon read it while completing his own *Memoirs of an Infantry Officer*. He felt it to be an attempt to sensationalise the war and noted also its failure to be specific with details of places, which left 'everything vague'. This of course had been intentional. By maintaining a narrow focus on a group of friends, Remarque magnified experience. His stated intention had been 'to give an account of a generation that was destroyed by the war – even those of it who survived the shelling'.

The experience of Paul Bäumer and friends is told in the first person, bluntly and with an attention to the trivial moods and details of life in the German army, which proves highly atmospheric. We are given ample evidence of the boredom and the horror but see nothing of the glory. For the most part the men battle poor conditions: near starvation, monotony, fears and rumours, brutality, artillery barrages and, occasionally, the unseen enemy. For naive boys who have just left school for war, the experiences are either fatal or ruinous. Their world view, their moral health is destroyed. Their jingoistic, self-involved teachers are revealed as shams, while their parents are simply bewildered victims. Witnessing the sufferings in a military hospital, Bäumer's response is, 'How pointless all human thoughts, words and deeds must be, if things like this are possible!' The novel ends with great pessimism: 'If we had come back in 1916 we could have unleashed a storm out of the pain and intensity of our experience. If we go back now we shall be weary, broken-down, burnt-out, rootless and devoid of hope.'

To a Guardian correspondent who interviewed Remarque in the Swiss Alps in June 1929, the author claimed that his success, 'made me feel inexpressibly sad and helpless. Suddenly I, the unknown, became an object of interest and curiosity. It all depressed me, and I had to escape from Berlin.' Yet far from questioning whether he would ever write another novel, he almost immediately set out to do just that. Shortly after, he began living in style in Porto Ronco, Switzerland, basking in his royalties, feuding in his marriage and driving fast cars.

The Way Back / Der Weg zurück – 'a worthy successor', according to *The New York Times Book Review* – appeared two years later. Effectively a sequel, it explores the *Weltshmerz* Paul Bäumer anticipated. It is a novel Remarque himself felt superior to the first. Again the authenticity and the atmosphere are telling, while the dialogue is convincingly idiomatic. The war grinds on and Remarque captures the monotony and resignation which accompany great moments of fear ('In the road a cockerel is treading a hen. We smoke, and our minds are blank.') Hence the sense of unreality, the emotional anti-climax after the Armistice. Bäumer's friend Ernst, the new narrator, does allow himself the observation that wars are inevitable 'because you can never completely share the suffering of other people' ('How can you expect a man who's warm to understand a man who's cold?' Solzhenitsyn said.)

In the weeks that follow Ernst's classmates discovers that the intense comradeship of the trenches breaks down in a civilian society no longer admiring of their sacrifice. Although he returns to school, nothing has changed in the teachers' attitudes; their world view is now redundant. The veterans suffer psychological damage, fury and bitterness. Unemployment is rife; social harmony is threatened; tensions lead to violence. Finally, at his friend Ludwig's grave, Ernst talks with guarded optimism of trying to find his way back to connection with the natural world and with happiness.

Remarque's wealth remained unassailable from the proceeds of these novels. In its first eighteen months in print, *All Quiet* had worldwide sales of two-and-a-half million copies (in twenty-two languages). Yet the economic climate had deteriorated. The Nazis made great political capital out of the Wall Street Crash of 1929 and the Great Depression, which promised economic ruin for Germany, imperilling loans promised it by the Treaty of Versailles. Although living in Switzerland, Remarque soon found himself *persona non grata* in his homeland, his books banned by the triumphant Nazis as defeatist. Ironically he had taken care to make no overtly political pronouncements. Publicly pacifistic and a humanitarian, he avoided speaking out against the Nazis until 1945 (no doubt partly to protect German relatives and friends).

With his next novel, *Three Comrades / Drei Kameraden* (1936), Remarque turned to more conventional plotting. He set his story in Berlin in 1928, where three veterans run an auto-repair workshop and live among prostitutes and bohemians during this period of social unrest. In dealing with the consequences, one of them falls in love in a world where survival is hardly assured. The modern reader may well be a little puzzled by the novel's thirty year old hero. There is nothing unusual about a self-reliant, two-fisted mechanic, though most would not have been pianists and former advertising managers. That, of course, is part of Remarque's point: the world has been shaken up by war and in its aftermath people are out of place:

> 'It wouldn't take much to make him happy, though,' said I. 'All he wants is a bit of work.'
> 'Not so easy,' replied Stefan, 'nowadays.'
> 'He'll do anything.'
> 'Everybody will do anything nowadays.' Stefan grew soberer.
> 'He only needs seventy-five marks a month.'
> 'Impossible. He couldn't live on that.'
> 'He does live on it,' said Lenz.

The catalyst to the story, and Remarque's most sympathetically realised heroine, is Patricia Hollmann, who shows the hero the limitations of his belief that 'everything can be there: a human being, love, happiness, life – and that yet in some terrible way it is always too little, and grows ever less the more it seems'. If the romance reminds one of Hemingway, its sanatorium scenes are reminiscent of Thomas Mann's *The Magic Mountain* (1924). In not ending well, the novel reflects what seems to have been Remarque's Turgenevian view of the human condition: 'It was the melancholy secret that reality can arouse desires but never satisfy them.' Interestingly, *The Way Back* was to become vastly influential on publication in Russia twenty years later. It was deemed the novel of a generation for its focus on male friendship and doomed love.

Remarque had his German citizenship revoked in 1938, his crime being association with 'Jews and Communists'. The following year he left Switzerland, uncertain as to its future. Remarrying his first wife for her safety, he left with her for America where his status as an enemy alien was made more palatable by wealth and connections. He had been an intimate friend of Marlene Dietrich for some time. The émigré community proved less welcoming – at least the Thomas Mann circle in Hollywood – perhaps because popular authors made the money his friends were often desperately in need of.

His early struggle aside, one wonders why Remarque, who led such a comfortable, starry life from the 1930s onward, could capture so well the angst of those *sans nationalité*, many of them Jewish. The answer seems to be that the author felt himself to be of them in spirit. An outsider by temperament and a pampered refugee by circumstance, he never quite settled outside a Germany to which he would not return.

Two years after his arrival in America, Remarque's 1939 novel *Flotsam / Liebe deinen Nächsten* was published. It had been serialized in *Collier's* magazine. The novel has a convincing sense of period, conveyed particularly by the dialogue which to the reader may be more important here than the narrative. The reason I say this is because in relating the experience of a group of itinerant refugees (would-be émigrés), the one constant is movement. Variations are worked on the same repeated situation: crossing a border, finding meagre employment, being discovered or betrayed, being arrested and briefly imprisoned, then expelled across a border ('Whenever anything happens in Germany to make the neighbouring countries nervous, the emigres are the first to suffer.')

Nowhere is safe; 'some places are simply more hostile than others'. Paris, if not the final destination of his characters, is the nearest they come to happiness: 'a spirit of toleration prevailed; one could starve to death in it but one was harried only as much as was absolutely necessary – and this meant a great deal to them'. In New York in 1943 Hannah Arendt observed ironically that the refugees in America were 'a new kind of human beings' who 'are put in concentration camps by their foes and in internment camps by their friends'.

This is not to suggest that *Flotsam* is a dull novel. Indeed it is one of Remarque's best. He has two likeable central characters, Steiner and Kern, and a number of interesting secondary figures. We learn a lot about survival at the time (from work permits to deportation) and something about human nature, also. When Steiner leaves his knapsack behind with an unfriendly landlady, for example, he does so to secure a lodging: 'he understood the extraordinarily persuasive effect that personal belongings exert upon people who lead regular lives'.

Another huge bestseller, *Arch of Triumph / Arc de Triomphe*, appeared in 1945. Hilton Tims, Remarque's biographer, describes the novel as 'personally challenging work, virtually self-analysis in which he penetrates deep into his own psyche'. If there is Remarque in his hero Ravi, then Joan Madoc was inspired by his on-again, off-again relationship with Dietrich ('our book' he referred to it in a note to her). The story is set in Paris in 1939 and focuses on the life of a stateless surgeon who makes a shadowy living performing operations, including abortions, for others less competent. In this noir thriller – with shades of the movie 'Casablanca' (1942) – the interest is in what happens when love surprises the central character: 'what other home existed for one who belonged nowhere, but the stormy one in the heart of another for a short time?' It is Ravi's misfortune that the woman he chooses has her own problems. They inevitably invade his.

Today the novel still makes gripping reading. Its hero has all the refined, world-weary appeal of a jaded Hollywood hero and the heroine has qualities of the classic *femme fatale* – which is as much as to say *Arch of Triumph* is romantic, at times melodramatic, and therefore another step away from the simple realism of Remarque's two first novels. Yet it is also excellent: a wise, ruminative book and a good point of entrance into the later novels.

Appallingly, Remarque learned after the war that his sister, Elfriede Scholz, had been arrested by the Nazis for defeatism in 1943 and beheaded. Although denounced, it is believed she was actually the victim of her brother's success. According to one source, her judge is said to have remarked, 'Your brother is unfortunately beyond our reach – you, however, will not escape us.' This barbaric murder contributed significantly to Remarque's fits of depression. Perhaps it also influenced the writing of his concentration camp novel, *Spark of Life* (1952).

He returned to his Swiss home in 1948, where he remained for the rest of his life. Six years later he published another fine bestseller, *A Time to Love and a Time to Die / Zeit zu leben und Zeit zu sterben*. The first fifty pages of this grim novel, set on the Eastern front, are as powerful as any of Remarque's writing. When Ernst Graeber, its protagonist, is rather surprisingly granted leave at a critical time in the war, he returns to find his home destroyed and his parents missing. Despite the chaos of regular allied bombings, some precarious order is maintained within the community, enough at least for him to find love there.

Graeber is a man toughened by horror, though compromised by his actions at the front and by his resumed friendship with a disarmingly welcoming Nazi school friend. However, he cares about his parents, loves his girl, has ethical quandaries which lead him to seek an old teacher's advice. Ultimately – for want of seeing an alternative – he behaves as a cog in the war machine. The heroine escapes the fate of other Remarque heroines, being uncharacteristically healthy. She possesses the same *carpe diem* attitude as Graeber. At the end her lover redeems himself.

Remarque married the Hollywood actress Paulette Goddard in 1958. He remained busy with his writing while suffering health issues throughout the 1960s. A screenplay, a stage play and another novel (*The Black Obelisk*) emerged before yet another big bestseller *The Night in Lisbon / Die Nacht von Lissabon* appeared in English in 1964. The last novel published in his lifetime is a romantic melodrama, in which one man is bribed to listen to another's story with the promise of passports (thereby assuring, for the giver, the continuity of memory). When the mercurial Helen asks her dogged lover Schwartz if he remembers the chateau they had briefly hidden in, he replies 'I remember as if someone had told me about it.' And that unfortunately is the distancing effect of Remarque's narrative structure here. There are many details, about passports, visas, streets, cafes and camps, but not the little moments that would bring them vividly to life.

Unlike his best work, this novel does not have the sense of being in the moment, relying greatly on the inherent drama of a couple on the run from the Nazis, who can only talk their lives away. That their pursuer is her sadistic brother is as unconvincing as the fact that the heroine, Helen, later enjoys remarkable freedom when interned. Not that it is not well done otherwise. Remarque rightly saw his dialogue as the source of his power as a novelist. The other strength here is the character of Helen. Fated, she is increasingly assertive, capable of irresponsibility and self-sacrificial love.

Remarque died in Switzerland in 1970. The unsatisfactory *Shadows in Paradise* appeared in English in 1972 at the instigation of Remarque's widow. Twenty years after his death Goddard bequeathed twenty million dollars to establish the Remarque Institute for European Studies at New York University, where that outstanding historian Tony Judd became its first director.

A better posthumous version of the novel first appeared in Germany in 1998. *The Promised Land / Das globe Land* – translated into English in 2014 by the poet Michael Hofmann – opens on Ellis Island in 1942, where immigrants with problems of documentation were held. It deals with the mysterious Ludwig Sommer and his introduction to America ('What a country, I thought as I emerged on to the street. Forty-two flavours of ice cream, war, and not a soldier in sight.') The members of his new community, mostly Jewish, are typically well-sketched, most haunted by the sufferings in their pasts ('We were saved', Sommer tells us, 'but not from ourselves.') Sommer has his own ghosts and has adopted the identity of his mentor, a Jewish antique dealer.

He is observations on trivia are interestingly idiosyncratic: how cigarettes do not taste as good in the dark; how women's voices are deeper when they are naked (Maria Fila, the heroine in the novel, is a model as often naked as dressed); that memories are more dangerous where danger is not present. Sommer is a shrewd observer of his country. He has learnt that even SS individuals can be intimidated by the unpredictability of their system and recognises, with news of the failed plot against Hitler's life, that it expresses the anxiety of patriotism and not a humanitarian impulse. He also declares that America's morals are 'set by the women's league'.

Sommer seems to offer something of his author's summation of life. American exile has afforded him 'a gift of time, a blue space between two clouds' in order to recognize that love proves the only consolation in life – but an evanescent one. Love-making offers 'the illusion of union and self-abandonment, whereas in fact one was never more remote from the other and never more alien'. It is part of Remarque's recognition that while in childhood we 'assumed happiness was a statue and not a cloud that was forever changing', in actual fact life has only moments to offer.

REVIEW: LOUIS MENAND, *THE FREE WORLD: ART AND THOUGHT IN THE COLD WAR* (2021)

James Russell Lowell sounded a note of caution when he wrote in 1867, 'Our culture is, as for a long time it must be, European; for we shall be little better than apes and parrots till we are forced to measure our muscle with the trained and practised champions of that elder civilization.' He could hardly have guessed just how much muscle the U.S.A. would be able to flex in Europe within a century, militarily, economically and artistically.

World War 11 brought isolationist America back to world affairs for the second time in forty years, ending the Depression. Peace, however, meant only a new front, the Cold War, which was to hamper the nation's psyche. This was the time, as Jill Lepore argued in *These Truths* (2018), 'when the United States built a national security state' because of its fear of Communism, and thus 'a peace dividend expected after the Allied victory in 1945 never came'. What came instead were cagey, proxy confrontations and years of aggressive rhetoric. It was a time of seriousness of purpose, but of devastating ill-judgement abroad (the Cold War, Vietnam) and at home (McCarthyism, institutional sexism, racism and homophobia). Beneath the conservatism of the period, cultural historians like Morris Dickstein (*Leopards in the Temple*, 2002), detected an energy radically at odds with conformism, initially manifest in literature and film, which would be given dramatic expression in the 1960s.

It is this postwar period that Louis Menand has chosen to document in *The Free World: Art and Thought in the Cold War* and he has done it splendidly, in a work epic in both ambition and achievement. Menand is a respected observer of the American historical scene, a Harvard exponent of intellectual history and culture, as compulsively readable as, say, our own Stefan Collini. Known widely for his pieces in *The New Yorker*, *The New Republic* and *The New York Review of Books*, he is also the author of

Discovering Modernism: T. S. Eliot and His Context (1987), his Pulitzer prizewinning study of pragmatism, *The Metaphysical Club* (2001), and a collection of essays, *American Studies* (2002).

The Free World is as stimulating as *The Metaphysical Club,* though that book's cast of intellectuals – John Dewey, Charles Sanders Peirce, Oliver Wendell Holmes, Jr. and the mercurial William James (James hated the idea of undifferentiated oneness; he didn't even like the fact that everyone was expected to spell the same way. He thought the universe should be renamed the "pluriverse") – is here multiplied considerably. *The Free World* involves everyone from artist Mary Abbott to Paramount boss, Adolph Zukor.

Menand has a well-known aversion to the term 'cultural criticism' ('it's related to no body of knowledge and names no actual calling, unlike, say, movie criticism or book reviewing' – *The New Yorker*, 2016). He does, however, share the cultural critic's disapproval of the notion of a privileged culture with a capital 'C' (Though one has to say that some sense of a 'high' culture did give many working class children the aspiration to transcend the felt limitations of their own culture). The line between high and low culture that gave way in the 60s, according to Morris Dickstein in *The Gates of Eden* (1977), resulted when 'Serious artists in all fields were attracted to the simplicity and emotional directness of popular culture *and* the complexities of modernist experimentation' (Dickstein did not, of course, approve of the 'anything goes' approach to evaluating taste – what he called 'easy pluralism' – that might eliminate the critic's role.)

Menand would agree with this. In his book of essays *American Studies* (2002) he wrote about the *New Yorker* film critic Pauline Kael (a subject here, also). He celebrated first his own *New Yorker's* commitment to egalitarianism, arguing that the magazine 'made it possible to feel… that any culture worth having could be had without special equipment or intellectual gymnastics'. He then celebrated Kael: 'The critical attitude Kael represented only means approaching a work of art without bias about what "a work of art" is supposed to be. It is predicated on the notion that modern culture is fluid and promiscuous, and therefore that nothing is gained by foreclosing the experience of it.'

Reading his new book, one is reminded of Benedetto Croce's dictum 'all history is contemporary history'. Under the destructive years of the Trump presidency, America practised a trumpeting, aggrieved and predatorial isolationism. This is perhaps the spur to *The Free World*. 'This book,' it begins, 'is about a time when the United States was actively engaged with the rest of the world.' In his preface, Menand sets out his stall. His focus is on the twenty years post-1945 when American dollars, via the Marshall Plan, helped regenerate war-ravaged Europe – at a price: the exportation of liberal democracy, American style. His intention is to explore the underlying social forces and the resultant cultural terrain by taking 'a series of vertical cross-sections', focusing on leading practitioners in their fields (almost exclusively men, given the times). Along the way he considers the reversals of respect and scepticism that politics and the arts endured in the period. For all its 'free world' emphasis, this is a book chiefly about American experience.

Menand is keen to stress that 'the existence of the Cold War was a constant but only one of many contexts' in his book. These contexts tended to produce cultural goods which, like Abstract Expressionism, could anyway be seen as capitalist propaganda, as instruments of Cold War foreign policy. Writing of the source of Pop Art, he observes that people had been taught 'to think of modern art as a story with a single narrative whose stages developed internally'. He avoids the approach, offering various narratives, linking contexts, themes and characters.

Among the most interesting of these are: Kennan and 'containment', the political manoeuvring that became the Cold War; the slow death of institutional anti-Semitism in American academia; scientific racism, civil rights and the fight for a black identity; the emergence of dissonance in dance, art and music; censorship and the paperback revolution; sexism versus second-wave feminism; Hollywood Americana and the influence of *La Nouvelle Vague*; and the Vietnam War's politicizing of students at home.

We can get some idea of the way this last was experienced from Peter Novick's book, *That Noble Dream* (1998). Novick quotes historian Mark Naison, who is recalling taking his Ph.D. orals during the 1968 Columbia strike:

> Fayerweather Hall [was] occupied at the precise moment my exams began… My orals board, composed of Richard Hofstadter and some equally uptight, but less renowned professors, began their questioning amidst the sounds of breaking furniture, shouts of rage and pride, fragments of falling plaster and chants of "shut it down."… The behavior of the faculty members was curious. They were not, as I expected, unusually hostile to me, but absolutely tickled pink at the prospect of keeping the institutional ritual alive amidst the surrounding chaos.

To take just one thread from Menand's book as an illustration of its strengths: 'Freedom and Nothingness' (Chapter 3), concerns a Paris well-known to us through the work of writers such as Robert Gildea, Julian Jackson, Tony Judt and Sarah Bakewell, and yet still Menand turns up eye-opening details which may not have lodged earlier, such as the fact that most of the Free French divisions were a majority non-white, hence Leclerc's Second Armoured Division (75% white) was chosen to liberate Paris. Similarly, he gives a context for de Gaulle's fears of the ongoing influence of the French Communist Party (the PCF) – recognized for its wartime resistance – in reminding us that postwar it had twelve daily newspapers and forty-seven weeklies in its control.

He then turns to Paris's intellectual star of the period, Jean Paul Sartre (who could do a great Donald Duck impersonation, as we learn from one of Menand's ironic digressions). Sartre's resistance credentials were underwritten by his belief that almost all French people had been *résistants* in wartime ('A free act made in the name of freedom, whatever the act is and whoever makes it, is by its nature an act of resistance.') Inevitably many celebrated figures have only walk-on parts: Camus and Paulhan in Paris, for instance, Aron in London and Benjamin dying in Port Bou. He has more to say on Hannah Arendt, who recognized in flight that 'The European tradition had destroyed itself' and who finally escaped to America to find – as Alexander Herzen had found in London in the previous century – that her adopted nation offered the protection of its institutions, but a conformism that stultified.

Most interesting in this chapter, perhaps, are Menand's comments concerning the French take on American fiction, an influence on Existentialism. He introduces the reader to Maurice-Edgar Coindreau, whose impact 'was enormous, not only on the Americans he translated, particularly Faulkner, whose French reception was almost certainly crucial to his receiving the Nobel Prize in 1949 but also on French literary culture itself'. As Menand explains, French translation 'largely bleached out markers of race, region, and class' in their novels. 'The effect was to classicize.' Influence came down to a matter of time displacement and characterization. From the movies (and *vice versa*) Americans had learnt to play with narrative (flashback, montage, techniques of ellipsis) and to focus on exteriority, on action rather than on analysis of character motive.

Menand practises a revealing dualism with his vast cast of characters: Orwell and Burnham, Baldwin and Wright, Cage and Cunningham, Friedan and Beauvoir, Rauschenberg and Johns, Trilling and Ginsberg, Langlois and Bazin, Warhol versus the *avant-garde*, and so on. He also has an eye for stripping off the mythical accretions on anecdotes. He does this with Kerouac's *On the Road*. Apparently, Kerouac was not actually making the novel up at the keyboard after being inspired by a letter from Neal Cassady, as is often told, but working from drafts and journals. Nor was he typing – as the image has it – on a continuous roll of teletype paper, but on ten twelve-foot rolls of drawing paper. Also, Cassady's letter itself was inspired by one from John Clellon Holmes.

Elsewhere Menand recounts Isaiah Berlin's formative experience in visiting the officially disgraced poet Akhmatova in Moscow in 1956 (her 'guest from the future'), revealing the implausibilities in the romanticized version of their meeting. The elisions in Berlin's account(s) were meant to protect this ideological enemy of the state. And yet the line 'She was a seducer, but so, very much, was he', reads a tad steamy for Berlin-watchers.

Similarly, when Menand writes of Orwell: 'He turned his life into an experiment in classlessness', he is telling half a story. He might have added that despite his rough living, the Etonian Orwell had a problem with this. As his niece recalled, 'I think a lot of Eric's [Orwell] hang-ups came from the fact that he thought he ought to love all his fellow-men; and he couldn't even talk to them easily.'

Finally, because Menand *is* so generously inclusive, we begin to miss people: we have Sontag but hardly the similarly abrasive Mary McCarthy; Cleanth Brooks is here but Allen Tate is barely mentioned, one of the great networkers. Further, certain figures who seem to have had an impact on the culture of the period at the time, are missing: Charlie Parker, Arthur Miller, Fred Zinnemann, John Wayne, to name a few.

One salient remark in *The Free World* – a book blessed with many – comes from Susan Sontag. In an interview for *The Paris Review* (1994) she said, 'I was assuming that a principal task of art was to strengthen the adversarial consciousness.' Menand's book illustrates just how and how many artists in all media felt this to be their mission.

***

Postscript: Sontag continued in that interview with a complaint with which I have some sympathy:

'But taste has become so debauched in the thirty years I've been writing that now simply to defend the idea of seriousness has become an adversarial act. Just to be serious or to care about things in an ardent, disinterested way is becoming incomprehensible to most people. Perhaps only those who were born in the 1930s – and maybe a few stragglers – are going to understand what it means to talk about art as opposed to art projects. Or artists as opposed to celebrities. As you see, I'm chock-full of indignation about the barbarism and relentless vacuity of this culture. How tedious always to be indignant.'

ACKNOWLEDGEMENTS

My thanks to John Lucas for his example and support. And to my wife, Chris. To Jim Burns, Paul Roberts and Mike Freeman for their reading of these pieces, and to the Book Typesetters. Further acknowledgements are due to the following editors and their magazines, which hosted versions of a good number of the essays: Michael Schmidt (*PN Review*), Steven O'Brien (*The London Magazine*), Patricia McCarthy (*Agenda*) and John Whale (*Stand*).

PART ONE: LOWELL & Co.

Lizzie, Cal & Dolphin *PNR* 253 2020

John Berryman & Robert Lowell: Letters from the Bottom of the World, *The London Magazine* December/January 2022

A Wary Friendship: Alfred Kazin and Robert Lowell, *PNR* 267 2022

Pioneers: The Iowa Writers' Workshop in the Early Fifties, *PNR* 266 2022

Delmore Schwartz: The Unravelling Man, *The London Magazine* Feb/March 2019

Intimate Distance: Berryman & Giroux, *PNR* 258 2021

The Enthralling Alfred Kazin, *PNR* 257 2020

James Atlas: The Shadow and the Poet, *PNR* 252 2020

Richard Hugo & James Wright: 'Make it scotch and dirty river water', *PNR* 272 2023

Robert Hass: A Voice in My Ear, *Agenda* Autumn/Winter 2020/2021

Dave Smith, *Looking Up: Poems 2010–2022 Stand,* April–June, 2023

Discovering F.T. Prince, *The London Magazine* Oct/Nov 2019

The Low Visibility of Norman Cameron, *The London Magazine* April/May 2022

PART TWO: ARNOLD & Co.

Matthew Arnold: A Bicentenary Portrait from the Letters, *The London Magazine* June/July 2023

PART THREE: CIVILIANS & WAR

Weltschmerz: The Remarkable Remarque *The London Magazine* Aug/Sept 2020
Louis Menand, *The Free World: Art and Thought in the Cold War*, *PNR 262* 2021